Richard Kirwan

Elements of Mineralogy

Richard Kirwan

Elements of Mineralogy

ISBN/EAN: 9783743343665

Manufactured in Europe, USA, Canada, Australia, Japa

Cover: Foto ©ninafisch / pixelio.de

Manufactured and distributed by brebook publishing software (www.brebook.com)

Richard Kirwan

Elements of Mineralogy

ELEMENTS
OF
MINERALOGY.

BY

RICHARD KIRWAN, Esq; F.R.S.

LONDON:

Printed for P. ELMSLY, in the *Strand*.

M.DCC.LXXXIV.

PREFACE.

WHEN we confider the degree of excellence which many of the practical arts bufied in the treatment of Minerals have reached in *England*, and alfo that in the merely fpeculative fciences, we are at leaft on a level with our neighbours on the continent, it cannot but be matter of furprize that, with refpect to Mineralogy, the parent of thefe arts, they fhould ftand confeffedly fuperior to us. That this inferiority on our fide does not originate in any want of ingenuity in our artifts evidently appears by the mafterly productions of a *Parker* and a *Wedgewood*. The true caufe lies deeper. Mineralogy is an art, whofe cultivation and improvement requires both fpeculation and practice: the mere theorift will never defcend into the laborious details of the practical part, without due encouragement or a degree of enthufiafm, in a country devoted to politics rarely to be met with, and the practical artift feldom poffeffes thofe general principles of fcience and extenfive acquaintance with the difcoveries of his cotemporaries that are indifpenfably requifite to eftablifh him on a footing of equality with them. On the continent Mineralogy is on a very different footing. In *Sweden* and *Germany* it is confidered as a branch of fcience worthy of the attention of government. There are colleges in which it is regularly taught; it forms a diſtinct and honourable profeſſion, like that of the ſoldier, the merchant, or the barriſter; its ſuperior officers form a part of the adminiſtration of the ſtate. Young ſtudents, fraught with the knowledge to be acquired in their own country, are ſent abroad to glean all that can be collected from a more diverſified view of nature, or a more improved practice of the arts. This example has been lately followed by the *French*, the *Ruſſians*, and even the *Spaniards*.

The French have erected a Mineralogical School at *Paris*, to which a conſiderable penſion is annexed. Subterraneous maps of the whole kingdom are now a tracing, and mineralogical voyages are from time to time undertaken at the public expence *. Chymiſtry, the Parent of Mineralogy, is cultivated by the moſt enlightened nations in *Europe*, and particularly in *France* with a degree of ardour that approaches to enthuſiaſm; it forms the favourite occupation, and even the moſt faſhionable object of attention not only of the middling, but even of ſome in the higheſt ranks of ſociety †.

In

* As that of Mr. *Jars*, &c.
† Among theſe we may reckon in *Ruſſia* prince *Gallitzen*; in *Germany* count *Sickengen*; in *Italy* the counts *de Saluces*
de

PREFACE.

In *England*, on the contrary, (a country far richer than *France* in mineral productions) it receives no encouragement from the public, and few apply to it except gentlemen in the Medical Line, whose transient attention is soon diverted by their more direct occupations. The consequences are obvious. The grossest blunders are daily committed in working our mines and extracting our ores; insomuch, that learned foreigners have remarked that were it not for their superior excellence, and the cheapness of fuel, their extraction would infallibly be attended with loss †, and many useful substances are daily rejected as useless.

Sensible of our inferiority in this respect, and well acquainted with the cause of it, the zealous and learned Doctor *Shaw*, and our late eminent Chymist Dr. *Lewis*, have laboured to promote and facilitate the study of Chymistry among us, and for this purpose transfered into our own language the most considerable improvements made in their time

---

de Morozzo, and the marquis *de Gironi*, governor of *Leghorn*; in *Geneva* Mr. *de Sauffure*; in *France* the dukes *de Chaulnes*, *Rochefoucault*, and *D'Ayen*; the counts *de Lauragais*, *la Garay*, *Milly*, *Treffan*, and *de la Tour d'Auvergne*; the marquisses *de Courtenvaux* and *de Courtivron*; the barons *d'Olbach* and *de Servieres*; madame *la Présidente d'Arconville*; messieurs *Trudaine*, *Lavoisier*, *Montigny*, and above all, Mr. *de Morveau*, one of the first chymists of the age.

† *Ferber, Reise Derbyshire.*

by foreigners. At a still later period Mr. *Keir* has poured upon us many valuable treasures in his excellent notes on Mr. *Macquer*'s Chymical Dictionary, a work generally known, and equally esteemed; yet since this work appeared, (the last of any note among us) such rapid advances have been made in the mineralogical art in particular, that it has put on quite a new face. Several new semi metals have been discovered, the number of primitive earths ascertained, many analyses accomplished heretofore attempted in vain, and the art itself of Mineral Analysis brought to a degree of certainty and precision of which it was scarcely thought capable. Actuated by the same views as the patriotic gentlemen just mentioned, I have endeavoured to collect in the ensuing treatise all that has been hitherto done in this science, with some few improvements of my own, modelled and digested in the method that seemed to me most useful.

The point which I principally laboured was not to present the reader with a minute detail of the various external appearances of minerals in various countries, nor of their situation, vicinity, or mixture with each other, circumstances ever contingent and fortuitous, much less to entertain him with prolix and plausible accounts of their origin,

enquiries

PREFACE.

enquires which appear to me to belong to another branch of the science of fossils, viz. *Natural History*, but rather to determine the characters by which fossils are invariably and permanently distinguished from each other in all times and places. In a word, rather to define the *species* than describe the *individual*; even among these permanent characters I have, for the sake of brevity, omitted all, except the most obvious, a compleat detail of them being in my opinion fitter for a treatise of Chymistry than of Mineralogy. The merit of this latter seeming to me to consist in presenting such *criteria* as may enable us to distinguish Minerals in the shortest, easiest, and surest manner; so that we may always apply the same names to the same substances, and being confident of speaking the same language, may always understand each other. What confusion hath heretofore arisen from the ambiguity of names is well known, and will, I fear, render many very interesting researches, even of modern date, intirely useless. Among these I shall only mention those of the celebrated *Canon Recupero*, who for many years, and with immense pains, has studied and described the Minerals in the neighbourhood of *Mount Ætna*, but committed such mistakes in their denomination as will, according to the remark of that excellent Mineralogist Mr.

Mr. *Sauffure*, render his work, if ever it appears, abfolutely unintelligible *.

Whether the characters of Minerals fhould be taken from external appearances only, or from their internal properties as difcovered by chymical agents, has long been controverted among Mineralogifts; though, indeed, at prefent the controverfy feems almoft at an end from the univerfal approbation with which the fyftem of the celebrated *Cronfted*, founded almoft entirely on chymical characters as far as they were known in his time, has been received by all *Europe*. However, fome able patrons of the former opinion have appeared of late, among whom I fhall mention only Mr. *Werner* and Mr. *Romé de Lifle*.

Mr. *Werner* is the author of an excellent treatife written in the *German* language on the external characters of foffils. Mr. *Romé* has lately publifhed a voluminous treatife on the external forms of cryftals, under which title he comprehends all thofe foffils that are fufceptible of a regular figure, all of which he pretends may be diftinguifhed by the angles which their planes make with each other, *if fome heterogeneous matter be not contained in them*; but fuppofing all this to

* *Voyages des Alps*, p. 67.

PREFACE.

be true, what a vast variety of figures are not these crystals subject to from a variety of accidents? How many indeterminate and confused crystallizations reducible to no certain figure? By how many external accidents may not these figures, though originally perfect, be altered and modified? What shall we say of his *macles* or agglutinated crystals? of the conic, spheroidal, cilyndrical shapes in which no angle can be discovered? and of the various amorphous appearances of most Minerals?

Mr. *Werner* has endeavoured to classify Minerals by the joint consideration of all their external properties, and yet, that even this re-union is insufficient to determine their nature, he himself gives us a clear proof in his notes on *Cronsted*, p. 217. There, on the faith of these characters, he ranges among *micas* a green foliated substance, which, being sent to Mr. *Bergman*, proved to be a compound of marine salt of copper and argillaceous earth, though the quantity sent him amounted but to one grain; so much surer are chymical tests! Every science must be founded on permanent principles. The only principles of this sort that Mineralogy affords are the relations of the bodies it considers with chymical agents. Without referring to these, it can be reckoned at most only a con-
jectural

jectural art. This will plainly appear by examining each of the external characters in particular; namely, colour, transparency, or opacity, coherence, texture, shape, and specific gravity.

And first as to *colour*, Mr. *Werner* ownes that white quartz, white lead ore, and white calcareous iron ore, have exactly the same *snow white* colour. Some species of the ores of iron, manganese, cobalt, and copper, the same *iron grey* colour, wolfram and blende the same *brownish black*, &c. in short it is well known, that the slightest change in the texture of bodies, frequently produces a considerable alteration in colour; thus a lump of cinnabar, whose colour is *dark red*, becomes of a beautiful *florid red*, by simply reducing it to a powder; besides it is difficult, if not impossible, to render the various shades of colour intelligible by any description.

Transparency and Opacity are qualities common to a vast variety of substances, different in all other respects. They are susceptible of numerous undiscribable degrees, and discover at most the mode of union, not the substances united.

Coherence and hardness are properties equally ambiguous: with respect to earths and powdered

PREFACE. ix

dered stones, their consideration is of no use, striking fire with steel, has often been given as a test of pure siliceous earths, but it is now known, that well baked clay, to say nothing of other compound substances, will exhibit the same appearance.

Texture, all its varieties as granular, lamellar, fibrous, scaly, equable, &c. are common to substances, widely different; thus the fibrous is found in some varieties of gypsum, in asbestos, shoerl, pumice, pyrites, antimony, hæmatites, malachite, cobalt, and arsenical ores, the scaly in lead and iron ores, mica, limestones, gypsum, the lamellar, granular, and equable, are still of wider extent.

Shape, the varieties of this even when regular and determinate, are endless, as may be seen in Mr. *De Lisle's* Treatise, and must be so, as they depend of various external accidents, thus he finds 32 varieties in the shape of calcareous spar, 14 in that of gypsum, 9 in that of fluor, 16 in that of quartz, besides its *monstrous* forms, equally regular as the rest, 19 in that of felt spar, &c. and not only the same specific substance is susceptible of various shapes, but various substances specifically different, assume the same shape. Thus the native calx of arsenic, blende, cinnabar, and grey copper ore, often appear in a tetrahædral form;

form; common salt, fluor, zeolyte, galena, in a cubic, &c. if the nature of any substance could be determined by its form, it would undoubtedly be that of salts, yet there is scarce any of these which in different circumstances, may not assume a different figure; Mr. *Pott* assures us, that microcosmic salt assumes the figure of almost all other salts, nitre, vitriol, salammoniac, allum, glauber's salts, &c. 4 *Pott*, 49. According to *Maquer*, if sublimate corrosive be crystalized, by cooling it forms needles, but if by mere evaporation, cubes or lozenges. *Mem. Par.* 1755, p. 540. Digestive salt will form cubes if it be exactly neutral, but if the alkali predominates quadrangular prisms, common salt is generally looked upon as the most constant in its figure, yet Mr. *Cadet* has found it crystalized in needles, 9 *Mem. Scav. Etrang.* p. 555. and *Gerhard*, 4 *Berlin, Schrift.* 292. Very many, if not most of the mistakes to be found in chymical writers on salts, arose from their having denominated them from their figure.

Lastly, *Specific Gravity*, which is certainly one of the best external tests, frequently varies, by reason either of the different texture of the same species of mineral, into whose interstices water cannot equally penetrate, or by reason of the greater proportion of some

PREFACE.

or other of the constituent parts, as is particularly observable in zeolytes, which differ exceedingly in the proportion of water which enters into them as one of their constituent principles: also in the sparry or calcareous iron ore, whose proportion of calcareous earth is subject to great variation; besides all this, various substances specifically different, possess very nearly the same specific gravity.

Nevertheless I am far from asserting, that the consideration of mere external properties is intirely useless; on the contrary, I am persuaded that from the consideration of these alone, a very probable conjecture may be drawn in most cases concerning the nature of fossils, whose specific properties are already known by analysis, but this conjecture must be formed by an experienced eye: for it is not possible by any description, to convey an adequate idea of those minute differences, or as I may say, the *physiognomies* of fossils, by which alone they are distinguishable. On this account I have been very succinct in this particular, rather hoping to help, than expecting to form the *coup d'œil*. Those who love to amuse themselves with a detailed description of these external forms, may consult with advantage Mr. *Romé de Lisle's* improved edition of his *Cryftallographie* *, though daily expe-

* Or the improved edition of *Cronsted*, which Mr. *Magellan* promises soon to publish.

rience evinces, that nature is still more varied than his descriptions.* But where any *new* substance occurs, or an intire certainty required, such as constitutes the foundation of a *science*, there chymical tests are absolutely requisite, and alone sufficient. Thus neglecting these, Mr. *Romé de Lisle* took that to be a zeolyte which Mr. *Pelletier* afterwards found to be an ore of zinc. 2 *Crystallogr.* p. 46, 20 *Roz.* 424.

Mineralogy must therefore, on the whole, be considered as a branch of Chymistry, and its progress, like that of other branches of that science, has been for many ages scarce sensible. In the earliest times, of which we have any account in history, mankind seem to have been of the same turn of thinking as the less enlightened and civilized nations of our own age. Satisfied with such information as casual experience threw in their way, they regarded the occupation of consulting nature by experiment as a childish, trifling and useless amusement, and neglected forming any theory whatsoever concerning its operations; but in succeeding times the generalizing spirit of Aristotelic Metaphysics extending itself to Natural Philosophy, soon suggested the notion of one common matter

* See *Roz.* journal for March, 1784, p. 206, 207, and 211.

being

PREFACE. xiii

being the *substratum* of all vegetable, animal and mineral substances, discriminated only by particular forms, which in the two former were held to be *substantial*, and in the latter purely accidental. From this ungrounded opinion (to which however some of the greatest men in the last century were much attached) that of the transmutability of metals into each other naturally arose; and to this notion, and some other equally false, the progress of Mineralogy, and every branch of Chymistry, is undoubtedly owing. To accomplish their favourite purpose experiments were multiplied without end, and by means of these the arts of dying, pottery, glass-making and metallurgy were insensibly improved.

The two last named arts necessarily required some knowledge of the chymical properties of stones and earths. Accordingly we find that all those that were useful in the former were called *vitrifiable*; those that were capable of burning to lime *calcareous*, and those on which fire could produce neither effect, *apyrous*. For a long time these three divisions were thought to comprehend all species of earths and stones. The same narrow spirit of referring every thing to what is already known, induced Mineralogists to class all metallic substances under some of the species

cies antiently known, denominating all thofe which difcovered any fingular properties *wild, rapacious* and *arfenical compounds.* Hence the oppofition which the introduction of the new femi-metals, cobalt, nickel, and manganefe ftill meets with among Mineralogifts of the antient ftamp.

However at laft, happily for fcience a few diftinguifhed characters appeared, who, rejecting all hypothetical delufions, determined, not only to fubmit to no other guide but actual experiment, and its neceffary confequences, but alfo to follow it wherever it led them. Of this truly philofophic band, Mr. *Margraaf* of *Berlin* led the van, followed by a few others, particularly in *Sweden*. Difcoveries now multiplied apace in the hands of a *Brandt, Swab, Cronfted, Gahn,* and particularly Mr. *Scheele,* until at laft Mr. *Bergman* of *Upfal,* by the folidity of his judgment, the ingenuity and accuracy of his methods, and the multiplicity of his experiments, brought Mineralogy to that degree of perfection at which we at prefent behold it.

CONTENTS

CONTENTS.

PART I.

OF EARTHS and STONES   P. 1

CHAP. I.
Of Simple Earths, their number and Characters — — — 3

CHAP. II.
Of the Affinities of Earths to each other   11

CHAP. III.
Of the Systematical Arrangement of Earths and Stones — — — 18

CHAP. IV.
Calcareous Genus — — 22

CHAP. V.
Barytic Genus — — 53

CHAP. VI.
Muriatic Genus — — 58

CHAP. VII.
Argillaceous Genus — — 71

CHAP. VIII.
Siliceous Genus — — 103

CHAP. IX.
Of Vegetable and Animal Earths   154

APPENDIX I.
Of Diamond and Plumbago — 157

APPENDIX II.
Of the general Examination and Analysis of Earths and Stones — 160

PART II,

CONTENTS.

PART II.
Saline Substances — 174

CHAP. I.
Of Acids — — 174

CHAP. II.
Of Alkalis — — 177

CHAP. III.
Of Neutral Salts — — 180

PART III.
Inflammables — — 208

PART IV.
Metallic Substances — — 226

CHAP. I.
Gold — — — 230

CHAP. II.
Platina — — — 238

CHAP. III.
Silver — — — 240

CHAP. IV.
Copper — — — 256

CHAP. V.
Iron — — — 269

CHAP. VI.
Tin — — — 291

CHAP. VII.
Lead — — — 297

CHAP. VIII.
Mercury — — — 306

CHAP.

TABLE III. continued.

100 Parts — *Siliceous Genus*.

	Silex.	Argill	Calcar.	Magn.	Iron.
Cryſtal	93	6	1	—	—
Flint	80	18	2	—	—
Petroſilex	72	22	6	—	—
Jaſper	75	20	—	—	5
Chalcedonian	84	16	—	—	—
Ruby	39	40	mild 9	—	10
Topaz	39	46	ditto 8	—	6
Hyacinth	25	40	dit. 20	—	13
Emerald	24	60	8	—	6
Sapphire	35	58	5	—	2
Chryſopraſium	95	—	1,7	1,2	0,4 *a*
Lapis lazuli	—	—	—	—	— *b*
Feltſpar	67	14	—	8	— *c*
Veſuvian garnet	55	39	6	—	—
Garnet	48	30	12	—	10
Martial Garnet	43,6	27,6	10	—	19
Shoerl tranſparent	48	40	5	1	5
Shoerl Black	58	27	5	1	5
Bar ſhoerl	61,6	6,6	21,6	5	1,6 *d*
Tourmaline	37	45	13	—	5 *e*
Baſaltes	52	15	8	2	25
Rowley ragg	47,5	32,5	—	—	20
Comp. and cellular lava	47	30	5	—	18
Vitreous ditto	49	35	4	—	12
Another from Lipari	69	22	—	—	9
Black agate of Iceland nearly as the above	—	—	—	—	—
Pumice ſtone	84 or 90	—	—	6 to 15	— *f*
Martial muriatic ſpat	50	—	—	30 mild	20 *g*
Turkey ſtone	70	5	mild 25	—	— *h*
Ragg ſtone	70	5	dit. 20	—	5 *i*
Siliceous grit with calcareous cement	62,5	—	d⁰ 37,5	—	—
Siliceous ditto with argillaceous cement	77	20	—	—	3 *k*
Ditto with ferruginous cement	80	5	—	—	15 *l*

a 0,6 copper, and ſparry acid.   *b* 80 martial fluor, 20 gypſum, as I
believe.   *c* 11 Ponderous.   *d* 5 water.   *e* At a medium.
f Remainder calcareous.   *g* As I believe.   *h* As I believe.
i As I believe.   *k* As I believe.   *l* As I believe.

TABLE III. *continued.*

Granite	Quartz, felt spar and mica. Quartz, felt spar and shoerl.
Stellsten, Granitello	Quartz and mica.
Rapakivi, Granitone	Felt spar and mica.
Murksten, Norka	Quartz, garnet and mica.
Porphyry	Jasper, chert, lava, shoerl containing quartz, felt spar, shoerl, mica, or serpentine in a crystaline form.
Pudding stone	Jasper, chert, siliceous grit, or lava, containing pebbles of an oval form
Siliceous breccias	The same ground and contents, but in angular forms.
Gneiss	Quartz, mica, steatites. Quartz, mica, serpentine. Quartz, mica, shoerl, steatites, or soap rock. Quartz, felt spar, mica, serpentine.
Amygdaloides	Jasper, or chert, containing spar or serpentine.
Metallic rock of Born	Quartz, clay and steatites, and felt spar sometimes.
Variolite	Serpentine, containing various stones.

Proportion of Ingredients in Natural Salts.

	Acids	Alka.	Earth	Water	
Tartar vitriolate	31	63	—	6	
Glauber's salt	14	22	—	64	
Vitriolic ammon.	42	40	—	18	
Epsom	24	—	19	57	
Alum	24	—	18	58	
Vitriol of iron	20	—	—	55	25 iron.
Ditto of copper	30	—	—	43	27 copper.
Ditto of zinc	22	—	—	58	20 zinc.
Nitre	30	63	—	7	
Cubic nitre	29	50	—	21	
Nitrous ammon.	46	40	—	14	
Nitrous selenite	33	—	32	35	
Ditto Epsom	36	—	27	37	
Salt of Silvius	30	63	—	7	
Common salt	33	50	—	17	
Sal. ammoniac	52	40	—	8	
Marine selenite	42	—	38	20	
Borax purified	34	17	—	47	

Inflammable.

Hepatic air—100 cubic inches of it united to water may contain 8 of sulphur.

Sulphur—60 acid and 40 of phlogiston.

Proportion of Ingredients in Metallic Ores.

100 Parts.   *Gold.*

Ore of *Adelfors* or *Norway*—99,59 martial pyrites 0,41 gold.

—— of *Salſburg* in *Tyrole*—$\frac{948}{1000}$ arsenical pyrites, and, 052 of gold.

—— of *Nagaya*—99 pyrites, galena and silver, 0,83 of gold.

Gold sand of *Africa*—0,22 at most.

---

100 Parts.   *Silver.*

Vitreous ore—25 sulphur, and 75 of silver.

Slightly arsenicated at *Quadanal-canal*—10 arsenic, and 90 of silver.

—— superarsenicated at ditto—ditto from 4 to 6 ozs. of silver per quintal.

Red ore—31 realgar, 8 sulphur, and 60 silver generally.

Black ore solid—40 sulphur, arsenic, and pyrites, and 60 silver.

Black

Black ore loose—75 sulphur and pyrites, and 25 silver at most.

Arsenico-martial ore—from 90 to 99 iron, and arsenic, and from 10 to 1 of silver.

White ore—from 70 to 90 of sulphurated copper, arsenic, and iron, and from 10 to 30 of silver.

Grey ore—from 12 to 24 of copper, from 1 to 12 of silver, and the remainder sulphur, arsenic, and a little iron.

Brown ore—mostly copper, sulphur, arsenic, a little regulus of antimony and iron, and from 1 to 5 per cent. of silver.

Plumose ore—pyrites, arsenic, antimony, and about 1 per cent. of silver.

Cobaltic ore—sulphur, arsenic, cobalt, iron, and from 40 to 50 per cent. of silver.

Vitriolic and *marine silver*—about 70 of silver.

---

100 Parts.　　*Copper.*

Red calx of copper—26 fixed air, 1 water, 73 copper.

Brownish red—pyrites, and from 20 to 50 of copper.

Malachite—29 aerial acid and water, and 71 of copper.

Mountain green—22 aerial acid, 6 water, and 72 of copper.

Mountain blue—29 aerial acid, 2 water, and 69 of copper.

Vitreous

CONTENTS.

CHAP. IX.
Zinc — — — 312

CHAP. X.
Regulus of Antimony — — 324

CHAP. XI.
Regulus of Arsenic — — 327

CHAP. XII.
Bismuth — — 332

CHAP. XIII.
Cobalt — — — 335

CHAP. XIV.
Nickel — — — 341

CHAP. XV.
Regulus of Manganese — — 345

CHAP. XVI.
Siderite — — 354

CHAP. XVII.
Molybdena. Molybdena membranacea Cronst. 154. Wasserbley of the Germans 357

CHAP. XVIII.
Of the Tungstenic Acid ——— 360

CHAP. XIX.
Saturnite — — 361

CHAP. XX.
Reflexions on the nature of Cobalt, Nickel, and Manganese — — 362

APPENDIX III.
Geological Observations — 373

TABLE

CONTENTS.

TABLE I.
The Quantity of Metal in a Reguline State afforded by 100 Grains, &c. — 398

TABLE II.
Of the Weight and Colour of Metallic and Earthy Precipitates, &c. — 399

TABLE III.
Of the Proportion of Ingredients in Earths and Stones — — 403

CORRECTIONS.

P. Line
- 12. 14. *Dele* they
- 16. 10. *Dele* and
- 34. for Species III. *read* Species IV. and correct the numerals of the other Species, as far as p. 46, where for Species XI. *read* Species XII.
- 36. 1. *read* if Iron be precipitated from the sparry acid by lime water, the precipitate will be white, &c.
- 36. 21. *read* commonly cubic, sometimes octagonal, or polygonal.
- 51. 6. *for* proceeds the shistus, *read* proceeds from the shistus.
- 75. 21. *for* 60 of, *read* 60 per cent of.
- 118. 6. *for* parallelipedal, *read* parallelopipedal.
- 120. 18. *for* parallelipeds, *read* parallelopipeds.
- 147. 4. *for* rnelian, *read* carnelian.
- 153. 14. *for* Metallic stone, *read* Metallic rock
- 200. 9. *for* selentine, *read* selenite.
- 384. 20. *for* 1000, *read* 10000.

ADDITIONS.
- 114. 3. Mr. *Greville* possesses an agate, speckled with yellow pyrites, which is called an *Avanturine*.
- 139. 17. Mr. *Dolomieu* has lately discovered at *Stromboli*, another sort of pumice, which seems to be a ferruginous granite altered by fire.

ELEMENTS

ELEMENTS
OF
MINERALOGY.

MINERALS in their strictest signification denote only such substances as are found in mines, such as Metals, Semi-metals, Sulphur and Salts; but in a more extensive sense, they denote all fossils that do not belong either to the vegetable or animal kingdoms, and consequently Stones and Earths, all of which are comprehended under the Denomination of the *Mineral kingdom.*

The mineral kingdom is therefore usually divided into four parts or classes, *viz.* I. *Earths, and Stones.* II. *Salts.* III. *Inflammable Substances.* IV. *Metallic Substances:* which naturally point out a similar fourfold division of this treatise.

PART I.
Of EARTHS *and* STONES.

By *Earths* are commonly underſtood taſteleſs, inodorous, dry, brittle, uninflammable ſubſtances, whoſe ſpecific gravity does not exceed 4,5. which are incapable of being metalized, are ſcarcely ſoluble in water, and give no tinge to Borax when melted with it. However Quicklime is uſually called an *Earth*, though it has a pungent taſte and is very perceptibly ſoluble in water, ſo alſo are limeſtone and gypſum, though they both contain a purely ſaline principle, and therefore in my opinion they and ſome other ſuch ſubſtances may be claſſed both among Salts and among Earths. Nay it appears that all Earths are ſoluble in ſome very large proportion of water. Hence I think with *Mr. Bergman*, that in the ſtricteſt ſenſe the term Earth, ſhould, excluſively of any other denomination, be appropriated to ſubſtances of the above deſcription, that require above one thouſand times their weight of boiling water to diſſolve them, and that thoſe which are ſoluble in between four hundred and one thouſand times their weight of water may be called either ſalts as technical, or Earths as common language requires.

Stones

Simple Earths.

Stones differ from Earths only in hardness and its consequences, and therefore are included under the same generical name. Yet diamond is also called a Stone, though it probably contains little Earth of any kind.

CHAP. I.

Of Simple Earths, their number and Characters.

By *simple* Earths, I mean those which possessing permanently distinct characters, are incapable of being further analyzed or changed into any other, by any means hitherto known. Of these, we know only five. The *Calcareous*, the *Ponderous*, the *Magnesian* or *Muriatic*, the *Argillaceous*, and the *Siliceous*. All Stones and Earths hitherto examined, are found to consist of these either singly, or mixed, or chymically united with each other, in various proportions, together with saline, inflammable and metallic substances; for in the Earth they are seldom or ever found perfectly pure.

Of the Characters of Calcareous Earth.

1st. When perfectly pure and free from all combination, it constitutes *lime*; its specific gravity is about 2,3. it has a hot burning taste, acts powerfully on animal substances, and when in lumps, heats with a moderate quantity of water.

$2^{d.}$ In the temperature of 60°. it requires about six hundred and eighty times its weight of water to diffolve it; its tafte is then pungent, urinous, yet fweetifh.

$3^{d.}$ It is combinable with all acids, and in particular eafily foluble in the nitrous or marine, but difficultly cryftalizes with them, as it forms deliquefcent falts, and is in great meafure precipitable from them by the vitriolic, to which it preferably unites, forming gypfum or felenite, which is wholly precipitable from them by the affufion of highly rectified fpirits of wine, or moderate evaporation, nitrous felenite eafily parts with its acid, when calcined in open veffels and a red heat; but marine felenite fcarcely. Both felenites have a bitter tafte.

$4^{th.}$ When in veffels on which it cannot act, it is infufible *per fe* (that is fingly;) in a heat that would melt iron: yet *Mr. Parker's* glafs feems to have induced a flight beginning of fufion in lime, even when it ftood on charcoal, but if mixed with argillaceous, magnefian or filiceous Earths, it will melt in a more moderate heat, and particularly if mixed with two or more of thofe Earths. And hence

hence it is fusible in earthen vessels, even of porcelain; it is scarcely affected by fixed alkalis, but easily melted and without effervescence by borax or microcosmic salt, or calces of lead.

Ponderous Earth.

1st. This may more conveniently be called *Barytes*, when pure it is also in the state of lime, which it perfectly resembles in taste, but it requires nine hundred times its weight of water to dissolve it in the temperature of 60°.

2d. It is combinable with acids, but with the nitrous and marine, it forms salts that do not deliquesce, and with the vitriolic, a salt much more difficultly soluble than gypsum, it decomposes tartar vitrolate, an effect which no other Earth can operate.

3d. It is precipitable from the nitrous and marine acids by the Prussian Alkali, a property which also distinguishes it from all other Earths.

4th. In the dry way it acts and is acted upon nearly as calcareous Earth, but it is something more fusible by the mineral alkali. Its specific gravity exceeds 4,000.

Magnesia or Muriatic Earth

1$^{ft.}$ Its specific gravity when perfectly pure is about 2,33.

2$^{d.}$ It requires about seven thousand six hundred and ninety-two times its weight of water to dissolve it in the common temperature of the air.

3$^{d.}$ It is combinable with acids, and though the vitriolic easily separates it from the nitrous and marine, yet it does not precipitate it, as it does calcareous Earth and barytes, but forms Epsom salt which is bitter and soluble in its own weight of water; whereas with the former Earths it forms insipid and very difficultly soluble compounds.

4$^{th.}$ Exposed to the strongest heat, it will neither burn to lime, nor melt *per se*, but loses much of its weight, partly by evaporation, and partly by the loss of a certain proportion of water, which it naturally retains. Neither will it vitrify in company with any other simple Earth, except the calcareous, of which, according to *Mr. Achard* 100$^{s..}$ will promote the fusion of from twenty-five to fifty of magnesia, it will also melt with argillaceous and siliceous Earths together, and much more readily if calcareous Earth be added to them. Like lime

Argillaceous Earth.

lime it is brought into fusion by borax or microcosmic salt, but is scarcely affected by fixed alkalis, or calces of lead.

Argillaceous Earth or Earth of Alum.

1st. This may more conveniently be called *Argill*, its specific gravity when pure does not exceed 2,000.

2^{d.} It is exceedingly diffusible, but scarcely more soluble in water than pure magnesia.

3^{d.} It is combinable with acids, and when combined with the nitrous or marine, like magnesia it is separable, but scarcely precipitable by the vitriolic acid* with which it forms Alum, which always contains an excess of acid and has an astringent taste; when combined with any of these acids, it is not precipitable by the acid of sugar, which distinquishes it from the foregoing Earths, all of which (except the ponderous united to the vitriolic acid) are precipitable from the vitriolic, nitrous and marine acids, by that of sugar, though the precipitation is not always apparent before the liquors are evaporated, nor at all, if there be an excess of the mineral acids.

* For if concentrated oil of vitriol be droped into a very saturate solution of nitrous or marine Alum, a greyish precipitate will immediately appear.

8 *Elements of Mineralogy.*

4th. The strongest heat barely hardens it, but does not give it the qualities of lime, nor melt it, while single, or accompanied only with magnesia or siliceous Earth; but mixed with calcareous, it runs into fusion very readily, and hence *Mr. Gerhard* has found it fusible in a crucible of chalk, but not in one of clay; fixed alkalis do not promote its fusion, but borax and microcosmic salt dissolve it; the first with scarce any, and the latter with a more notable effervescence. Calces of lead affect it something less than they do calcareous Earths.

Siliceous Earth.

1st. This is by some called crystaline, quartzy, or vitrifiable Earth, as it is that of which glass is usually formed; its specific gravity is 2,65, and consequently it is the heaviest of all the simple Earths, except the barytes.

2d. It seems less soluble in water than any other, yet in the common temperature of the atmosphere ten thousand parts of water may contain one of this Earth; and in very high degrees of heat, much exceeding that at which water usually boils, it seems soluble in a much greater proportion.

3d. It

3ᵈ· It combines with no acid hitherto known, except the sparry, which either in a liquid or aerial state, but particularly in the latter, is capable of holding much of it in solution, which it deposits either on cooling or coming in contact with water, or substances with which it has a greater affinity. But caustic fixed alkalis may even in the liquid way take up from $\frac{1}{10}$ to $\frac{1}{6}$ of their weight of this Earth, according as it is more or less subtilly divided, and hence it is not improbable that even lime-water has some action on it.

4ᵗʰ· It is infusible *per se* in the strongest heat, neither does argillaceous or magnesian Earths promote its fusion, the effect of calcareous Earth is somewhat more doubtful, for *Mr. Achard* * and Mr. *Scheffer*,† assert that these Earths do not melt together, but *Mr. Darcet*,‡ and also Mr. *Bergman*,§ and Mr. *Swab*, ‖ say that two parts lime melt one of quartz; at least there is no doubt but this may be effected in vessels of clay, for an admixture of this will make the other two Earths immediately yield. Fixed alkalis, particularly the mineral, readily melt double their weight of this Earth with effervescence, borax affects it more difficultly, and with scarce any effervescence, and microcosmic salt has hardly any action

* Mem. Berlin, 1780, p. 32. † Foreles. § 175, b.
‡ 22 Roz. p. 27. § Scheff. Foreles, § 175, b. 2 Anmerk.
‖ 2 Memoires d'Upsal, p. 443.

on it; calces of lead act on it more powerfully than on argill, but less than on calcareous Earth, and melt from $\frac{1}{3}$ to $\frac{1}{2}$ their weight of it.

The calcareous, ponderous magnesian and argillaceous Earths being combinable with all acids, may be called *absorbent* Earths, in contradistinction to the siliceous, which unites only to the sparry acid.

Besides the general characters of these Earths, here given, *Mr. Bergman* has observed and noted their different powers of absorbing and retaining water; after moistening equal weights of siliceous sand, chalk, magnesia, and Earth of alum, with as much water as they could take up without dropping, he found that the sand took $\frac{1}{4}$ of its weight, chalk $\frac{1}{2}$, magnesia $1\frac{1}{20}$, and Earth of alum $2,\frac{1}{2}$, and when all these moistened Earths were exposed to the same heat, the sand lost its water first, then the chalk, then the magnesia, but the argill, not until red-hot.

Again one of the characters of argillaceous Earth is the extreme subtility and fineness of its integrant parts, which render it smooth to the touch, and slowly separable from water when diffused through it, also a certain viscidity

Affinities of Earths. 11

dity and ductility which proceed from its power of retaining water, and of these properties magnesia also participates though in a lesser degree. Siliceous Earths on the contrary are characterised by roughness, hardness, sharpness to the touch, and a total want of flexibility and adherence to each other, when minutely divided, and a ready separation from water; of these properties calcareous and ponderous Earths participate, though in a lesser degree.

CHAP II.

Of the Affinities of Earths to each other.

The above mentioned Earths are never found in nature perfectly pure, but always combined or mixed either with a saline or inflammable principle, or with each other, or with some metallic principle, particularly iron, besides water; when mixed with any notable proportion of the inflammable or metallic principles, or even of the saline, so as to exhibit the characters of such principles, they shall be treated of under those particular heads; I shall here consider only such compounds as retain the general characters of Earths, and as in conformity with *Mr. Cronsted*, I intend deducing the various *species* of Earths from their union either with saline principles or with each other, it will be necessary to indicate the affinities on which such unions are founded;

founded; the affinities of Earths to acids are generally known, but those of Earths to each other and to calces of iron have no where been treated of; and therefore require some developement.—The efforts of art can scarcely exhibit in the *humid* way, the affinities of Earths to each other, if this could be effected, we should probably find the same election and preference take place among them as among Earths and acids, we are therefore obliged to have recourse to the *dry* way, which is much more imperfect: for as they are all reduced by fire to a state of liquidity, they differ but little in specific gravity, and can difficultly be examined while in fusion, when cold they are all found so mixed that it is not possible to judge of their affinities by the way of preference and exclusion; but if we judge of these affinities as we do of that of water to salts, by the greater or the lesser quantity which one of them considered as a menstruum, can take up of another or what proportion of the one determines the fusion of another, we may in that manner form a tolerably accurate idea of their different attractive powers.

Among the simple Earths, the calcareous alone,* can be looked upon as the menstru-

* Perhaps the ponderous may also have this property, but it being scarce, no experiments have yet been made with a view to determine this point.

um

Affinities of Earths. 13

um of other Earths, for according to the important difcovery of *Mr. D'Arcet*, they are all rendered fufible by a proper proportion of this Earth, though infufible of themfelves. A difcovery which throws the greateft light, not only on mineralogy, but alfo on metallurgy and the arts of vitrifaction and pottery; now calcareous Earth requires for its fufion half its weight of magnefia, and only $\frac{1}{4}$ of its weight of argillaceous Earth, according to the experiments of *Mr. Achard*.† He did not indeed obferve that it had any effect on filiceous Earth, but this appears to be owing to his having ufed too fmall a proportion of the calcareous, for *Mr. Gerhard*‡ having expofed filiceous Earth to a violent heat in a crucible of chalk, found it vitrified in the edges where it touched the chalk, but we may infer that this Earth is lefs acted upon and more difficultly than the foregoing; even in the liquid way, calcareous Earth in fome cafes manifefts the fame affinities, thus if Earth of alum perfectly pure be added to lime water, it will precipitate the lime as *Mr. Scheele* has fhewn in the Memoirs of Stockholm, for 1776, and the precipitate is foluble in the marine acid, which fhews that the precipitation does not arife from any remains of the vitriolic acid in the Earth of

---

† Mem. Berlin, 1780.   ‡ 2 Gefch. Mineral Reich.

alum,

alum, as gypsum in that case would be formed, which is insoluble in the marine acid, but pure magnesia, that is, free from aerial acid, does not precipitate lime water.

Siliceous Earth seems also to have some affinity to the argillaceous, for although it cannot be brought into fusion by the argillaceous, yet when melted by fixed alkalis it acts on the argillaceous Earth of the crucibles and dissolves it; now fixed alkalis singly, cannot melt argillaceous Earth; to say nothing of the hardening power of argill and siliceous Earths, when mixed together and heated.

Iron in a more or less dephlogisticated state, being found in some proportion mixed or united with almost all sorts of Earths and Stones, deserves also to have its affinities to them mentioned, it is much more fusible than any of them, and may therefore be considered as a menstruum. *Mr. Achard* has found that an hundred parts of calx of iron are capable of melting four hundred of calcareous, fifty of argillaceous, thirty-three of siliceous and twenty-five of magnesian Earths, it acts still more powerfully on lesser proportions of these Earths.

Hence,

Affinities of Earths.

Hence the affinities of these Earths, and calces of iron to each other, seem to me to stand in the following order.

Lime,	Magnesia,	Argill,	Silex,	Calx of Iron.
Calx of Iron,	Lime,	Calx of Iron,	Calx of Iron,	Lime,
Argill,	Calx of Iron,	Lime,	Lime,	Argill,
Magnesia,		Silex,	Argill,	Silex,
Silex,				Magnesia.

When substances are dissolved and at liberty, their affinities whether in the moist or dry way, are exactly the same, they being equally divided; and the only difference is, that in one case, they are dissolved by fire, in the other by a liquid. We may also observe, 1st, that the less calces of iron are dephlogisticated, the greater is their power of attracting Earths as *Mr. Rinman* has discovered, and when dephlogisticated to a certain degree, they lose this power, their colour according to the degree of their dephlogistication is as follows, whitish, pale yellow, yellow, red, brown, green, and blue. 2dly. That when once lime or calces of iron have acted as menstruums upon any Earth, a compound menstruum arises, which acts much more powerfully on other Earths; thus, though one hundred parts of lime can dissolve or liquify very little of silex, yet when these hundred parts of lime have taken up fifty of magnesia, they are enabled to dissolve one hundred of silex, and

this

this laft compound forms a menftruum ftill more compound, which is able to diffolve ftill more of magnefia, for equal parts lime, magnefia, and filex form a perfect glafs; and hence equal parts of any three of the fimple Earths will vitrify in a fufficient heat, fo that calcareous Earth be one of the three; nay one part lime and one of argill will melt 2 or 2½ of filex, and other mixtures are more or lefs fufible as they approach to this proportion.

The principal marks of Chymical Union are the following.

1$^{ft.}$ *A fpecific gravity* exceeding that of the heavieft of the ingredients of the compound, or even greater than the intermediate. But it does not follow that, where fuch denfity is wanting, a chymical union does not exift, for the peculiar ftructure of the compound which does not admit water into its vacuities may hinder this property from being obferved, fo may alfo a certain quantity of water which enters into the compofition, and cannot always be made fenfible.

2$^{d.}$ *Tranfparency*, when this property is found in combinations of Earths with each other, or with faline fubftances, it indicates a chymical union; but fuch an union is alfo
consistent

consistent with opacity, as this may arise from a mere mechanical arrangement of the parts, or the interposition of some that are not chymically combined, too great thickness, &c.

3ᵈ· *Cryſtalization.* This proves that the parts of the chryſtalized ſubſtances have been at ſome period very minutely divided; and in general that they have been chymically combined with the menſtruum, in which they chryſtallized; though I agree with *Mr. Bergman* that a chymical union with ſuch a menſtruum is not always requiſite; but it does not prove that they were chymically combined with any other ſubſtance which chryſtallizes with them, except ſome other mark of ſuch union appears, and particularly a denſity greater than could be expected from the proportion and denſity of the component parts.

4ᵗʰ· *A more difficult Solubility* in their common menſtruums, and of courſe a ſtill greater difficulty of ſolution in menſtruums, that act only on one of the component parts. Of this there are numberleſs inſtances, yet there is one exception, viz. where one of the component parts is reſolvable by the action of the menſtruum into an elaſtic fluid, which by its eruption ſo powerfully agitates and

divides

divides the compound, as to render it more soluble. Thus lime-stone, and mild magnesia, are more easily dissolved than either lime or calcined magnesia. On the other hand, some metallic calces are more easily dissolved in certain acids, than they are when furnished with phlogiston, though this also be resolvable into an elastic fluid; but this I have elsewhere explained. The calces of iron are so much the more difficultly dissolved, as they are more dephlogisticated; hence the whitish calx is most difficultly dissolved; and next to that the yellowish and red; but the brown, green, and blue, most easily; and hence, stones which contain dephlogisticated calces of iron and unareated Earths, are most difficultly dissolved, though the calces are not so strongly attracted by the Earths, nor consequently the stones so hard, as those that contain iron in a more phlogisticated state. This accounts for the difficult solubility of talc, mica, &c.

CHAP. III.
Of the Systematical Arrangement of Earths and Stones.

All Earths may be divided into simple and compound. Simple are the five unalterable kinds already described, which constitute five sorts or *genera*, under which all terrene compounds may be ranged.

By

By *Compound Earths*, I underſtand thoſe that are combined or mixed in a *notable* proportion, either with each other, or with a ſaline, inflammable, or metallic principle, yet not in ſufficient proportion to require them to be arranged under ſuch foreign principles. Such compounds being permanent, and being the foundation of a peculiar denomination, I call *ſpecies*, and ſimple ſpecies, in order to diſtinguiſh them from ſuper compounds, which will preſently be mentioned. Thus *gypſum* is a compound Earth, conſiſting of calcareous Earth, and a ſaline principle, not accidentally, but permanently mixed with it. So alſo tourmaline is a compound Earth, conſiſting of the argillaceous, ſiliceous, and calcareous, and iron, in proportions determined within certain limits, and forms a ſimple ſpecies. I ſaid a *notable* proportion, becauſe it is difficult to aſſign this proportion with preciſion; for it relates to denominations of ſubſtances, and theſe are founded on the neceſſity of diſtinction, ariſing ſometimes from the uſefulneſs of ſubſtances to mankind, and ſometimes from caprice. Thus, a compound Earth, which ſhould conſiſt of calcareous Earth, and only two per cent. of gold or ſilver, would be denominated an *ore*, whereas, if it contained only two per cent. of iron, or of another Earth, it would ſtill retain the name of, and be reckoned among, calcareous Earths. However, in general we may

may fay, that any proportion which produces peculiar effects, or is the foundation of some particular use, is *notable*. When iron is found in any Earth or Stone, in the proportion of 14 or 15 per cent. it commonly renders it magnetic, either before or after torrefaction, according to its state of phlogistication; and if it be found in the proportion of 30 per cent. or more, it gives the compound the denomination of an *ore*. To stones that contain a greater quantity of iron than is essential to them in the purest state, I add the denomination *martial*, or *ferruginous*.

When simple Earths, belonging to different *genera*, are mixed or combined with each other, I generally place them under that *genus* of which the compound contains the largest proportion, yet not always, for if the compound possesses the peculiar characters of the component part, which is in a smaller proportion; or if it attracts the attention, and is subservient to the uses of mankind, merely on account of the less copious ingredient, I range it under the *genus* of that ingredient. Thus, though common clay contains much more of siliceous than of mere argillaceous Earth, yet, as it possesses smoothness, viscidity, and softness, in a high degree, it would appear ridiculous to place it under the siliceous genus, whose characters are the very reverse. For the same reason, I place the precious

Earths and Stones.

precious stones under the siliceous genus, though the argillaceous be, in point of proportion, predominant in their composition.

By *super-compound* Earths or Stones, I mean aggregates of *visibly different simple species*, in a notable proportion, whether these species belong to the same, or to different *genera*. Thus I would call a compound of gypsum and fluor spar a super-compound, though both belong to the calcareous genus; and *a fortiori* granites and porphyries, which form aggregates of simple species belonging to different *genera*. Super-compounds, therefore, form *compound species*, which may be ranged under that genus which is found in them in greater proportion. In general they may be known by the eye, at least when aided by a lens.

In strictness, Earths of different *genera*, each of which contain the aerial acid, should, when mixed with each other, constitute a compound species, yet, as this acid is easily expelled, and causes no great difference in the properties of the compound, and as in fact absorbent Earths, when combined with no other saline principle, are seldom without it, I shall rank those compounds among the simple species, and so I shall quartz and silex, though seldom absolutely pure.

CHAP.

CHAP. IV.

Calcareous Genus.

SPECIES 1.

Calcareous Earth, uncombined with any Acid.

This ſtone is of a grey colour, moderately hard, or rather ſoft, found near Bath; it is mixed with calcareous Earth combined with fixed air; and hence it efferveſces with acids, but at the ſame time it is ſoluble in water, to which it communicates the taſte of lime; and if this ſolution be mixed with ſulphur, it diſſolves it, and forms a calcareous liver of ſulphur, with the aſſiſtance of heat; whence it is plain that part of the calcareous earth is in an uncombined ſtate. See *Falconer* on Bath Waters, vol. i. p. 156 and 257. When expoſed to the air for ſome time, it hardens, by attracting a ſufficiency of the aerial acid. I have obſerved ſeveral lime-ſtones to have the ſame property of hardening ſome time after they have been dug. *Mr. Monnet* alſo found this Earth in a looſe, dry, powdery form, of a yellowiſh colour, in the mountains of Auvergne, and ſuſpected it to be of volcanic origin. *Mineralogie*, p. 515.

SPECIES

Species II.

Combined with the Aerial Acid.

This species comprehends a great variety of external appearances, the most remarkable of which are transparency and opacity, hence I shall divide it into two series, the transparent and opake; all effervesce with acids; none give fire with steel; the chrystalized decrepitate when heated.

Series I.

Transparent Spars.

These are of a lamellar texture, and mostly break or split into rhomboidal laminæ; and this structure is generally called spathose, or sparry. They are found crystallized in various forms, rhomboidal, hexangular, triangular, polyangular; but the most common is the rhomboidal, of which sort is the Iceland crystal, which possesses a double refracting power.

Their specific gravity is generally about 2,700, when pure from metallic particles; and they generally contain from 34 to 36 per cent. of the aerial acid, from 53 to 55 of mere Earth, and the remainder water.

24   *Elements of Mineralogy.*

These spars when pure are always colourless, but sometimes they are found green, brown, reddish, yellowish, and even black, from a mixture of metallic particles.

De la Hire and *Huygens,* denote rhomboidal spar under the name of talc.

SERIES II.

Opake.

Under this series I range a variety of stones of the same species, but which are known under various denominations arising from external properties, or the apparent mode of their origination; such as opake-spars, stalactites, tophuses, incrustations, petrifactions, agaric-mineral, chalk, limestone, marble.

Opake Spars.

These are chrystalized under the same regular forms as the transparent spars, and sometimes appear in a globular form; their texture is also lamellar, they are of different colours like the foregoing; the red frequently receive that tinge from manganese. 16 *Roz.* 15.

Stalactites,

Stalactites, Sinter Calcareum, Stiria.

These are found suspended from vaults, being formed by the oozing of water charged with calcareous particles, and gradually evaporating, leaving those particles behind; this deposition can scarce be called a chrystalization, as the calcareous particles do not appear to have been dissolved, nor even very minutely divided, though this sometimes happens, whereas transparent spars appear to have been formed from a solution in water, by means of the aerial acid. Stalactites are of a lamellar or granular texture, and either in a branchy form, or in that of perforated cones, or globular, and then called *stalagmites, oolithes, pisolites*, &c. Most of these stones contain a slight mixture of argill and calx of iron. And hence are of a grey, brown, yellow, or blackish colour.

Tophi, Duckstein of the Germans, Pori.

These differ from the former, not only in shape, but principally in this, that they have been formed by a gradual deposition of Earths, chiefly of the calcareous kind, barely diffused through water, within the water itself and not in air. Hence they are of a soft and porous texture, and of the same colour

colour as the foregoing, the pureſt ſorts alone are placed here.

Calcareous Incruſtations.

Theſe are generally found on branches or roots of trees, and ſometimes on ſtones of different kinds, the moſt remarkable of theſe incruſtations is that found on the roots of pines, called *Oſteocolla,* which Mr. *Margraaf* found to conſiſt chiefly of calcareous Earth, mixed with a ſmall proportion of ſiliceous, and volatile alkali, together with ſome vegetable parts.

Calcareous Petrifactions.

Theſe conſiſt of calcareous ſtones, in the form of animal or vegetable ſubſtances, the former are called *Zoophytes,* the latter *Phytholites.*

The moſt remarkable of the former are, 1ſt, Thoſe of the *Coral* claſs, of a ramified and tubular form as coral, madrepores, millepores, aſtroites. 2d, Thoſe of the claſs of ſea worms, belemnites, which are of a conic or cylyndrical form. *Aſteriæ* and *Entrochi,* which have a ſtarry appearance. 3d, Thoſe of the teſtaceous claſs, as *nautilites, ammonites, echini,* &c.

Agaric

Agaric Mineral, Guhr.

This fanciful name denotes only a loose calcareous Earth found in the clefts or cavities of rocks, mostly white, but sometimes red or yellow, from a mixture of clay or ochre.

Chalk, Craie, Craie de Champagne, blanc d'Espagne of the French.

This substance is too well known to need any description, the purest is *white*, yet it contains a little siliceous Earth, and about two per cent. of argill. Mr. *Rinman's* History of Iron, § 201, mentions a blue chalk found in the neighbourhood of *Upsal*, which contains iron. Mr. *Beaumé* says that the purest calcareous Earths he has met with contain some small proportion of iron, which deposits from solutions long made. 1 *Beaumé* 255. however I have frequently used chalk, in whose solution neither galls nor Prussian alkali could discover any. Dry chalk contains more aerial acid than any other of the calcareous class; generally about forty per cent. its specific gravity is from 2,4, to 2,65.

Limestones, *Albarese of the Italians.*

All stones which are usually burned to lime, are comprehended under this name; some are of a lamellar and some of a granular texture; their colours are various, the purest are white, grey, or bluish grey, their proportion of aerial acid is something greater than that in spars, and all contain some small proportion of argill, quartz and iron. 18 *Roz.* 345, Mr. *Meyer* asserts, that in the purest limestones he has examined, these foreign ingredients amounted to about four per cent. he also says that he has found marine Epsom and sea salt in some small proportion in all of them. 1 *Meyer*, 5, 20, and 21. Some limestones found in *Scania*, contain orpiment according to *Scheffer's* account. Among limestones we may reckon, that called St. Stephen's stone by *Cartheuser* and *Vogel*, because it has some red spots on its surface resembling blood; the lamellar limestones usually contain petrifactions, chiefly of marine animals and also shells; the specific gravity of limestones is from 2,65, to 2,70, generally.

Ketton Stone is a remarkable species of limestone, consisting of very small globules like the roe of fish, concreted together. Hence

Calcareous Genus.

Hence its specific gravity is only 2,456, and it is called *Hammites*, it contains ninety per cent. of mild calcareous Earth, and ten per cent. of argillaceous Earth so firmly united to red calx of iron, as to be difficultly soluble even in aqua regia; the proportion of iron is not above one per cent. in this stone, and yet it sensibly colours it.

Portland Stone, and *Purbeck* Stone belong also to this class, the specific gravity of the former is 2,533, and of the latter 2,680, according to the experiments of Dr. *Watson*, who accordingly found that the latter afforded more lime, 2 *Watson's* Essays, 190. Portland Stone is of a dull white colour, loose open porous texture, easily cut, and contains a small proportion of silex. *Bath* Stone resembles the Portland, but its texture is more granular and open; its specific gravity 2,494.

Calcareous Flag-stone, otherwise called calcareous schistus. That found near *Woodstock*, and used for covering houses, is of a yellowish white colour and moderately hard, its specific gravity is 2,585, contains a little clay and more iron than the *Portland* Stone.

Marbles.

Marbles.

Opake ſtones of any ſort, ſomething harder than limeſtones, more compact, of a cloſer grain and ſuſceptible of a good poliſh, have been called *Marble* by ſtatuaries, but this name is now appropriated to ſtones of the above deſcription, of the calcareous genus only. The ſpecific gravity of Marbles is from 2,7 to 2,8, their texture like that of limeſtones is either lamellar or granular and their colours various, not only in different maſſes, but in one and the ſame piece; theſe laſt will be mentioned among the compound ſpecies: when the different ſpecies are in large diſtinct maſſes they are called *Breccias*, Marbles of three colours, grey, yellow, and black; which abound in petrifactions, are called *lumachellis*; thoſe of four colours, white, grey, yellow and red, are called *Brocatello's*. I ſhall here only mention the purer ſorts that contain the leaſt mixture of foreign genera.

White Marble, particularly that of *Carrara*, is the pureſt with which we are acquainted; it is of a granular texture and ſparkling in its fracture like ſugar; its ſpecific gravity is 2,7175, of this ſort is the *Pietra Elaſtica* of *Rome*. Ferber, *Italy*, 130. Other white marbles are not ſo pure, many are of a lamellar texture.

Black.

Black. This colour is commonly owing to a flight mixture of Iron. Mr. *Bayen* found one fpecimen of it to contain five per cent. of iron, yet the lime made of it was at firft white, but in time acquired an ochry, or reddifh yellow colour, 11 Roz. 496.

Mr. *Bergman* remarks, that all calcareous ftones which grow black or brown by calcination, may be fufpected to contain manganefe, in that cafe the lime they form is excellent as a cement. 2 *Bergman*, 229. And according to *Rinman* (Hiftory of Iron, § 189,) white calcareous ftones, that grow black by calcination, contain about ten per cent. of iron.

Grey. This fort of marble contains lefs iron, only one or two per cent. according to Mr. *Bayen.*

Blue and *Green* marbles derive their colour from a mixture of fhorl, according to Mr. *Rinman, Hiftoria ferri.* § 201. 206.

Species III.

Combined with the Vitriolic Acid.
Gypfum, Selenite, Plaifter of Paris.

This fpecies is of different colours, moftly white or grey, of a lamellar, granular, or fibrous

fibrous texture, of a moderate hardnefs, not fo great as to give fire with fteel; fometimes opake, fometimes pellucid, fometimes regularly chryftalized, and fometimes amorphous.

Its fpecific gravity is 2,32 generally, fometimes only 1,87.

It is foluble in about five hundred times its weight of water, at the temperature of fixty. It does not effervefce with acids, and is difficultly foluble in any, particularly in the marine.

When heated a little below ignition, it undergoes a motion fimilar to that of ebullition, from the diffipation of its aqueous part, and falls into powder; if taken up when this motion ceafes, and fprinkled over with water, it foon concretes and hardens, by reafon of its fudden chryftalization.

If calcined with ¼ of its weight of charcoal, it yields a liver of fulphur, and the Earth thus feparated, treated with black flux, frequently yields a little of Iron: it is fufible *per fe* by the blow pipe. 2 *Bergman*, 469, or in a long continued porcelain heat, 22 *Roz.* 26, though Mr. *Gerhard* fays this does not happen in crucibles of chalk, but only in thofe of clay. 2 *Gerh. Gefch.* 16.

It

It contains about 30 per cent. vitriolic acid, 32 of mere Earth, and 38 of water; of which it parts with about 20 by calcination. The beſt method of decompoſing it is to boil it, well pulverized, in a fixed alkaline lye.

The varieties of its external appearances may be preſented under two ſeries, the tranſparent and opake.

Series I.

Tranſparent.

Lapis Specularis, Vitrum Ruthenicum, Glacies Mariæ, Stirium Pellucidum, Gypſum Spathoſum Diaphanum.

This is either colourleſs, or yellowiſh, green, or reddiſh; which laſt colour is from iron, as *Mr. Morveau* has, by means of vinegar, completely ſeparated it. Its form is either amorphous, or regular, generally cubic; its texture lamellar, ſcaly, or fibrous.

Series II.

Opake.

The colour of this is either white, grey, yellowiſh, greeniſh, or black; its texture ſcaly,

scaly, fibrous, or granular; its shape either regular as cubic, rhomboidal, or prismatic, consisting of three or five sides; or amorphous, of which sort is *alabaster*, whose texture is granular, with shining particles, and its specific gravity 1,87.

Species III.

Combined with the Sparry Acid.

Fluor, Spathum fusibile, Petunse of Margraaf, 2 *Theil.* p. 45, *Blue John.*

Its colours are various, being either white, yellow, blue, green, reddish, purple, brown, or colourless; its texture sparry or shattery; its form either amorphous or regular; its hardness not so great as to give fire with steel; its specific gravity from 3,14 to 3,18; if greater it proceeds from a large proportion of metallic or other foreign particles.

It is insoluble in water, does not effervesce with acids, and is scarcely soluble in them without decomposition.

When heated it decrepitates and bursts, but does not yield lime, nor harden by the affusion of water, as gypsums do. The coloured fluors become phosphorescent when heated slowly,

slowly, below ignition, but lose this property when made red hot, and also on cooling. It melts *per se* in a strong heat, and violently attacks the crucibles, as it powerfully promotes the fusion of argillaceous Earths. It is also fusible with mineral alkali, borax or microcosmic salt, and without effervescence. It consists of the sparry acid, water, and calcareous Earth. According to Mr. *D'Arcet,* the acid is in the proportion of 16 per cent. 22 *Roz.* 24. and according to Mr. *Scheele,* 100 gr. of fluor contain about 57 of mere Earth, and consequently about 27 of water; but I believe it contains much less water, and much more acid, for a great deal of the acid pierces through the luting during distillation.

It is decomposed by distilling it with three times its weight of concentrated vitriolic acid, but to obtain the sparry acid pure, it should be distilled with its own weight of that concentrated acid pure and colourless, at first with a gentle, and towards the end with a strong heat, placing water in the receiver, in the proportion of 10 or 12 times the weight of the spar. The nitrous and marine acids decompose it if dilute, but not when these acids are concentrated.

Blue fluors derive their colour mostly from iron, but sometimes from cobalt. 2 *Berlin. Beschaft.*

Beschaft. 330; and in fact, iron, precipitated from the sparry acid by lime water, is white, with blue specks. Green fluors owe also their colour to iron. *Rinman,* § 206.

Most fluors contain a mixture of argillaceous and siliceous Earths, and some marine acid. The siliceous Earth, which sublimes in distilling these spars, arise, from the solution of that pre-contained in the spar, or from the corrosion of the glass vessels, as Messrs. *Mayer* and *Wiegleb* have shewn; this acid possessing the singular property of dissolving siliceous Earths, and consequently glass.

The varieties of this species may be reduced to two, the transparent and opake; of which there are necessarily many intermediate shades.

Series I.

Transparent.

These are generally of a regular shape, cubic, rhomboidal, polygonal, and of different colours; and hence called pseudo-emeralds, sapphires, topazes, amethysts, &c.— Some are amorphous.

Series II.

Series II.

Opake.

These are distinguished by the same colours; their texture also is generally the same, but it is said to be sometimes granular; their form is also regular, or amorphous, like the foregoing.

The phosphorescent property of fluors seems to arise not from the acid singly, otherwise all fluors would possess it, but from the acid, in contact with metallic particles, and consequently from the acid and phlogiston.

Species IV.

Combined with the Tungsten Acid.

Tungsten, Lapis Ponderosus, Schwerere Zingraupen of the Germans.

When pure it is of a grey colour and lamellar texture, gives fire with steel, and is very weighty, its specific gravity being from 4,99 to 5,8.

It is insoluble in acids, except by peculiar management; when powdered and digested with

with the nitrous or marine, it assumes a yellow colour, as Mr. *Woulfe* first observed. *Phil. Transf.* 1779, p. 26.

When heated it bursts, becomes reddish, melts very difficultly *per se*; nay, according to Mr. *Bergman*, it is infusible with the blow pipe, and not totally fusible even with the assistance of fixed alkali, but easily by borax, and without effervescence. It also easily melts with its own weight of fluor.

Its constituent parts were discovered by Mr. *Bergman* and Mr. *Scheele*, nearly at the same time, but first published by Mr. *Scheele* in the Swedish Memoirs for 1781. It appears to contain about ½ its weight of calcareous Earth, and the remainder a peculiar acid of an earthy appearance, and iron.

This acid is separated from its earthy basis, by digesting the powdered stone in three times its weight of nitrous acid, and after pouring off this acid, and edulcorating the residuum, digesting it again in caustic volatile alkali, after some time the alkali is also poured off, and the residuum being edulcorated, is again digested in nitrous acid, and afterwards in volatile alkali: These successive digestions are continued until the greater part of the stone disappears, the nitrous acid constantly taking

Calcareous Genus. 39

taking up the calcareous Earth, and the volatile alkali uniting to the tungſten acid; at laſt the tungſten acid is precipitated from the volatile alkali in the form of a white powder, by ſaturating the alkali with any other acid. This powder is ſoluble in 20 times its weight of boiling water, and then reddens litmus, has an acid taſte, and with lime water produces a regenerated tungſten; its ſpecific gravity is about 3,600.

Species V.

Mild Calcareous Earth mixed with a notable Proportion of Magneſia.

I. Variety.

Compound Spar.

This ſtone is deſcribed by Mr. *Woulfe. Phil. Tranſ.* 1779, p. 29. It is there ſaid to be either white and ſemitranſparent, or of a pearl colour, or reddiſh, or of different ſhades of brown or yellow, of a peculiar gloſs or brightneſs, like gold, braſs, or copper; and to conſiſt of flat, ſolid, and rhomboidal chryſtals, and harder than calcareous ſpars. It effervesces with acids.

One hundred parts of it contain 60 of mild calcareous Earth, 35 of mild muriatic, and

5 of iron: the iron appears to be accidental, and its quantity greater or smaller, according to the colour of the stone.

II. Variety.

Creutzenwald Stone.

This stone is mentioned, but not described by Mr. *Bayen*. 13 *Roz.* 59. It is probably of a brown, or yellowish colour, and great weight; it contains by Mr. *Bayen*'s account, 75 *per cent.* mild calcareous Earth, 12 mild magnesia, and 13 of iron. It is found near *Creutzenwald*, and there used as a flux for iron ores.

Species VI.

Mild Calcareous Earth mixed with a notable Proportion of Clay.

I. Variety.

In a loose Form. Calcareous Marl.

Marl is well known from its use in agriculture. I distinguish two sorts of it, the calcareous and the argillaceous; it is of various colours, grey, yellow, red, brown, or bluish; these arise from a mixture either of iron or pyrites. The calcareous strongly effervesces

Calcareous Genus. 41

fervefces with acids; it is of different degrees of hardnefs, and readily burfts and falls into powder in water, or by expofure to the air. When the calcareous Earth is in large proportion it burns to lime, and even vitrifies in a ftronger heat. The proportion of mild calcareous Earth is from 50 to 75 or 80 per cent. if greater it fhould rather be claffed among chalks. Hence any Earth of this fort, that lofes from 16 to 27 parts of its weight per cent. by folution in acids, may be deemed a calcareous marl, this being the weight of the volatilized fixed air which correfponds with the above proportion of calcareous Earth. Note alfo, that by *clay* I mean common clay, that is, a mixture of argill and filiceous Earth, in which this latter moftly predominates. See Dr. *Withering's* Differtation. *Phil. Tranf.* 1773, p. 161, and 3. *Edinb. Effays*, p. 4.

II. VARIETY.

In a Stony Form.

Travertino, Pietra Forte, Pietra Fongaia of the Italians. Margodes.

The two firft differ only in hardnefs; they are of a grey, blue, or yellow colour; the firft loofe and porous, the fecond harder; the third is a tufa, which, containing the feeds of mufhrooms, produces them yearly, on being fprinkled sprinkled with water. *Ferber Italy,* 117, 159. They are often formed of volcanic ashes, indurated by water, and evidently contain some proportion of iron; the two first are used as lime stones. The *pietra colombina,* and *turchina,* are said to be of this sort.

Analogous to these is the *margodes,* a bluish grey stone, entirely resembling clay in its outward appearance, but so hard as to cut spars, or even zeolytes, but not to such a degree as to give fire with steel; dull in its fracture, its texture thick laminæ, and of a conchoidal form; its specific gravity 2,877; it effervesces with acids. I found it to contain 50 per cent. of calcareous Earth, about 32 of argill, 15 of silex, and 2 of iron.

Mr. *Bergman,* in his remarks on the mountains of *West Gothland, Memoirs of Stockholm,* 1768, mentions a sort of red marble found near *Roloock,* which contains so much clay that it hardens in fire, and even melts in a strong heat,

Species VII.

Mild Calcareous Earth mixed with a notable Proportion of Ponderous Earth.

Barytical Limestone, or *Marl.*

This is said to be found both in a stony and loose form in *Derbyshire;* the former is said

said to be of a grey colour, and heavier than common lime-stones, but I have seen none of them.

Species VIII.

Mild Calcareous Earth mixed with a notable Proportion of Siliceous Earth.

I. Variety.

Stellated Spar, Stern Spath, Stern Schoerl of the Germans.

This is opake, and of a radiated form, found in limestone by Mr. *Fichtel* on the *Carpathian Mountains*. It effervesces with acids, and according to Mr. *Bindheim*, 100 parts of it contain 66 mild calcareous Earth, 30 of siliceous, and 3 of iron. 3 *Schrift. Naturforsch. Freunde*, p. 454.

II. Variety.

Calcareous Grit, Calcareous Sand-stone, Calcarius Arenarius, Pierre de Taille Calcaire, Moellon, Pierre de Liais. Monnet *Mineralogie*, p. 216.

Its colour is various, but mostly white, grey, brown, or of different shades of yellow: it effervesces with acids, and is more or less soluble in them, according to the proportion

portion of mild calcareous Earth, which alfo varies, from 50 to 70 or 80 per cent. when lefs, it fhould be reckoned among the filiceous fand-ftones.

It frequently contains alfo a fmall proportion of argill, and a ftill fmaller of iron. Its furface is generally rough; its texture moftly granular, but fometimes fcaly: it does not ftrike fire with fteel; it is fometimes ufed as a limeftone; it hardens by expofure to the air; it is frequently fprinkled over with mica, but not in fuch proportion as to alter its genus or fpecies. The fand-ftone of *St. Helena*, which is very brittle, and burns to lime, is of this fpecies.

SPECIES IX.

Mild Calcareous Earth mixed with Petrol in fmall Proportion.

Swine-ftone, Pierre Puante, Stinkfteine, Lapis Suillus, Orften of the Swedes.

The colour of this ftone is either white, grey, yellowifh, brown, or black, with glittering particles; its texture granular, fcaly, or lamellar; its form either round or prifmatic, and polygon or amorphous; its grain compact and equable, or loofe and open; its fpecific gravity confequently from two to three;

three; its hardness not so great as to give fire with steel.

It is soluble with effervescence in acids, but its most distinctive character is the offensive urinous smell it gives when rubbed: it loses this smell when heated sufficiently, and gives a slight flame when surrounded with burning coals, and at last burns to lime.

It affords little or no oil by distillation.

It frequently contains a little argillaceous Earth and Iron, and moulders by exposure to the air.

Species X.

Mild Calcareous Earth mixed with a notable Proportion of Pyrites.

Pyritaceous Limestone, Pierre de St. Ambroix.

This stone was analysed by Baron *Servieres*, 21 *Roz.* 394. 22 *Roz.* 207. Its colour is iron grey, interspersed with shining particles. Its texture compact; its hardness such as scarcely to give fire with steel; its specific gravity 2,7034.

It is soluble in acids, and mostly with effervescence.

It

46   *Elements of Mineralogy.*

It calcines in a strong heat, and makes nitre slightly detonnate. If distilled, it affords a small portion of vitriolic acid, and some sulphur sublimes.

It consists of about 75 per cent. mild calcareous Earth, and 25 of pyrites, which contains 14 of argill, 7 of quartz and sulphur, and 4 of iron.

Species XI.

Mixed with a notable Proportion of Iron.

I. Variety.

Mild Calcareous Earth mixed with Iron.

These stones are either yellowish white, or red: the former are of a scaly texture, and grow black when exposed to the air, very weighty, effervesce with acids, and contain about 25 per cent. of iron; the latter are of a coarse grain, slightly effervesce with acids, lose 30 per cent. by calcination, and contain 10 per cent. of iron. Some stalactites also contain from 20 to 27 per cent of iron. *Rinman Mem. Stock.* 1754. Other iron stones of this species, containing more iron, belong to the calcareous iron ores.

II. Variety.

II. Variety.

Tungsten intimately mixed with Iron.

Red or Flesh-coloured Tungsten.

It does not effervesce with acids, scarcely gives fire with steel; is of a coarse texture, easily pulverized: its specific gravity from 4,9 to 5,8; becomes magnetic after calcination; easily melted with its own weight of fluor; with great difficulty affords about 30 per cent. of iron. *Cronsted. Mem. Stock.* 1751. Hence it is never used as an iron ore.

Compound Species, in which the Calcareous Genus predominates.

Species I.

Compounds of the different simple Species of the Calcareous Genus.

Here I place all the different compounds of mild calcareous Earth and gypsum, or fluor, or tungsten, &c. which may occur; also those of gypsum and fluor, gypsum and tungsten, or fluor and tungsten, &c. which may be placed as varieties of this compound species.

Species II.

Species II.

Compounds of Calcareous and Barytical Species.

I have seen yellowish stones of this species from *Derbyshire*, consisting of lumps of chalk interspersed with nodules of baroselenite: many more may occur, as compounds of gypsum and baroselenite, fluor and baroselenite, &c.

Species III.

Compounds of the Calcareous and Muriatic Species.

Under this head I range all the compounds of mild calcareous Earth, or fluor, or gypsum, which contain steatites, serpentine, talc, amianthus or asbestos. Of this species the following varieties have been observed.

I. Variety.

White Marble interspersed with Spots of Steatites, or Soaprock Kolmord Marble. Cronsted. § 261.

This is of a scaly texture, and the steatites and soaprock either green or black.

II. Variety.

II. Variety.

1. *Pietra Talchina.*

This confifts of white fpar, with veins of talc.

2. *Verde Antico.*

A light green marble, with deep green, black, white, and purple fpots; 100 parts of it contain, according to Mr. *Bayen*, 62 mild calcareous Earth, 30 of green talc, 1 of magnefia, and 1 of femiphlogifticated iron. 12 *Roz.* 56.

Species IV.

Compounds of the Calcareous and Argillaceous Species.

I. Variety.

Mild Calcareous Earth and Argillaceous Shiftus.

1. *Green Campan from the Pyrenees.*

This is a marble of a green colour, and flightly magnetic. According to Mr. *Bayen*, 100 parts of it contain 65 of mild calcareous Earth, 32 of argillaceous, and 3 of femiphlogifticated iron, 11 *Roz.* 499. Since this stone

stone is something magnetic, it is plain that the shistus must contain at least 10 parts iron; and also, that this iron is not much dephlogisticated. Hence also, the colour is green, which colour, or blue, is always, when it proceeds from iron, a sign that the iron is not much dephlogisticated; on the contrary, a red or yellow colour from iron, denotes it to be in a dephlogisticated state.

2. *Red Campan.*

A red marble, not magnetic; 100 parts of it contain 82 of mild calcareous Earth, 11 of argillaceous shistus, and 7 of dephlogisticated iron. 11 *Roz.* 501.

3. *Yellow figured Marble from Florence.*

Mr. *Bayen* found 100 parts of it to contain 75 of mild calcareous Earth, 13 or 14 of shistus, and 4 or 5 of dephlogisticated iron.

4. *Griotte.*

A red marble from *Autun*; contains 67 of mild calcareous Earth, 26 of reddish shistus, 2 of iron, and 1 of magnesia, per cent. according to Mr. *Bayen.*

5. *Amandola.*

Calcareous Genus. 51

5. *Amandola.*

A green honeycomb-like looking marble, containing white spots: 100 parts of it contain 76 of mild calcareous Earth, 20 of shistus, 2 of semiphlogisticated iron; the cellular appearance proceeds the shistus. 12 *Roz.* 56.

6. *Cipolin from Rome.*

A green marble, with white zones. It gives fire with steel, though difficultly; 100 parts of it contain 67,8 of mild calcareous Earth, 25 of quartz, 8 of shistus, 0,2 of iron, besides the iron contained in the shistus. 22 *Roz.* 52.

II. VARIETY.
Calcareous Earth and Mica.

1. *Cipolin from Autun.*

A green marble, consisting of 83 parts mild calcareous Earth, 12 of green mica, and 1 of iron. 12 *Roz.* 55.

2. *Micaceous Limestone.*

This is of a glittering appearance, of various degrees of hardness, and effervesces with

with acids; the proportion of mica is various. The *macigno* of the Italians is of this species. Ferber, 116. The yellow sort is called *pietra bigia*, the blue *pietra colombina*, or *turchina*.

Species V.

Compounds of the Calcareous and Siliceous Species.

I. Variety. With Quartz.

1. *Calcareous Quartz and Puddingstone.*

This consists of lumps of quartz, and sometimes felt spar, in a calcareous cement.

2. *Limestone with Veins of Quartz, Saxum Sahlbergense.*

Also several marbles in Sweden and Siberia, that strike fire with steel.

II. Variety. With Lava.

1. *Calcareous Volcanic Puddingstone, Cierchina.*

In this, lumps of spar and lava are found in a calcareous cement. Ferber Italy, 115.

2. *Marble mixed with Veins of black or green Lava.* Ferber Italy, 67.

Species VI.

Species VI.

Compounds of Calcareous Earths with Species of two or more Genera.

I. Variety.
Calcareous Porphyry.

This confists of quartz, felt fpar, and mica, in feparate grains, united by a calcareous cement.

II. Variety.
Limeftone interfperfed with Shoerl and Mica.

CHAP. IV.
Barytic Genus.

Species I.
Ponderous Earth combined with the Aerial Acid, aerated Barofelenite.

Dr. *Withering* prefented me with a very pure fpecimen of this fpecies from *Alfton Moor,* in *Cumberland.* It much refembles alum, but its texture is ftriated: its fpecific gravity is 4,331, though when this compound is artificial its fpecific gravity is only 3,773, according to Mr. *Bergman*; evidently becaufe it contains much water, for

for 100 parts of it contain 65 of pure Earth, 28 of water, and 7 of the aerial acid; whereas 100 parts of the native contain about 20 of aerial acid and 78 of Earth, a little of the vitriolic barofelenite, and no water. It effervefces with acids.

The artificial, when calcined, burns to lime, which has the properties of pure barofelenite already defcribed; but the natural will not burn to lime, for it will not part with its fixed air, but rather melts, as Dr. *Withering* has difcovered. He alfo found that cauftic alkalis precipitate this Earth from the nitrous and marine acids, which happens, as I think, from their taking up the excefs of acid requifite to keep it in folution.

Species II.

Combined with the vitriolic Acid.

Barofelenite, Marmor Metallicum, Cronft. 182, *Lapis Bononienfis, Selenitic Spar, Gypfum Spathofum, Spathum Fufibile, Margraf* 2, *Theile* p. 44, *Weigel O ferv. Mineral.* p. 65 and 66. *Cawk, Petunfe of fome, Ponderous Spar.*

This ftone is of a white, grey, or yellowifh white colour, and fometimes reddifh; sometimes

Barytical Genus.

times not harder than chalk, but mostly very compact, and of a stony hardness, though never so hard as to give fire with steel. Its texture lamellar or fibrous; its shape either amorphous, orbicular, tabular, or cristated, that is, jagged like a cock's comb, or chrystalized in polygon prisms: it is also found opake, semi-transparent, or transparent; this last sort is an electric *per se*.

Its specific gravity is generally from 4 to 4,6, though sometimes, as Mr. *Wiegleb* remarks, it is not so great. 11 *Nev. Endeck*, 15.

It is insoluble, or nearly so, in water, as well as in acids.

The harder sorts decrepitate in fire; it does not burn to Plaster of Paris as gypsum does; it is infusible *per se* with a blow-pipe, yet Mr. *D'Arcet* found the semi-transparent sort fusible in a long continued porcelain heat. 22 *Roz.* 26; probably because it was placed in an argillaceous vessel: but it is fusible by the help of the mineral alkali, with effervescence, and also with borax and microcosmic salt, according to Mr. *Bergman*.

It is often mixed with calcareous Earth, 6 *Roz.* 222. 13 *Roz. Supplement*, p. 408.

Elements of Mineralogy.

Mr. *Morveau* obferves that it accompanies the ores of moſt metals. Mr. *Margraaf* alſo frequently found maſſes of it mixed with gypſum. 1 *Margr.* 332.

The eaſieſt method of decompoſing it, is that practiſed by Mr. *Wolfe* and Mr. *Wiegleb*, viz. by calcining it in a ſtrong red heat for 1 or 2 hours, with $1\frac{1}{2}$ or twice its weight of fixed alkali; the neutral ſalt and ſuperfluous alkali are then waſhed of, and the Earth is found combined with fixed air. Mr. *Morveau's* method is cheaper. He calcines the ponderous ſpar with $\frac{1}{6}$ of its weight of charcoal for 1 hour, in a crucible, well luted, and a ſtrong red heat: he then diſſolves the Earth in the acetous acid. The ſulphur is thus ſeparated. *Mem. Dijon*, 1782. Mr. *Margraaf* decompoſed it in the liquid way, by mixing two parts of the ſtone with one of fixed alkali; then pouring hot water on it, and keeping it boiling for ſome hours. 1 *Margr.* 366. The decompoſed part, well edulcorated, is ſoluble in acids.

This ſpecies often forms the ſtony matter of petrifactions. *Mem. Dijon*, 1782. 1 *Semeſt.* p. 163.

According to Mr. *Bergman*, 100 parts of it contain 84 of Earth, 13 of the moſt concentrated

Barytical Genus. 57

centrated acid, and 3 of water. 100 parts of artificial barofelenite contain about 33 of vitriolic acid and water, and 67 of Earth.

Some fpecies, particularly the red, contain 1 or two gr. of iron per cent.

Species III.
Combined with the Sparry Acid.

This combination has not yet been found in nature; that formed by art is nearly infoluble in water.

Species IV.
Combined with the Tungften Acid.

This combination is alfo infoluble in water, but it has not as yet been found.

Species V.
Mild Barytes intimately mixed with a notable Proportion of Silex and Iron.

I mention this fpecies on the authority of Mr. *Bindheim.* 4 *Berlin Schrift.* 397. It is infoluble in acids, and of a fparry texture; but, as he fays it becomes foluble after calcination with oil, I fhould be inclined to judge it rather a barofelenite.

Species VI.

Species VI.

Barofelenite mixed with a notable Proportion of Silex, Mineral Oil and Terrene Salts, Liver Stone, Lapis Hepaticus.

It's colour is white, grey, yellow, brown, or black; it is generally compact, but not fo hard as to give fire with steel; its texture is either equable or laminar, scaly or sparry, and it takes a polish as alabaster.

It does not effervesce with acids.

When calcined, it is partially reduced to a fort of Plaister of Paris.

It emits a smell of hepar sulphuris, at least when rubbed.

According to Mr. *Bergman*, 100 parts of it afford 33 of barofelenite, 38 of silex, 22 of alum, 7 of gypsum, and 5 of mineral oil. The increase proceeds from the water of chrystalization.

CHAP. VI.

Muriatic Genus.

Under this genus I include not only those Earths and Stones in which magnesia predominates, but also those in which the siliceous genus

Muriatic Genus.

genus predominates, if magnefia be, next to the filiceous, the moft copious ingredient, and the compound poffeffes the characters of the muriatic, and not thofe of the filiceous genus.

Species I.

Combined with the Aerial Acid, and barely mixed with other Earths, in an earthy, or semi-indurated Form.

Pure magnefia has no where yet been found, nor even magnefia, barely combined with fixed air, and free from all mixture of other Earths. When combined with fixed air by art, 100 patts of it contain at a medium 30 of aerial acid, 48 of mere Earth, and 22 of water; but thefe proportions are variable within certain limits, the fixed air being found in the proportion of from 25 to 37, the Earth from 40 to 48, and the water from 20 to 30. in general when the proportion of fixed air is greateft, that of water is fmalleft, and *vice verfa.*

I. Variety.

Mixed with Siliceous Earth.

Spuma Maris, Meerfhaum of the Germans. Keffekill.

This is found in various parts of the world, particularly in the Eaft, in veins of moderate thickness,

60 *Elements of Mineralogy.*

thickneſs, and is the ſubſtance of which the large Turkey tobacco-pipes are formed: it is probably found alſo in *North America*, being the ſubſtance called in *Canada, Terre a chalumeau*. It is of a white or yellow colour, ſoapy feel, and moderately hard. It hardens eaſily in fire without requiring a great heat. In the ſtate in which we receive it, that is baked, it does not effervesce with acids, and is difficultly ſoluble therein.

According to Mr. *Wiegleb's* analyſis, it conſiſts of equal parts, magneſia and ſilex. 5 *Crell. Nev. Entdeck*, p. 3.

II. Variety.

Mixed with Calcareous Earth and Iron.

It appears like an olive-coloured, or blue clay: the olive-coloured contains no argillaceous Earth: the blue ſort contains moſt calcareous Earth, alſo iron, a little argill, and petrefactions. Both are found near *Thionville*. The former ſort is uſed in pottery. 13 *Roz.* p. 60.

III. Variety.

Mixed with Clay, Talc, and Iron.

This is a greeniſh yellow, looſe Earth, of a greaſy feel, found in *Sileſia*. It contains

tains $\frac{1}{3}$ of its weight of magnesia. *Margraaf*, 2 *Theil.* p. 18.

SPECIES II.

Combined with Aerial Acid, above four times its weight of Silex, and a smaller proportion of Argill.

I. VARIETY.

Steatites.

This is always of a green or greenish colour, and so soft as to be scraped by the nail; of a soft soapy feel: its texture undistinguishable; its specific gravity from 2,433 to 2,78. It is not easily diffusible in water, nor rendered ductile by mixture with it.

It does not effervesce with acids, and is very slowly and only partially soluble in the three mineral acids.

In fire it hardens, but is infusible *per se*, and becomes whiter. It is imperfectly melted by mineral alkali and microcosmic salt, but more perfectly by borax. It is apt to corrode the crucibles.

According

According to Mr. *Bergman*'s analyſis, 100 parts of it contain 80 of ſilex, 17 of mild magneſia, 2 of argill, and nearly 1 of iron in a ſemiphlogiſticated ſtate.

II. Variety.

Soap-rock, Lapis Ollaris, Pot-ſtone, Speckſtein of the Germans, Spaniſh Chalk. 2 Margr. 14.

This is of a *yellow* colour, and ſometimes whitiſh, and but rarely black: it is alſo ſomewhat harder than the former variety, and probably the proportion of argill is ſomewhat greater, but in other reſpects it perfectly reſembles it. The black contains a mineral oil.

This ſtone is eaſily worked and turned, inſomuch that pots and mortars are often made of it.

Mr. *Gerhard* remarks, that the Swediſh *ſpeckſtein* often effervesces with acids, and contains calcareous Earth, but that of *Saxony* and *Sileſia* never. The limeſtone is merely an accidental mixture. 4 *Berlin, Schriſt*. 300.

Species III.

Species III.

Mild Magnesia combined with Silex, Calcareous Earth, and a small proportion of Argill and Iron.

I. Variety.

Fibrous Asbestos, Alumen Plumosum.

The colour of this stone is generally greenish, and it consists of filaments either parallel to, or interwoven with each other. It is rough to the touch, and brittle and uneven in its fracture, hence it does not strike fire with steel. Its specific gravity is from 2,5 to 2,8.

It does not effervesce with acids, and is soluble in them but partially, and by particular management.

When sufficiently heated, it becomes somewhat whiter and more brittle, but is infusible *per se* by the blow-pipe, unless it contains a notable proportion of calx of iron. It is difficultly fusible with mineral alkali, more easily with borax and microcosmic salt, and with scarce any effervescence. It is never transparent, and in that respect, and in the unevenefs of their fracture only, some sorts
of

of martial afbeftos differ in external appearance from fome forts of fhoerl.

According to Mr. *Bergman*, this variety contains from 53 to 74 parts of filex, from 12 to 28 of mild magnefia, from 7 to 14 of mild calcareous Earth, from 2 to 6 of argill, and from 1 to 10 of iron *per cent*. 100 parts martial afbeftos contain 62 of filex, 13,7 of magnefia, 12 of calcareous Earth, 1,7 of argill, and 10,6 of iron; yet it gives in fufion a white flagg.

II. Variety.

Coriaceous Afbeftos, Suber Montanum, Aluta Montana, Mountain Cork, Leather, &c.

This fort of afbeftos refembles in texture thofe fubftances from which it borrows thefe fanciful appellations. It is eafily diftinguifhed by its elafticity and lightnefs, for it floats a long time on water. In other refpects it refembles the former fpecies, except that its colour is either white, yellow, brown, green, or black.

100 parts of it contain from 56 to 62 of filex, from 22 to 26 of mild magnefia, from 10 to 12 of mild calcareous Earth, from 2 to 2,8 of argill, and about 3 of iron.

Species IV.

Species IV.

Mild Magnesia combined with Silex, mild Calcareous Earth, Barytes, Argill and Iron.

Amianthus.

In structure this species resembles the first variety of the foregoing; consisting of long parallel fibres, in some degree flexible, and soft to the touch. The surface of its fracture is also uneven. Its colour, white, grey, greenish or reddish: its specific gravity 2,913.

It does not effervesce with acids, and is difficultly, and but partially soluble therein.

It is fusible *per se* in a strong heat, and also with borax, microcosmic salt, and mineral alkali, with effervescence. In fusion it again chrystalizes in filaments, but in a still stronger heat it forms a green glass, which corrodes the crucibles, as Mr. *Sauſſure* has observed.

100 parts of the *Amianthus* of *Tarentaise* examined by Mr. *Bergman*, afforded him 64 of silex, 18,6 of magnesia, 6,9 of calcareous Earth, 6 of barytes, 3,3 of argill, and 1,2 of iron.

Species V.

Species V.

Pure Magnesia combined with something more than its own weight of Silex, about ⅓ of its weight of argill, nearly ⅓ of its weight of water, and about 1 or 2 tenths of its weight of Iron.

Serpentine, Lapis Nephriticus, Gabro of the Italians.

In respect to colour, as well as composition, this stone is susceptible of great variety, for it is found either white, green, brown, reddish brown, yellow, light blue, black, spotted, or streaked with veins of different colours. Its texture is either indistinct, obscurely laminar, or fibrous. It is harder than soap-rock, but not so hard as to give fire with steel, and less smooth to the touch, but susceptible of a good polish, looks like marble, and is often in thin pieces semi-transparent.

Its specific gravity is from 2,4 to 2,65.

It does not effervesce with acids, but is slowly and partially soluble in them.

It melts *per se* in a strong heat, and preys on the crucibles. *Vogel*, 103. In a lower degree of heat it hardens.

According

According to the analysis of Mr. *Bayen*, 100 parts of it contain about 41 of silex, (which he takes rather to be mica) 33 of magnesia, 10 of argill, 12 of water, and about 3 of iron. The serpentine of Corsica contains a larger proportion of argill and a smaller of silex.

The greener sorts of this stone have been called *nephritic*.

Species VI.

Pure Magnesia intimately mixed with nearly twice its weight of Silex, and less than its own weight of Argill.

Venetian Talc.

Its colour is white, grey, yellowish, or greenish: it is soft and soapy to the touch, and in thin pieces semi-transparent: it is composed of very thin laminæ disposed in a laminar or filamentous form, much tenderer and more brittle than those of mica, but like this it has a metallic lustre: its hardness is so inconsiderable that it may be scratched with the nail: its specific gravity is 2,729.

It does not effervesce with acids, and is soluble therein very difficultly by particular management, and only in part.

In fire it becomes more brittle and whiter, but is infusible *per se* by the blow-pipe, and scarcely fusible by fixed alkalis, but more completely, and with little effervescence, by borax or microcosmic salt.

This talc contains something less than 50 per cent. of silex, and about 2 per cent. of iron. The magnesia is in smaller quantity, but it exceeds the argill: the exact proportion I have not found.

Muscovy talc consists of broad, elastic, flexible, transparent leaves, and differs externally from mica only in being softer and more soapy to the touch.

Species VII.

Combined with the Sparry Acid.

This combination is scarcely soluble in water, but has not yet been discovered in nature.

Species VIII.

Combined with the Tungsten Acid.

This compound when artificial is also infoluble, but has not as yet been observed native.

Compound

Compound Species in which the Muriatic Genus predominates.

Species I.

Compounds of the different simple Muriatic Species with each other.

I. Variety.

1. Steatites mixed with Talc, *Craie de Briançon.* It is generally grey, yellow, or greenish: it seems more argillaceous than pure steatites, and contains more iron. Mr. *D'Arcet* found it fusible in a porcelain heat.

II. Variety.

1. Serpentine mixed with veins or spots of green Steatites.

2. Red Serpentine mixed with veins of Asbestos.

Species II.

Compounds of the Muriatic and Calcareous Species.

1, Red, green, yellow, or black Serpentine, with veins or spots of white Calcareous Spar *Potzevera.* The black is called *Nero di prato;*

the green *Verde di Suza*; but thefe names are not reftrained to this fpecies.

2. Serpentine with veins or fpots of Gypfum.

Species III.
Compounds of the Muriatic and Barytic Species.

I. Variety.

Serpentine with veins or fpots of barofelenite.

Species IV.
Compounds of the Muriatic and Argillaceous Species.

I. Variety.

1. Steatites mixed with a notable proportion of indurated Clay. It is lefs foft to the touch, and fomething harder than the pure fteatites: its colour is grey or greenifh brown: it frequently contains alfo mica or talc, and fometimes a notable proportion of iron, and then it is red. The talcofe is frequently called French chalk, or *Craie de Briançon*.

2. Steatites,

Muriatic Genus.

2. Steatites mixed with Shiftus, or bituminous Shiftus. This is blue or black, and rougher to the touch than pure fteatites.

3. Serpentine mixed with veins or fpots of Shiftus.

4. Soap-rock mixed with Mica. *Cronft.* § 265. Grey, yellow, or greenifh.

SPECIES V.

Compounds of the Muriatic and Siliceous Species.

1. Serpentine with veins of Quartz or Feltfpar, or Shoerl.

CHAP. VII.

Argillaceous Genus.

SPECIES I.

Saturated with Aerial Acid.

Lac Lunæ.

This fanciful name was heretofore thought to denote a very fine fpecies of calcareous Earth, but Mr. *Schreber* has lately fhewn that the Earth to which this name is given, is a very uncommon fpecies of argill. It is generally found in fmall cakes of the hardnefs

hardnefs of chalk, and like that, it marks white: its hardnefs is nearly as that of fteatites, and does not feel as fat as common clay does: its fpecific gravity is 1,669: its colour is fnow white. When examined with a microfcope, it is found to confift of fmall tranfparent cryftals; and by his experiments it plainly appears to be an argill faturated with fixed air. It effervefces with acids, and contains a very fmall proportion of calcareous Earth, and fometimes of gypfum, and fome feeble traces of iron. It is found near *Halles*. 15 *Naturforfch*. 209.

Species II.

Combined but not faturated with Aerial Acid, in a loofe or femi-indurated form, and mixed with fine Quartz or Silex in various proportions, a fmall quantity of Water, and generally of Iron.

Clay, Creta of the Italians.

This fpecies receives a number of different denominations, arifing from its hardnefs, fufibility or infufibility, or the different ufes it is applied to, or relative to its colour, or origin; fuch as ftone clay or lithomarga, fufible or apyrous clay, marl, Fuller's earth, pipe clay, kaolin, brick clay, umber, coloured clays, boles, pouzzolana, terras, tripoli, &c. All clays

Argillaceous Genus. 73

clays are more or less easily diffusible in water, which they imbibe with more or less avidity, according to their previous compactness, and if they contain much air they froth with water, burst and fall to pieces: when they have imbibed it they are more or less ductil and vicid, according as the sand they are mixed with is more or less fine. They contract in drying, and crack when heated, they contract still more, and harden to such a degree as to give fire with steel. They do not effervesce with acids, unless they contain magnesia or calcareous Earth. The finer clays have a smooth, and in some measure, a soapy feel.

These are the properties of pure argillaceous Earths; yet most clays contain but from 25 to 48 per cent. of this Earth, the remainder consists of fine siliceous Earth, and a little water. On the subtility and purity of the siliceous part, the fineness of clay principally depend.

Many clays contain a little volatile alkali, and some the vitriolic acid; probably this latter is united to the argill in the state of embryon allum, that is, in such proportion as not to render it soluble in water. Most of them contain also a small proportion of iron.

Fusible

Fusible Clays.

All clays, which, besides argillaceous and siliceous Earths, contain a mixture of calcareous or muriatic Earths, or gypsum, or fluor, or felt spar, or iron, are more or less fusible, according to the proportion of these foreign ingredients.

Apyrous Clays.

Clays that consist of argillaceous and siliceous Earths singly, without any mixture of iron or other metallic substance, or at least only in an inconsiderable proportion, are infusibl. Such is that found near *Plombiere*. *Mem. Par.* 1778, p. 433.

Argillaceous Marl.

Any clay that contains from 20 to 50 per cent. of mild calcareous Earth, comes under this denomination. It differs prodigiously in point of hardness and colour: the hardest is called *lithomarga*, or stone marl. The best for agriculture is the grey or white; the coloured generally contain metallic particles: when it contains 20 or 30 per cent. of calcareous Earth it is fusible *per se*. The coloured marls, as they contain more iron, are still

more

more fufible. This fpecies of marl falls to pieces more difficultly, either in water or air, than calcareous marl.

Indurated marls, of a quadrangular form, have been called *Ludi helmontii*.

Fuller's Earth.

This is moftly of a white, grey, bluifh, or yellowifh colour, compact, femi-indurated, of a lamellar texture, and often conchoidal in its fracture; confifting of very fine particles, fmooth and fomewhat foapy to the touch: it burfts and is diffufible in water, with which it often froths like foap: it does not effervefce with acids; in a ftrong heat it melts into a flag. Microcofmic falt affects it but flightly; mineral alkali more powerfully, and with much effervefcence, but borax melts it moft completely.

Different fpecimens of it, from various countries, afforded Mr. *Bergman* from 47 to 60 of filiceous Earth, from 11 to 25 of argillaceous, from ¼ to 6 parts of magnefia, from 3 to 7 of mild calcareous Earth, from 3 to 5,5 of dephlogifticated iron, and from 15 to 18 of water, mixed with a very minute proportion of marine acid; but this laft was found only in a few of them. Its fulling power

power arises from the property of clay to absorb oils, the fineness of its particles, which do not injure the cloth, and its easy diffusibility in water, which renders it capable of being washed off.

Terra lemnia is a yellowish or flesh-coloured clay of this sort.

Pipe Clay.

Any moderately pure and fine white clay, which retains its colour in fire, is distinguished by this appellation. That of *Cologne* is the purest, and is infusible in the strongest heat. Many of these clays become grey in a weak degree of heat, because the mineral oil with which they are mixed burns to a coal, but in a stronger heat they again become white, this coal being consumed.

Porcelain Earth, or Kaolin.

This differs from the former chiefly in the fineness or subtility of the siliceous ingredient. It sometimes effervesces with acids, either because it contains crystalized argill, or magnesia, or calcareous Earth: it also abounds in talcose particles. It never contains any oily matter, and therefore retains its colour in every degree of heat.

Brick

Brick Clay.

Its colour is various, reddiſh, bluiſh, or yellowiſh: it always contains iron, and melts into a ſlag. The beſt ſort contains little or none of calcareous Earth, but a good deal of a coarſe ſiliceous ſand.

Coloured Clays.

Yellow, red, and *brown* clays contain moſt iron, ſometimes diſperſed through them, and ſometimes united to the ſiliceous part: in this caſe they are more difficultly fuſible. The yellow calx of iron is more dephlogiſticated than the red, and the red more ſo than the brown. When theſe clays contain about 14 or 15 per cent. of iron, they become magnetic after calcination.

Red chalk, Rubrica fabrilis, is, according to Mr. *Rinman,* either a clay intermixed with the red calx of iron, which hardens in fire, and then becomes magnetic and browner, and in a ſtronger heat melts into a black glaſs, and contains from 16 to 18 per cent. of iron, (but ſometimes it contains but 7 or 8 per cent. of iron, and then does not become magnetic by roaſting) or it is an impure ſteatites, mixed with clay and calx of iron. *Hiſtoria Ferri,* § 189.

Blue

Blue Clays.

These sometimes lose their colour and become white when heated, and consequently contain but little of iron, but owe their colour to an oily matter, which is dissipated by heat; others owe their colour, according to Mr. *Monnet*, to a mixture of pyrites. *Mineralogie*, p. 339. Mr. *Beaumé* says, that blue clays contain the vitriolic acid, but he probably found it only in the pyritical clays, for in other sorts Mr. *Woulfe* could discover none. *Phil. Transf.* 1779, p. 20. Mr. *Bergman* found some which contained copper and a little of cobolt. *Rinman* mentions a blue lithomarga, which contained 13 per cent. of iron, 4 of lead, and some vestiges of zinc. *Hist. Ferri*, § 201, p. 712.

Umber.

A brown or blackish substance, which stains the fingers, and is very light; it has long been taken for a clay, but Mr. *Hupsch*, *Mem. Berlin*, 1777, has discovered it to consist of particles of decayed wood, mixed with bitumen; yet it is certain that this name hath also been given to a sort of brown ochre, of the same colour, which becomes red when slightly heated, but in a stronger heat is again brown and magnetic, and in a still stronger melts into a black glass. It does not effervesce with acids before

before roasting, but after that the martial part is soluble.

Green Clays.

Some sorts are said to redden in fire, and contain iron. Mr. *Bergman* has found some which contain copper and cobalt; to separate which he precipitated the copper by iron, and digested the residuum in distilled vinegar. Other sorts are said to contain nickel.

Black Clays.

These are said to be bituminous.

Variegated.

The most remarkable of this species is the *Terra miraculosa Saxoniæ*, which is a beautiful indurated clay, of a purplish colour, with white, yellow, red, or brown veins or dots.

Bole.

Is a term of uncertain signification, and should therefore be banished. Some bestow this name on very smooth compact clays, consisting of the finest particles: others require besides, that their colour should be red, yellow, or brown, and that they should contain iron. The red generally blacken in fire, 2

Bergm.

Bergm. 476, yet do not become magnetic. *Rinman,* § 189. The yellow, when heated, become firſt red, and in a ſtrong heat, brown or black. *Calamita bianca* of the Italians is a white bole, ſtriated like aſbeſtos. *Ferber, Itally,* 122. *Terra figillata rubra* contains calcareous Earth, and becomes magnetic after torrefaction. *Rinman,* § 189.

Of Volcanic Origin.

Pouzzolana.

This is of a grey, brown, yellowiſh, or blackiſh colour, looſe, granular, or duſty, and rough, porous and ſpungy, reſembling a clay hardened in fire and then reduced to a groſs powder. It contains, mixed with it, various heterogenous ſubſtances: its ſpecific gravity is from 2,5 to 2,8, and it is in ſome degree magnetic: it ſcarcely effervesces with acids, though partially ſoluble in them: it melts eaſily *per ſe*: but its moſt diſtinguiſhing property is, that it hardens very ſuddenly when mixed with ¼ of its weight of lime and water, and forms a cement, which is more durable in water than any other. According to Mr. *Bergman's* analyſis, 100 parts of it contain from 55 to 60 of ſiliceous Earth, 19 or 20 of argillaceous, 5 or 6 of calcareous, and from 15 to 20 of iron. 3 *Bergm.* 193. It is evidently a martial argillaceous marl that

Argillaceous Genus.

that has suffered a moderate heat. Its hardening power arises from the dry state of the half-baked argillaceous particles, which makes them imbibe water very rapidly, and thus accelerates the desication of the calcareous part; and also from the quantity and semiphlogisticated state of the iron contained in it. It is found not only in *Italy* but also in *France*, in the provinces of *Auvergne* and *Limoges*, and also in *England*, and elsewhere.

Traass, or Terras.

This differs but little in its principles from pouzzolana, but is much more compact and harder, porous and spungy. It is generally of a whitish yellow colour, and contains more heterogenous particles, as spar, quartz, shoerl, &c. and something more of calcareous Earth: it effervesces with acids, is magnetic, and fusible *per se*. When pulverized, it serves as a cement, like pouzzolana. It is found in *Germany* and *Sweden*.

Tufa.

Volcanic ashes concreted with various other species of stone, but in which argill predominates, forms the stone thus called: it is harder than traafs, but still porous and spungy.

White Volcanic Earth.

That of *Solfatera*, examined by Mr. *Bergman*, was found to confift chiefly of filex, mixed with about 4 per cent. of argill, and 8 per cent. of allum. 3 *Bergm.* 198.

Tripoli.

Its colour is either white, grey, yellow, reddifh, or brown, either indurated and brittle, or loofe, powdery, and rough: it does not foften in water, nor effervefce with acids. According to Mr. *D'Arcet*, it is vitrifiable *per fe* in a porcelain heat long continued; and according to Mr. *Bergman*, it yields to borax and microcofmic falt, but fcarcely to fixed alkali.

Mr. *Haafe*, who has lately analyfed it, found 100 parts of it to contain 90 of filiceous Earth, 7 of argill, and 3 of iron; but the red fort probably contains more iron. According to Mr. *Gerhard*, magnefia has fometimes been extracted from it.

It is evidently a volcanic product; for a coal-mine near *St. Eftienne* having accidentally taken fire, and the fire in its progrefs having extended to fome ftrata of fhiftus and bitumen, tripoli was found in thofe parts of the ftrata that

Argillaceous Genus. 83

that the fire had acted upon, but not in any other. *Mem. Par.* 1769, p. 276.

The *rotten stone* of *Derbyshire* is, according to Mr. *Ferber*, a tripoli mixed with calcareous Earth.

Species III.

Barely saturated with Vitriolic Acid.

Embryon Allum.

This species was first discovered by Mr. *Beaumè*; it forms small scaly chrystals like mica, which require 1450 times their weight of water to dissolve them in the temperature of 60°. It is no where found single, but generally mixed with clays, from which it may be separated by boiling, and dissolved in water, to which it gives an earthy taste, and is separable by the affusion of lime water, which precipitates the argill.

Species IV.

Barely saturated with Marine Acid.

Embryon Marine Allum.

As a solution of marine alum, completely saturated with argill, forms also a very difficultly soluble compound, and as many clays are found to contain the marine acid, it is probable that this species exists in them, though it hath not yet been noticed.

In a stony Form.

'Under this head I comprehend all those stones which, although the siliceous genus predominates in their composition, and the argillaceous, with respect to quantity, obtains only the second place, yet do not possess the character of siliceous stones, as they do not strike fire with steel; and on the contrary, I exclude those which possess the characters of siliceous Earths, though they contain the argillaceous in greater quantity.

SPECIES V.

Argill combined with 1,36 its weight of Silex, 0,7 of its weight of pure Magnesia, and 0,5 of its weight of highly dephlogisticated Iron.

Pure Mica.

This stone, in its purest state, is colourless; but either from a less intimate combination, or from a mixture of some superfluous ingredient, principally iron, it is found of different colours, white, red, yellow, green, brown, or black, (the white and yellow sort have

Argillaceous Genus. 85

have a splendid metallic appearance) smooth, but not greasy to the touch, which distinguishes it from talc. Its texture is always lamellar or scaly, and the lamellæ, or scales, are slightly flexible and often elastic; these scales are sometimes parallel to each other, sometimes interwoven, sometimes wavy, or undulated, and sometimes they represent filaments. Its specific gravity is from 2,535, to 3,000 when loaded with iron.

It does not effervesce with acids, and is insoluble in them without particular management, but after it has been calcined with 4 times its weight of fixed alkali, it effervesces strongly, and is in great measure soluble.

The pure colourless mica is infusible *per se*, and scarcely melts even with mineral alkali, but yields more readily to borax or microcosmic salt, with scarce any effervescence; but the coloured sorts were found by Mr. *Sauſſure* to be fusible *per se*, though with difficulty, for they require a stronger heat than shoerl does.

100 parts of the colourless kind contain 38 of silex, 28 of argill, 20 of magnesia, and 14 of the most dephlogisticated calx of iron. Martial mica contains besides, 10 or 12 per cent. of a more phlogisticated calx

86   *Elements of Mineralogy.*

calx of iron, from whence its various colours are derived, and a proportionably fmaller quantity of the other ingredients.

Argillaceous Fiffile Stones.

Thefe and many other of different genera, have been comprehended under the denomination of *Schifti*, but to avoid ambiguity, I think it expedient to confine this name to ftones of the argillaceous genus.

Species VI.
Roof Slate, Shiftus Tegularis.

Of this fpecies there are many varieties, none of which have been hitherto analyfed, except the bluifh purple flate chiefly ufed here, which I have lately examined, and to which, as to a ftandard, I fhall refer the other forts.

I. Variety.

Argill intimately mixed with 1,77 *of its weight of Siliceous Earth,* 0,3 *of its weight of Magnefia,* 0,15 *of Calcareous Earth, both flightly aerated, and nearly* 0,54 *of its weight of Iron, befides a flight admixture of Mineral Oil.*

Bluifh Purple Slate.

It does not ftrike fire with fteel, and may be flightly fcraped with the nail; it is very brittle,

brittle, and of a lamellar texture: its specific gravity is 2,876: when in pieces of ⅛ of an inch thick, or less, it gives a clear sound if struck: its grain is moderately fine: it is never transparent: it slightly effervesces with acids when reduced to powder, otherwise not: when heated red, it loses something more than 2 per cent. of its weight, slightly detonnates with nitre, and then assumes a brownish red colour, but calcination does not render it magnetic: in a stronger heat it is fusible *per se*, and forms a black scoria: it is difficultly dissolved by mineral alkali in the dry way, more easily by borax, though with little effervescence, and also by microcosmic salt with some effervescence. Mr *Gerhard* remarks, that it melts with equal ease in chalk or clay vessels.

Dephlogisticated spirit of nitre, after standing on it two months in cold, assumes a green colour.

I found 100 gr. of it to contain about 46 of silex, 26 of argill, 8 of magnesia, 4 of calcareous Earth, and 14 of iron. Part of the iron seems to be in a phlogisticated state, from its union with the oil, and part in a dephlogisticated state, or that of a red calx. This is united to the argillaceous part and silex, and is very difficultly separated.

II. Variety.

II. Variety.

Pale, flightly Purple, or bluish Shiftus.

This ftone is harder than the foregoing, its laminæ thicker, and its texture coarfer: it feems to contain a larger proportion of the filiceous and a fmaller of the martial ingredient.

III. Variety.

Blue Shiftus.

The proportion of the earthy ingredients being the fame as in the firft variety, that of the martial ingredient feems to be fmaller.

Other ftones are alfo ufed for covering houfes in various countries, but they are eafily diftinguifhed; as their laminæ are much thicker, their furface more uneven, and their texture coarfer. They chiefly belong to the clafs of fand-ftones, or to the calcareous genus.

IV. Variety.

Dark Blue Slate, Shiftus Scriptorius.

It effervefces more brifkly with acids, and feems to contain more magnefia, and lefs iron, than

than the firſt variety: its ſpecific gravity is
2,701.

Species VII.

*Argillaceous Earth mixed with a variable
Proportion of Pyrites, with a little Magneſia and Calcareous Earth.*

Pyritaceous Shiſtus.

Its colour is grey, brown, blue, or black:
it is more or leſs decompoſable by expoſure to
the air, according to the quantity of the pyritous ingredient and the ſtate of the iron in
the pyrites: if the iron be in a ſemiphlogiſticated ſtate it is eaſily decompoſed, but if the
calx of iron be already much dephlogiſticated,
it will be decompoſed but ſlowly, if at all.
Aluminous ſchiſtus is of this ſpecies, but will
more properly be mentioned in treating of
alum.

Species VIII.

*Slate, or Pyritaceous Shiſtus, intimately mixed
with a notable Proportion of Mineral Oil or
Bitumen.*

Bituminous Schiſtus.

It is generally black, of a lamellar texture,
of different degrees of hardneſs, but never
gives

gives fire with steel. it emits a strong smell when heated, and sometimes without heat; does not shew white when scraped.

Species IX.

Argill mixed with from 3 to 4 tenths of its weight of Silex, and a little of the yellow or red Calx of Iron.

I. Variety.

Argillaceous Shistus, Flag-stone.

This is of a grey, yellowish, or reddish white colour; does not give fire with steel, nor effervesce with acids: its specific gravity is from 2,6 to 2,78: it is in some places used for covering of houses, but mostly for flooring: it is sometimes compact, and sometimes sandy, like the next variety, and then its specific gravity is smaller.

II. Variety.

Argillaceous Grit, Free-stone, or Sand-stone.

It is called free-stone because it may be cut easily in all directions: its texture is more or less porous, equable and rough to the touch: it exhales an earthy smell when fresh broken and breathed upon: it does not give fire with steel, nor effervesce with acids.

That

Argillaceous Genus: 91

That from *Hollington*, near *Utoxeter*, is of a whitish or yellowish grey, and its specific gravity 2,288. That from *Kniperſly*, in *Staffordſhire*, is of a bluish grey, and so infusible as to be used for a fire-stone: its specific gravity is 2,568.

Species X.

Argillaceous Earth intimately mixed with 1,7 of its weight of Silex, about 0,7 of its weight of mild Magneſia, 0,09 of its weight of mild Calcareous Earth, and about its own weight of ſemiphlogiſticated Calx of Iron.

Horn-ſtone, Hornblende of Cronſted, and Talcum Striatum of Rinman, Mem. Stockh. 1754.

The general characters of this stone, besides a partial solubility (though without effervescence) in acids, and a hardness never sufficient to strike fire with steel, properties which are common to it with the former species,) are $1^{ſt.}$ a specific gravity never less than 2,66, and frequently rising to 3,88. $2^{d.}$ a strong earthy smell which it exhales on being breathed upon, or having hot water poured on it: $3^{d.}$ a toughness or viscidity perceived in pounding it in a mortar, like mica or horn, from whence it derived its name: $4^{th.}$ its affording a greeniſh grey powder when pounded:

ed; 5$^{th.}$ fusibility *per se,* as it is said, though I could not melt it with the blow-pipe. It is frequently mixed with pyrites.

I. Variety.

Black Horn-stone, Corneus Nitens Waller,
Sp. 169.

Its texture is lamellar or granular; the former is sometimes so soft as to be scraped with the nail; its surface frequently as glossy as if it had been greased: its specific gravity is from 3,6 to 3,88; it possesses besides all the specific properties above-mentioned in a high degree: it does not detonate with nitre: it becomes of a snuff colour when heated, and then slightly effervesces with diluted nitrous acid: its solution in this acid is of a greenish colour.

In order to discover the principle on which its smell depends, I boiled its powder in water, but did not find the water altered in taste, nor did any test I applied shew any change in it.

I found 100 gr. of the lamellar sort to contain 37 of silex, 22 of argill, 16 of magnesia, 2 of calcareous Earth, (both in a mild state and 23 of calx of iron, not much dephlogisticated.

II. Variety.

Argillaceous Genus. 93

II. Variety.

Greenish Grey Horn-stone.

This is of a granular texture, or ftriated; the fpecific gravity of the pureft fpecimen I examined is 2,683: it is not fo foft as the fofteft of the former variety.

I fufpect the common pale greenifh grey whetftone to be of this fpecies: it is of a clofe granular texture, exhales an earthy fmell, affords a greenifh powder, does not effervefce with acids, nor give fire with fteel; its fpecific gravity is 2,664; it contains 65 per cent. of filex.

III. Variety.

Killas.

This ftone is chiefly found in *Cornwall*; its colour is pale grey or greenifh grey; its texture either lamellar or coarfely granular: the lamellar is fofter and lefs martial than the roof fhiftus: its fpecific gravity from 2,63 to 2,666.

I found 100 grains of the lamellar fort to contain about 60 of filex, 25 of argill, 9 of magnefia,

94 *Elements of Mineralogy.*

magnefia, and 6 of iron. The greenifh fort contains more iron and gives a greenifh colour to the nitrous acid.

Species XI.

Argillaceous Earth intimately mixed with 4 times its weight of Siliceous, ½ its weight of pure Calcareous, and fomething more than its weight of Iron.

Toad-ftone.

Dr. *Withering*, who has given us an analyfis of this ftone, defcribes it as being of a dark brownifh grey colour, of a granular texture, not giving fire with fteel, nor effervefcing with acids: it has cavities filled with chryftalized fpar: it is fufible *per fe* in a ftrong heat. *Phil. Tranf.* 1782, p. 333.

100 parts of it contain 63 of filiceous Earth, 14 of argillaceous, 7 of calcareous, and 16 of dephlogifticated iron: it differs but little from bafaltes; it is fofter, contains a fmaller proportion of iron, and a larger of filex.

Species XII.

Species XII.

Argill united to 2, 3, *or* 8 *times its weight of Silex, about half its weight of pure Calcareous Earth, and from once to twice its weight of Water, without any Iron, except accidentally.*

Zeolyte.

This stone is found of different degrees of transparency, or perfectly opake, either colourless, whitish, yellowish, greenish, or reddish; its shape is either pyramidical, columnar, tabular, oval, capillary, or amorphous; its texture either granular, scaly, or radiated; the filaments diverging as from a central point, or indistinguishable.

It does not give fire with steel.

Its specific gravity is from 2,1 to 3,15, but this last is very rare.

It does not effervesce with acids, though it is partially soluble in them, but if inserted into a proper proportion of concentrated nitrous acid, it forms a gelatinous mass, arising from the suspension and diffusion of the siliceous Earth contained in it; but this property is not peculiar to *zeolyte*, as Mr. *Pellatier* has shewn,

shewn. 20 *Roz.* 429. And some few zeolytes do not become gelatinous. 3 *Bergm.* 228.

When exposed to a strong heat it dilates and swells, more or less, according to the proportion of water contained in it, and afterwards melts *per se*, more or less easily, according to the proportion of calcareous Earth, into a frothy slag; in the moment of fusion it is said to become phosphorescent; it also melts easily, and with effervescence, with mineral alkali; something more difficultly with borax, but microcosmic salt has scarce any effect on it. When in fusion, it scarcely injures the crucibles. 22 *Roz.* p. 29. This dilatibility is the surest criterion whereby to distinguish zeolytes. The Upland zeolytes are difficultly fusible.

According to Mr. *Bergman's* analysis, the red zeolyte of *Adelfors* contains 80 per cent. of siliceous Earth, 9,5 of argillaceous, 6,5 of pure calcareous Earth, and 4 of water. *Van Troil's Letters,* p. 370.

The white, oval, radiated zeolyte of *Fero,* contains, according to Mr. *Pelletier,* 50 of silex, 20 of argill, 8 of pure calcareous Earth, and 22 of water. 20 *Roz.* 420. Mr. *Meyer* found another of the radiated sort to contain

Argillaceous Genus.

contain 58,33 per cent. of filex, 17,5 of argill, 6,66 of lime, and 17,5 of water. 4 *Berlin Befchaft.* p. 330. In general the cryftalized forts contain more water than the amorphous. Mr. *Bergman* found the zeolyte of *Jemptland* to contain 16 per cent. of calcareous Earth, and that of *Fero* to contain 25 per cent. of argill, fo that the proportions are very variable.

SPECIES XIII.

Of Volcanic Origin.

Argillaceous Earth imperfectly united to 4 times its weight of Siliceous, and $\frac{1}{5}$ of its weight of Iron.

Pitch-ftone, Lava.

It is of a greyifh, greenifh, black, red, or brown colour, has the glaffy appearance of a femi-vitrified fubftance, and melts eafily *per fe:* it often contains fubftances feemingly heterogenous: fome pieces of it do not give fire with fteel, and therefore belong to this genus, others do, and belong therefore to the filiceous genus.

According to Mr. *Wiegleb's* analyfis. 11 *Nev. Endeck,* p. 18, 100 parts of it contain

65 of filex, 16 of argill, 5 of iron, the remaining 14 gr. were diffipated.

Species XIV.

Argill mixed with a notable Proportion of red Calx of Iron, and fometimes Steatites.

Red Chalk.

It hardens in fire, and then often becomes magnetic, in the ftrongeft heat it melts into a black glafs, which does not corrode the crucibles, as calcareous ores do: it affords 16 or 18 per cent. of iron; if it does not become magnetic it affords only from 7 to 14 per cent. *Rinman Hiftoria Ferri,* § 189.

Compound Species in which the Argillaceous Genus predominates.

Species I.

Compounds of the different Species of the Argillaceous Genus.

I. Variety.

Micaceous Marl.

II. Variety.

Micaceous Shiftus, either Slate or Flag-ftone.

III. Variety.

Argillaceous Genus.

III. VARIETY.
Micaceous Sand-ſtones.

IV. VARIETY.
Micaceous Horn-ſtone.

Green hornſtone mixed with mica. *Gronſtein* of *Cronſted*, § 267, frequently contains pyrites, and 20 per cent. of iron.

V. VARIETY.
Shiſtus and Argillaceous Grit mixed in various Proportions.

VI. VARIETY.
Shiſtus and Hornſtone mixed in various Proportions.

SPECIES II.
Compounds of the Argillaceous and Calcareous Genus.

I. VARIETY.
Bituminous Shiſtus mixed with Limeſtone.

Marmore Nero Antico.

100 parts of this contain 18 of mild calcareous Earth, the remainder ſhiſtus, from which

which 18 parts of oil were extracted by distillation, also argill, and magnesia, and 6 parts of iron, besides much that was not separated. 12 *Roz.* 63.

Species III.

Compounds of the Argillaceous and Barytical Genus.

Species IV.

Compounds of the Argillaceous and Muriatic Genus.

I. Variety.

Shistus mixed with Steatites or Soap-rock.

II. Variety.

Shistus mixed with Serpentine.

III. Variety.

Hornstone mixed with Mica and Serpentine.

IV. Variety.

Hornstone mixed with Mica and Steatites, or Soap-rock.

V. Variety.

V. Variety.

Mica mixed with Soap-rock, Schneideſtein.
When the mica prevails the texture is ſlaty.

Species V.

Compounds of the Argillaceous and Siliceous Genus, none of which gives Fire with Steel.

I. Variety.

1. *Mica mixed with Quartz, Stellſtein, Cronſt.*
§ 262

It is of a ſlaty texture and eaſily divided.

2. *Mica and Quartz, and a little Argill, Saxum Novaculum Linnei.*

II. Variety.

1. *Hornſtone and Mica mixed with Quartz.*

2. *Hornſtone and Shoerl.*

This is alſo called *Gronſtein*, when the hornſtone is green.

3. *Hornſtone, Mica and Shoerl, Binda of the Swedes.*

It sometimes contains also quartz and pyrites. Its specific gravity exceeds 3,000.

III. Variety.

White Clay mixed with Mica and Quartz, and of no particular texture. Greiss, *of the Germans, or Growan of the Cornish Miners.*

When the texture is lamellar and the stone harder, it is called *Gneiss*.

IV. Variety.

Sandstone mixed with Mica, and Feltspar.

Species VI.

Compounds of the Argillaceous with two or more Genera.

I. Variety.

Micaceous Porphyry.

This consists of a greenish grey, micaceous ground, in which red feltspar and greenish soap-rock are inserted. *Saussure Voyage dans les Alpes*, p. 111, even the mica is not pure, he suspects it contains hornstone, p. 127.

II. Variety.

Hornstone mixed with Veins of Spar and Quartz.

Mentioned by Mr. *Saussure*, p. 120.

CHAP. VIII.

Siliceous Genus.

All the stones I place under this genus give fire with steel, except opals, and yellow carnelians; and none effervesce with acids, except *Lapis Lazuli* in powder, Barshoerl, martial muriatic spar, and Turky hone.

Species I.

Quartz, Crystal.

The stones of this species are in general the purest of the siliceous genus, though most contain a slight mixture of other Earths; the most obvious distinction among them, arises from their transparency or opacity.

Series I.

Transparent Quartz, Crystal.

This is either *colourless* and crystalized in hexagonal pyramids, and then called *mountain crystal*, or in various other forms, or amorphous. Its specific gravity is from 2,65 to 2,7; its texture lamellar and generally shattery, its appearance glassy; it cracks and loses its transparency when heated; it possesses all the other properties of pure siliceous Earth.

Earth. Mr. *Bergman* has extracted from 100 parts of mountain cryftal, about 6 of argill, and 1 of calcareous Earth. 2 *Bergm.* 112. So alfo has Mr. *Abilgaard. Denfk. Shrift.* 1781. Yet Mr. *Gerhard* fays, that fome are fo pure as to contain neither. *Gerh. Beytrage*, 78 and 85. He alfo fays that the amorphous cryftals, though colourlefs, being long digefted in acids, afforded when treated with pure pruffian alkali, fome traces of iron, *ibid.* 85.

The pureft and moft tranfparent of thefe cryftals form the falfe diamond, called briftal, or kerry ftone, diamant d'*Alençon*, &c.

The coloured tranfparent cryftals derive their tinge generally from metallic particles in exceeding fmall proportion; they all loofe their colour when heated; thefe form the falfe Gems. The moft remarkable are the *red*, from *Oran*, in *Barbary*; falfe rubies.

Yellow. From *Bohemia*; falfe topazes.

Green. Falfe emeralds and prafius.

Violet
Blue. } From *Bohemia* and *Saxony*.

It is faid that brown cryftals may be cleared by boiling them in tallow. 7. *Roz.* 360.

Mr.

Mr. *Bergman* has formed perfect cryſtals by diſſolving ſiliceous Earth in the ſparry acid, and ſuffering it to cryſtalize ſlowly. It is probable that nature forms them in a long courſe of time from a ſolution or diffuſion of this Earth in pure water, or water that holds a little argill or calcareous Earth which probably enable it to take up more of the ſiliceous Earth than it otherwiſe could. Perhaps the experiment which once ſucceeded with Mr. *Achard,* was owing to ſome ſuch cauſe.

Series II.

Opake Quartz, or Pebbles.

Thoſe are alſo cryſtalized, or amorphous, either white, grey, or yellowiſh, or tinged of other colours by metallic particles. The former are leſs pure than thoſe of the firſt ſeries, containing a larger proportion of argill, or at leaſt the argill is leſs perfectly united with the ſiliceous part. Their ſpecific gravity is from 2,4 to 2,7; their ſurface either rough, or ſmooth and ſhining, the laſt are called *fat quartz*: the texture either lamellar or granular; they crack like the former in fire, and become of a duller colour; when rubbed againſt each other they emit a phoſphoric ſmell. They are often found in round maſſes in the beds of rivers.

The Coloured Opake Quartz are either.

Black, being mixed with a large proportion of iron.

Red, according to *Cronsted* they contain copper, but Mr. *Bergman* could find none in them. 2 *Bergm*. 430.

Blue, from *Uto* in *Sweden.*

Green, found at *Adelsdorf* in *Sweden*,

Series III.

Arenaceous Quartz or Sand.

Though the powdery state of other stones does not deserve any particular notice: yet that of quartz or silex does, from the great use that is made of it, and from its seeming to possess properties which are incompatible with it in a grosser state. It is of various colours and incapable of forming a mass or hardening with water, the purest is white, the minute particles of which, when inspected through a lens are transparent. It is seldom perfectly pure; Mr. *Achard* says that the fine white sand of *Freyenwald*, which is used for the porcelain manufactories contains $\frac{1}{4}$ of its weight of argill and calcareous Earth, but this I should rather take to be a petro-silex

in

in powder. The fineness of some species of sand is so great as to pass through sieves, that contain 10,000 vacuities in the space of an inch, as Mr. *Wedgewood* one of the most celebrated manufacturers of earthen ware in Europe, has assured me. Hence this Earth has been found suspended in some waters in the quantity of 1 grain in a gallon. See 2 *Bergm.* 47, and *Cadet* in the Memoirs of the French Academy for 1767.

Species II.

Siliceous Earth intimately mixed and partly combined with about $\frac{1}{4}$ of its weight of Argill, and $\frac{1}{40}$ of its weight of Calcareous Earth.

Common Flint or Pebble, Hornstein, Kiesel of the Germans.

This stone is found of all colours, or variegated with veins of different colours; it is commonly covered with an opake white crust, which seems of the same nature, but more imperfectly combined; this crust adheres to the tongue like clay, yet strikes fire with steel, so that probably it contains a larger proportion of argill than the kernel. Flint is always semi-transparent in thin pieces; its hardness is various, though it always gives fire with steel; its texture is solid,

whereas,

whereas that of quartz is shattery; it breaks with smooth surfaces, one of which is convex, the other concave; it is never found crystalized, but rather in separate irregular nodules, scattered through other strata, and plentifully in *England* in beds of chalk; it has seldom any fissures, with which quartz abounds; its specific gravity is from 2,65 to 2,700.

Flints are infusible *per se* in the strongest fire, but generally become white and brittle by reiterated calcination, which seems to indicate that they all contain a little water; and hence also, their decrepitation, when heated; The same may be said of quartz; they are affected by fluxes in the same manner as the purest stones of this genus.

The common brown flint exhibited on Mr. *Wiegleb's* analysis 80 per cent. of siliceous Earth, 18 of argill, and 2 of calcareous. 6 *N. Act. Natur. Curiof.* p. 408. Coloured flints undoubtedly contain metallic particles.

To this species we must also annex the finer flints commonly called *Egyptian pebbles*, hæmachates, stigmites, silex sardus. These differ from common flints; 1^{ft}· in this, that they are less, if at all transparent; 2^d. that their texture is finer, harder, and closer, and

their

Siliceous Genus.

their specific gravity greater; 3$^{d.}$ that they are always covered with an ochry crust; but they break with conchoidal surfaces, as flints do. Their colour is reddish, yellow, black, brown, or grey, or beautifully variegated. They probably contain metallic particles.

Species III.

Siliceous Earth intimately mixed with from $\frac{1}{4}$ to $\frac{1}{3}$ of its weight of Argill, and from $\frac{1}{13}$ to $\frac{1}{12}$ of its weight of Calcareous.

Petro-silex, Chert.

This stone differs but little from the former in external appearance, only it is duller and less transparent; it is found of all colours, but generally dark blue, or yellowish grey; it breaks with conchoidal surfaces like the former, but is generally softer; it runs in veins through rocks, and hence derives its name; its specific gravity is from 2,59 to 2,7: in fire it whitens and decrepitates like silex, but is generally more fusible, for it commonly melts *per se*: it is not totally dissolved in the dry way by mineral alkali, but borax and microcosmic salt dissolve it without effervescence.

From a reddish petro-silex used in the *Count de Lauragais* Porcelain Manufactory, and

and there called a felt-fpar, I extracted 72 per cent. of filex, 22 of argill, and about 6 of mild calcareous Earth, but could not melt it by the blow-pipe. I believe the calcareous Earth was not in a mild ftate in the ftone. It fhewed no fign of iron notwithftanding its flight reddifh colour, nor of any other metal.

Species IV.

Siliceous Earth intimately mixed with about $\frac{1}{3}$ of its weight of Argill, and $\frac{1}{6}$ or $\frac{1}{7}$ of its weight of Calx of Iron.

1. *Jafper, Diafpro of the Italians.*

This fpecies alfo borders on the former, but it has a ftill duller, lefs glaffy, and more earthy appearance in its fracture, and its granular texture is more diftinct; it alfo often breaks with conchoidal furfaces; it is capable of a fine polifh; its colour is generally reddifh or green, or ftriped; but it is alfo found blue, grey, or whitifh; its fpecific gravity is from 2,68 to 2,778, or more, when it contains more iron. In fire it retains its colour much longer than petro filex, never decrepitates, but grows rather harder, as Mr. *Wedgewood* affured me, and does not melt *per fe* in clay crucibles, though it does in thofe made of chalk. Alkalis borax and microcofmic
salt

Siliceous Genus.

salt affect it like the former species. Mr. *Gerhard* says that some sorts of jasper melt *per se*: these contain an over proportion of iron, or else calcareous Earth, and then form the link betwixt cherts and jaspers.

The green jaspers contain iron in a semi-phlogisticated state, and have often been confounded with malachites, but these latter never give fire with steel, to say nothing of the entire difference of their composition. Red jaspers contain iron more dephlogisticated.

Sinople is a dark red jasper or flint, which strikes fire with steel, and affords in the dry way 10 per cent. of iron, and melts into a black slag. *Rinm. Hist. Ferri*, § 189. If tried with the Prussian alkali, it would probably shew 18 or 20 parts of iron, as this always separates nearly double the quantity of iron that can be extracted in the dry way.

Of the spontaneous Decomposition of Stones by long Exposure to the Air.

Flints, jaspers, petro-silex, felt-spar, granites, lavas and ferruginous stones, have frequently been said to be decomposed by long exposure to the air, and the observations of Mr. *Greville* and Sir *William Hamilton* have removed every doubt I entertained on this head.

With

With regard to ferruginous stones in which the calx of iron is not much dephlogisticated, this decomposition is easily understood, for this calx gradually becomes more dephlogisticated by the action of water and air, attracts water and fixed air, and loses its adherence with the siliceous or other stony particles: this is seen to happen to basaltes, toadstone, ferruginous limestone, &c. In other stones this decomposition may arise from their containing calcareous Earth in a caustic state, or manganese, for these will gradually attract water and fixed air, and then swell, burst and loosen the whole texture of the stone, as we see happen to bricks that contain lime. Thus also glass is decomposed by long exposure to the air, the alkali attracting water and aerial acid. Mortar, on the contrary hardens by long exposure to the air, because, though the aerial acid be attracted, yet a great part of the water exhales.

Species V.

The finer Flints mixed with various Proportions of other Earths and Iron.

Precious Stones of the second Order.

I. Variety.

Agates.

The oriental agate is almost transparent, and of a glassy appearance, but whitish, with inward

Siliceous Genus.

inward protuberances. The occidental is of various colours, and often veined with quartz or jasper; it is mostly found in small pieces covered with a crust, and often running in veins through rocks, as flints and petro-silex, to which it is analogous, but more transparent, the Earths being better combined and the grain closer; its specific gravity is 2,64; it often forms the stony matter of petrifactions.

Agates that present arborisations are called mochoes.

Alkalis, borax and microcosmic salt affect this stone in the same manner as they do flints.

II. VARIETY.

Opal, Oculus Mundi, Lapis Mutabilis.

This stone is of different colours, white, yellowish, or greenish brown; its peculiar characteristic is to reflect different colours, according to the different positions of the eye; it is mostly of a spungy texture, and admits water into it, and generally too soft to strike fire with steel; its specific gravity is from 1,7 to 2,24.

The usual fluxes act on it as on flints. Mr. *Bergman* has extracted argill from it.

Pseudopal

Pseudopal is opake, and reflects green and yellow rays, and hence called cat's eye.

Avanturine resembles an opal with gold specks, but is a product of art.

III. Variety.

Chalcedonian.

Its colour is a bluish cloudy white, or grey, with shades of other colours, and transversely inspected presents an iris; when white and opake it is called *chachelong*: its specific gravity, according to Mr. *Bergman*, is from 2,5 to 4,36. Stones of this latter weight must be very different from those of the former. These stones sometimes contain water. It is affected by the usual fluxes, as flint.

According to the experiments of Mr. *Bergman*, the chalcedony of *Fero* contains 84 per cent. of silex and 16 of argill. Mr. *Bindheim* found another sort to contain 83,3 of silex, 11 of calcareous Earth, and 1,6 of argill, besides a minute portion of iron. 3 *Schrift. Nuturfor. Freunde*, p. 429.

Opals and chalcedonies, which by admitting water within their pores become transparent, are called *hydrophanes*. This phœnomenon

nomenon is well explained in the second volume of Mr. *Bergman's* works.

IV. Variety.

Onyx.

This is a very hard stone of the colour of the human nail, with straight or circular zones of another colour; if the zones themselves be of different colours, it is more esteemed, and called *camehuya*: it is almost opake; its specific gravity is from 2,5 to 2,6; it is affected by fluxes as the former varieties.

V. Variety.

Carnelian.

Its colour is of different shades of red; it is also of different degrees of transparency and hardness: the best is of an orange or yellow red, and gives fire with steel; the whitish or yellowish are too soft to give fire with steel, and less esteemed; its specific gravity is from 2,6 to 2,7; it loses its colour in fire. Fluxes affect it like the above.

VI. Variety.

Sardonyx.

It consists of chalcedony and carnelian, united either in zones, strata, or spots.

Species VI.

Siliceous Earth perfectly united to, from an equal to 3 times its weight of Argill, and from $\frac{1}{8}$ to an equal weight of Calcareous Earth, together with from $\frac{1}{18}$ to an equal weight of Iron.

Precious Stones of the first Order.

I derive the denominations of these stones from their colour and hardness, and not from their hardness singly, as Jewellers mostly do, as this property, though it contributes to their splendor and value, has but little or no connexion with their composition. I also omit many sub-denominations of each sort of these stones, which are to be found in treatises expressly written on that subject. The specific gravity of all of them exceed 2,76, whereas that of coloured crystals never does. Their singular lustre and transparency are well known.

I. Variety.

Red.

Ruby, Oriental.

It is commonly found crystalized in an octohedral form; its texture is foliated; its hardness

Siliceous Genus.

hardnefs much greater than that of any other ftone, and yields only to that of diamond; its fpecific gravity from 3,18 to 4,283.

In fire it is invitriable *per fe*, and does not yield even to the focal rays of a burning glafs, but a flame excited by dephlogifticated air, directed by a blow-pipe, readily melts it; it does not lofe its colour in a heat that would melt iron. Borax and microcofmic falt effect its fufion, but mineral alkali fails.

100 parts of it contain, according to Mr. *Bergman*, 40 of argillaceous, 39 of filiceous, 9 of mild calcareous Earth, and 10 of iron.

Or, according to Mr. *Achard*, 41,66 of filiceous Earth, 36,66 of argill, 8,33 of calcareous Earth, and 10,83 of iron.

Brazil rubies are paler, and faid to be found in hexangular or polyangular cryftals.

Jewellers, among whom hardnefs and tranfparency are the chief characteriftics, mention alfo white and amethyft coloured rubies, but thefe have not been analyfed.

Oriental rubies are chiefly found in *Pegu*, *Ceylon*, *Bifnagar*, and *Cambuya*. A bafer fort is found in *Finland, Bohemia, Silesia, Saxony* and *Hungary.*

II. VARIETY.

Yellow.

Topaz, Hyacinth.

Topas is of a gold colour; its texture foliaceous; its form cubic, parallelipedal, or prismatic; its specific gravity from 3,46 to 4,56; it loses its colour only in a very strong heat, and of the usual fluxes it yields only to borax and microcosmic salt.

According to Mr. *Bergman,* 100 parts of it contain 46 of argill, 39 of siliceous Earth, 8 mild calcareous, and 6 of iron. Its great specific gravity shews these Earths to be very perfectly united.

Oriental *hyacinth* is of a reddish yellow colour, generally crystalized in a prismatic form; in a strong heat it becomes paler, and according to Mr. *Achard,* may be melted in a wind furnace in 2 hours.

According to Mr. *Bergman,* 100 parts of it contain 40 of argill, 25 of silex, 20 of mild calcareous Earth, and 13 of iron; and according

Siliceous Genus.

according to Mr. *Achard*, 41,33 of argill, 21,66 of filex, 20 of calcareous Earth, and 13,33 of iron.

Hyacinths are found in *Poland*, *Bohemia*, and *Saxony*.

III. VARIETY.

Green.

Emerald, Chryfolite, Beryl.

The colour of emerald is pure green; it is fometimes found in round flat pieces, but moftly cryftalized in hexagonal prifms; its fpecific gravity is from 2,78 to 3,711. It is the fofteft of all the precious ftones.

According to Mr. *Achard*, it preferves its colour in a porcelain heat, and only becomes more opake; in a ftronger heat it melts into a flag. *Mem. Stock.* 1768. Like the foregoing it eludes the force of mineral alkali, but yields to borax and microcofmic falt. With the former, according to Mr. *Quift*, it gives a colourlefs glafs.

100 parts of it contain, by Mr. *Bergman*'s analyfis, 60 of argill, 24 of filex, 8 of calcareous Earth, and 6 of iron; and by that of Mr.

Mr. *Achard*, 60 of argill, 21,66 of filex, 8,33 of calcareous Earth, and 5 of iron.

It was antiently found in *Egypt*, now chiefly in *Peru*.

Chryfolite, or *Beryl*, is of a light yellowifh green; it melts *per fe* into a flag; it is fofter than cryftal; it yields only to borax and microcofmic falt, and is fcarcely affected by alkalis: when ready to melt it becomes phofphorefcent.

Aqua Marine (augites) is of a bluifh green; it melts *per fe* by the blow-pipe.

IV. VARIETY.

Blue.

Sapphire.

Its colour is fky blue; its texture foliaceous; its form hexangular or polyangular prifms or parallelipeds; its fpecific gravity from 3,78 to 3,994; the oriental preferves its colour in a porcelain heat, and will not melt *per fe*, but that of *Brazil* lofes its colour; it is affected by fluxes as the other varieties.

Mr. *Bergman* found 100 parts of this ftone to contain 58 of argill, 35 of filex, 5 of
mild

Siliceous Genus.

mild calcareous Earth, and 2 of iron; and Mr. *Achard* 58,33 of argill, 33,33 of filex, 6,66 of calcareous Earth, and 3,33 of iron.

Jewellers mention white, green, and yellow fapphires, or pale red.

Species VII.
Amethyft.

Some of this fpecies are as tranfparent as the former ftones, others duller; its fpecific gravity, which reaches only from 2,6 to 2,7, makes me judge it to be very different from them; its colour is pale bluifh red; its texture nearly granular, and generally cryftalized in hexangular prifms; it lofes its colour in a ftrong heat, but does not melt *per fe,* though with borax it gives a colourlefs glafs; its compofition has not yet been examined.

Species VIII.

Siliceous Earth united to $\frac{1}{55}$ of its weight of Calcareous Earth, ftill lefs of Magnefia, with an exceeding fmall Proportion of Iron, Copper, and Sparry Acid.

Chryfoprafium.

It is of an apple green colour, and femitranfparent; it has never been found cryftalized;

ſtalized; it is much harder than green fluors or green quartz.

When diſtilled, a little of its Earth ſublimes; it loſes its tranſparency and colour in fire, but does not melt *per ſe*.

Mr. *Achard* found 100 parts of it to contain 95 of ſiliceous Earth, 1,7 of calcareous Earth, 1,2 of magneſia, 0,4 of iron, and 0,6 of copper.

Species IX.

Siliceous Earth intimately mixed with blue martial Fluor, and a ſmall Proportion of Gypſum.

Lapis Lazuli.

The colour of this ſtone is a beautiful opake blue, which varies a little in intenſity, and is generally ſprinkled over with yellow, bright, pyritaceous ſpecks or ſtreaks: it obſtinately retains its colour in a ſtrong heat, which diſtinguiſhes it from other blue ſtones: it is of an equable or very fine granular texture, and takes a beautiful poliſh: its ſpecific gravity is 3,054.

If powdered and not calcined, it effervesces very ſlightly with acids, but if calcined,

cined, it does not effervesce, but becomes gelatinous.

In a strong fire it melts *per se* into a *whitish* glass.

This stone has been examined by Mr. *Margraaf* only with a view of finding whether it contained copper. He found none, but only calcareous Earth, gypsum, iron, and silex. Mr. *Rinman* lately found it to contain the sparry acid.

Species X.

Jade.

Jade is found in scattered masses like pebbles, semi-transparent, of a greasy look, and exceeding hard: its colour is either white, grey, olive, green, or yellowish: its specific gravity from 2,97 to 3,389. According to Mr. *Sauſſure*, it is scarcely soluble in acids, at least without particular management, and also infusible in fire. However, he seems to have extracted iron from it.

May it not be a compound of silex and magnesia?

Species XI.

Species XI.

Siliceous Earth intimately mixed and partly united with 0,209 of its weight of Argill, 0,164 of its weight of ponderous Earth, and 0,12 of its weight of Magnesia.

Felt-spar, Spathum Pyromachum, Rhombic Quartz, Quartzum Spathosum, Spathum Durum, Petunse.

This stone, which is generally opake, is found of all colours, white, red, yellow, brown, green, violet, or iridescent; sometimes crystalized in rhombic, cubic, or parallelipedal forms, and often amorphous: its texture close but lamellar, and breaks like spar: its specific gravity is from 2,4 to 2,6, and Mr. *Gerhard* says he found it even 3,5; but it was then probably loaded with metallic particles: it is harder than fluors, but not so hard as quartz.

It melts *per se* more quickly and perfectly than fluors, into a whitish glass, and does not, like them, attack the crucibles. Borax and microcosmic salt entirely dissolve it without effervescence, but it does not easily enter into fixed alkalis. When crystalized, it decrepitates in a moderate heat, otherwise not.

Siliceous Genus.

It never conſtitutes veins or ſtrata, but is either found in looſe maſſes at moſt 2 inches long, or mixed with ſand or clay, or imbodied in other ſtones, as granites, &c.

100 parts of the white contain about 67 of ſiliceous Earth, 14 of argillaceous, 11 of ponderous, and 8 of magniſia.

The ſpecific gravity of the ſpecimen I tried was 2,542.

Labrador ſtone is of this ſpecies; it reflects the colours of the rainbow, is ſomewhat ſofter than common felt-ſpar, and is found in pretty large pieces, generally of a dark grey colour: its ſpecific gravity is 2,755.

Felt-ſpar is undoubtedly the ſtone which the Saxons uſe as petunſe in their porcelain manufactories. 3 *Berlin Beſchaftig.* p. 471.

Species XII.

Siliceous Zeolyte.

This differs from that deſcribed under the argillaceous genus only in this, that it gives fire with ſteel. It is white, and found at *Mæſſiberg.* 3 *Bergm.* 224. It is very rare.

Species XIII.

Species XIII.

Siliceous Earth imperfectly united to about 0,7 of its weight of Argill, and $\frac{1}{9}$ of its weight of Calcareous Earth, without Iron.

Vesuvian Garnet.

It is improperly called a garnet, as it contains no iron, and it differs from zeolyte in containing no water, and also in texture and hardness: its colour is white, sometimes opake and sometimes transparent, and very hard: it is difficultly acted on by any of the fluxes.

According to Mr. *Bergman*, it contains 55 per cent. of siliceous Earth, 39 of argill, and 6 of calcareous Earth.

Species XIV.

Siliceous Earth more or less perfectly united to 0,63 of its weight of Argill, about 0,4 of its weight of Calcareous Earth, and from 0,28 to about 0,41 of its weight of dephlogisticated Iron.

Garnet.

When not over-loaded with iron it is transparent, though, from the intensity of its colour,

Siliceous Genus.

lour, which is a bluish or yellowish red, its transparency is often obscure, except it be held to a strong light: it is generally crystalized in various polygon forms, but it is frequently amorphous: its texture is granular; its specific gravity from 3,6 to 4,188.

It melts *per se*, though difficultly, into a black slag. Mineral alkali does not attack it so powerfully as borax or microcosmic salt.

It retains its colour in a strong calcining heat.

It is often found in small grains, imbodied in stones of the commonest kind.

100 parts of it contain, according to Mr. Achard, 48,3 of siliceous Earth, 30 of argill, 11,6 of calcareous Earth, and 10 of iron.

Opake garnets, over-loaded with iron, scarcely give fire with steel, are sometimes crystalized and sometimes amorphous, and either red, yellowish, or blackish. They afford about 20 per cent. of iron. Sometimes they contain tin and even lead, but very rarely. 2 *Bergm.* 106.

SPECIES XV.

Species XV.

Siliceous Earth more or less perfectly united to from 0,46 to 0,83 of its weight of Argill, from $\frac{1}{14}$ to $\frac{1}{9}$ of Calcareous Earth, and to $\frac{1}{5}$ or $\frac{1}{6}$ of semiphlogisticated Calx of Iron, and from $\frac{1}{48}$ to $\frac{1}{38}$ of Magnesia.

Schoerl.

Its distinguishing properties are, 1st. either a sparry or semi-vitrified appearance, like an enamel or a flag; 2d. a filamentous or scaly texture, which distinguishes it from garnets; the filaments either separate from each other, or conjoined and plated; 3d. fusibility *per se* in a moderate heat; 4th. a specific gravity from 3, to 3,6, rarely 4,000, and only when loaded with iron; 5th its hardness nearly as that of crystal.

I. Variety.

Transparent.

This is always crystalized in some polygon form: its texture obscurely sparry: its colour brown, reddish brown, greenish or yellowish brown, or violet: its specific gravity from 3, to 3,6.

A reddish brown, prismatic shoerl of this sort, from *Vesuvius*, contained, according to Mr. *Bergman*, 48 per cent. of siliceous Earth, 40 of argill, 5 of calcareous, 1 of magnesia, and 5 of iron. The usual fluxes affect this species, as they do the foregoing.

The filamentous sort resembles asbestos, and differs externally only in transparency and breaking with an even surface.

II. VARIETY.

Opake.

These are of all colours, white, black, red, brown, greenish, and violet; the filaments are conjoined and parallel, or diverge, as from a common center. Those of a scaly or sparry appearance are generally greenish or black, and are called *Hornblende*. They are frequently crystalized in regular forms, and often so soft as to be scraped with a knife.

100 grains of the black crystalized sort from *Albano*, afforded Mr. *Bergman* 58 of silex, 27 of argill, 5 of calcareous Earth, 1 of magnesia, and 5 of iron. 3 *Bergm.* 207. Other sorts have afforded 50 per cent. of sili-

ceous Earth, 30 of argill, 1 or 2 of magnesia, and 18 or 20 of iron.

The white sort probably contains less iron.

All these sorts become reddish by calcination.

Species XVI.

Siliceous Earth imperfectly united with 0,34 of its weight of Calcareous Earth, 0,107 of its weight of Argill, 0,08 of Magnesia, 0,026 of Iron, and about 0,048 of Water.

Bar Shoerl, Stangen Shoerl of the Germans.

This was lately found in the Carpathian Mountains by Mr. *Fichtel,* imbodied in limestone, and crystalized in prisms: it slightly effervesces with acids.

According to Mr. *Bindheim,* 100 parts of it contain 61,6 of siliceous Earth, 21,6 of calcareous Earth, 6,6 of argill, 5 of magnesia, 1,6 of iron, and 3 of water. 3 *Schrift. Naturforsch. Freunde,* p. 452.

Species XVII.

Species XVII.

Siliceous Earth imperfectly united with from 1,05 to 1,47 of its weight of Argill, from 0,3 to 0.4 of its weight of mild Calcareous Earth, and from 0,15 to 0,243 of its weight of Iron.

Tourmaline.

Tourmaline has hitherto been found only in *Ceylon, Brazil,* and the *Tyrol.* A specimen of each has had the advantage of having been particularly examined by Mr. *Bergman.* That of *Ceylon* is of a dark brown, or yellowish colour, its specific gravity 3,065, or, 3,295; that of *Brazil* is green, blue, red, or yellow, and its specific gravity 3,075 or 3,180; that of *Tyrol,* by reflected light, is of a blackish brown, but by refracted light, yellowish, or in thin pieces, green; its specific gravity 3,050; mostly crystalized in polygon prisms, but sometimes amorphous. The thickest parts are opake: the thin more or less transparent.

All are electric when heated to about 200 of *Fahrenheit.* Their texture is lamellar, and their surface has a glassy appearance.

In fire none of them decrepitate; but those of *Ceylon* and *Tyrol* melt *per se* into a black

black frothy flag. That of *Brazil* forms only a brittle scoria. Of the usual fluxes, borax dissolves them best, microcosmic salt and mineral alkali partially.

The proportion of their constituent principles is thus exhibited by Mr *Bergman*:

Tourmaline of Tyrol.

Argill,	42
Silex,	40
Calcareous Earth,	12
Iron,	6
	100

Tourmaline of Ceylon.

Argill,	39
Silex,	37
Calcareous Earth,	15
Iron,	9
	100

Tourmaline of Brazil.

Argill,	50
Silex,	34
Calcareous Earth,	11
Iron,	5
	100

SPECIES XVIII.

Siliceous Genus.

Species XVIII.

Siliceous Earth mixed with 0,3 *of its weight of Argill,* 0,17 *of mild Calcareous Earth,* 0,04 *of Magnesia, and* 0,5 *of Iron.*

Basaltes, Trapp of the Swedes, Saxum Danemorense.

A dark grey or black stone, generally invested with a ferruginous crust and crystalized in opake triangular or polyangular columns, is called basaltes; that which is amorphous, or breaks in large, thick, square pieces, is called *trapp*. Their constituent principles, and relation to acids and fluxes, are exactly the same. The texture of this stone is either coarse, rough, and distinct, or fine and indiscernable. This latter sort is often reddish; it is always opake, and moulders by exposure to the air; some specimens give fire with steel very difficultly, though it is always very compact; sometimes it is sprinkled over with a few minute shining particles: its specific gravity is 3,000.

When heated red hot, and quenched in water, it becomes by degrees of a reddish brown colour: it melts *per se* in a strong heat into a compact slag. Borax also dissolves it in fusion, but mineral alkali not intirely.

According to Mr. *Bergman,* 100 parts of the bafaltes contain 52 of filiceous Earth, 15 of argill, 8 of calcareous, 2 of magnefia, and 25 of iron. 3 *Bergm.* 213. And with this Mr. *Meyer* very nearly agrees. 14 *Naturforfh.* 5.

Species XIX.

Siliceous Earth mixed with 0,69 of its weight of Argill, and 0,41 of its weight of Iron in a femiphlogifticated ftate.

Rowly Ragg.

This ftone is alfo of a dufky or dark grey colour, with numerous minute fhining cryftals; its texture granular; by expofure to the air it acquires an ochry cruft; its fpecific gravity 2,748.

Heated in an open fire it becomes magnetic. In a ftrong heat it melts *per fe,* but more difficultly than bafaltes.

According to Dr. *Withering's* analyfis, 100 parts of it contain 47,5 of filiceous Earth, 32,5 of argill, and 20 of iron.

Species XX.

Species XX.

Siliceous Earth more or less perfectly united to from $\frac{1}{3}$ to $\frac{9}{10}$ of its weight of Argill, 0,3 or 0,4 of its weight of Iron, and a small proportion of pure Calcareous Earth, but this is sometimes wanting.

Lava.

By *Lava* I understand the immediate product of liquefaction or vitrification by volcanic fire, which should carefully be distinguished from the subsequent productions affected by the water either in a liquid or fluid state, which generally is ejected at the same time.

All lavas are more or less magnetic, give fire with steel, are of a granular texture, and fusible *per se*. Most are decomposable by long exposure to the air, sooner or later, according to the proportion of iron and calcareous Earth, and according as they were more or less perfectly melted or vitrified.

Mr. *Bergman*, in his elaborate treatise on volcanic products, distinguishes three varieties of lava; the cellular or frothy, the compact, and the vitreous.

I. Variety.

I. Variety.

Cellular Lavas.

These underwent only the first and lowest degree of fusion, being just mollified and heated sufficiently to expell the fixed air contained in the argillaceous particles; hence they abound in small cavities arising from the expansion of that air after it had recovered its elastic state. Their specific gravity is various: some are so light, by reason of their internal cavities, as to float for some time on water, and hence, have been mistaken for pumice stones, but they differ from these in this, that their texture is never filamentous.

Their colour is black, grey, brown, or reddish brown, and their cavities are often filled with cryftalizations.

Of this sort is the black cellular mill-stone of the *Rhine*.

These stones contain from 45 to 50 per cent. of silex, and from 15 to 20 per cent. of iron, 4 or 5 per cent. of pure calcareous Earth, and the remainder argill.

II. Variety.

II. Variety.

Compact Lavas.

These have undergone the 2d or more perfect degree of fusion, yet they are not entirely destitute of cavities which contain finer crystals, or pieces more perfectly vitrified; their colour is black or brown; their fracture is still obscure, and not glassy, as the stones themselves are opake: if not cracked, they give a clear sound when struck.

The proportion and quality of their constituent parts are the same as in the foregoing variety. The usual fluxes attack them with difficulty, and microcosmic salt has scarce any power over them.

III. Variety.

Vitreous Lavas.

These have been more completely melted, and form vitrifactions of different colours, generally black or ash-coloured, rarely blue or greenish.

A specimen of this glass, examined by Mr. *Bergman*, afforded 49 per cent. of silex,

35 of argill, 4 of pure calcareous Earth, and 12 of iron. Another specimen from the *Lipari Islands* afforded 69 of silex, 22 of argill, and 9 of iron. This must have been exposed to a very strong heat, for they melt very difficultly *per se*.

The *black Agate of Iceland*, *(Lapis obsidianus, Piedra de Galinaço)* is of this sort, and its principles and their proportions nearly the same.

The harder sort of pitch stones, already described, which give fire with steel, belong to this species.

Mr. *Sauffure* has ingeniously imitated all these species of lava, by melting more or less perfectly the compound argillaceous species into which hornstone enters as the most copious ingredient, and which he therefore calls *Hornrock*, *Roche de corne*, and which are already described. *Voyage dans les Alpes*, p. 127. And hence he justly conjectures that this stone, marl, and the schisti (Species 6, 7, and 8 of the Argillaceous Genus) are the principal materials of lava. *Ibid*, 131, 132.

SPECIES XXI.

Species XXI.

Siliceous Earth mixed with 0,11 *or* 0,17 *of its weight of Magnesia, and a little of Calcareous Earth.*

Pumice-stone, Pierre Ponce, Bimstein.

This seems rather a volcanic ejection than a volcanic product; its colour is grey, white, reddish brown, or black: it is hard, rough, and porous, and consists of slender fibres parallel to each other; very light, for it swims on water, and difficultly gives fire with steel. It seems to have originally been an asbestos decomposed by the action of fire.

100 parts of it contain, according to Mr. *Bergman,* from 6 to 15 of magnesia, with a very small proportion of calcareous Earth, the remainder silex.

Species XXII.

Siliceous Earth mixed with less than its own weight of Magnesia and Iron.

Martial Muriatic Spar.

Mr. *Monnet,* a Mineralogist of considerable note, lately discovered this stone at *St. Marie aux Mines,* and called it *pisolites;* but as a
very

very different compound is generally denoted by this name, I have called it martial muriatic fpar, a name which agrees better with its properties.

It is of a hard, folid, and fparry texture; of a grey, ochry, dull colour, but internally bright: it gives fire with fteel, yet effervefces with acids.

In a ftrong heat it grows brown, but at laft melts *per fe*.

100 parts of it contain 50 of filex, the remainder mild magnefia and iron, but in what proportion is not mentioned. 13 *Roz. Suppl.* 416.

Species XXIII.

Siliceous Earth intimately mixed with $\frac{1}{7}$ of its weight of mild Calcareous Earth.

Turky Stone, Cos Turcica.

This is of a dull white colour, and uneven texture; fome parts appearing more compact than others, fo that it is in fome meafure fhattery: it hardens with oil; its fpecific gravity is 2,598; it gives fire with fteel, yet effervefces with acids.

I

I found 100 parts of it to contain 25 of mild calcareous Earth, and no iron. There probably are two forts of ftone known by this name, as Mr. *Wallerius* affirms that which he defcribes, neither to give fire with fteel, nor effervefce with acids.

Species XXIV.

Siliceous Earth mixed with mild Calcareous Earth and Iron.

Ragg-ftone.

Its colour is grey; its texture obfcurely laminar, but the laminæ confift of a congeries of grains of a quartzy appearance, coarfe and rough; its fpecific gravity is 2,729; it effervefces with acids, and gives fire with fteel. I found it to contain a portion of calcareous Earth, and a fmall proportion of iron. It is ufed as a whetftone.

Species XXV.

Arenaceous Quartz confolidated by a fmaller proportion of Calcareous Earth, or Argill, and ftill a fmaller of Iron.

Silicevus Grit, Sandftone, Freeftone, Cos Arenarius, Grais.

Under this fpecies I comprehend only fuch as ftrike fire with fteel, and when pounded,

pounded, form a sand rather than a powder.

I. Variety.

Grit with a Calcareous Cement, Quadrum.

A stone of this sort hath been already described under the calcareous genus. When it contains about 50 per cent. or more of silex it belongs to this species; it commonly contains also a small proportion of argill and iron; it hardens by exposure to the air, and then strikes fire with steel, and effervesces slightly with acids: it is sometimes crystalized in rhomboids, as at *Fontainbleau*. 100 parts of this contain, by the experiments of Mr. *Laſſone*, 62,5 of silex and 37,5 of mild calcareous Earth. *Mem. Par.* 1777, p. 43.

The *Saxum margariticum* of *Linneus* belongs also to this species: it consists of quartz in a calcareous cement.

II. Variety.

With an Argillaceous Cement.

These do not effervesce with acids, but they strike fire with steel, though some sorts are too soft to do so until exposed for some time to the air. The free-stone from *Keredge*, near *Macclesfield*, which is of a close grain, is of this species. Its specific gravity is 2,544.

So

So also that of *Brownedge*, in *Staffordshire*, which is so perfect a sand-stone that its specific gravity is only 2,397; and the whitish grey freestone from *Uttoxeter*. All these contain a little of iron.

Stones of this species are used for whetting tools, and for filtring water, and in some countries as slates. The principal distinction among them arises from the fineness or coarseness of their grain and texture. Their colours are various, receiving different tinges from iron.

Species XXVI.

Siliceous Sand consolidated by semiphlogisticated Calx of Iron.

This stone does not fall into sand when powdered, and in this respect differs from the foregoing. It is generally of a brown or black colour, but grows reddish or yellowish, and moulders by exposure to the air; its specific gravity is from 2,8 to 3,6; it gives fire with steel, and does not effervesce with acids, unless it contains testaceous particles, as it frequently does: it is even often covered with shells.

The agglutinating power of solutions of iron has been shewn in an ingenious paper in the

the Philofophical Tranfactions for 1779, p. 35, by Mr. *Edward King*, who found a ftony concretion of this fort round iron, which had been long buried in the fea.

Mr. *Gadd*, in the Swedifh Memoirs for 1770, relates, that Mr. *Rinman* had found a fimilar concretion round an old anchor that had long been depofited in the fea. He alfo adds, from his own experiments, that dephlogifticated calces of iron, and particularly folutions made by the mineral acids, have not the fame binding power, but, on the contrary, make loofe concretions, as Dr. *Higgins* has alfo fhewn in a late very ufeful treatife on cements.

To this fpecies may be added the *black, heavy, gloffy Quartz* of *Cronfted*, § 53, which he fays is found in the mine of *Staf*, in *Sudermanland*, and contains a large proportion of iron.

Compound Species in which the Siliceous Genus predominates.

Species I.

Compounds of the different Species of the Siliceous Genus with each other.

I Variety.

I. Variety.
Quartz and Shoerl.

This stone consists of distinct grains of each compacted together in various proportions. The quartz is generally white, or reddish; the shoerl, black, brown, white, or green: by some it is called a *granite*. Some of the paving-stones of *London* are of this sort.

II. Variety.
Quartz and Felt-spar.

The quartz is generally white; the felt-spar red, yellow, or brown: found in the *Alps* by Mr. *Saussure*, from whose excellent work many of the following descriptions are taken. Mill-stones and whet-stones are often of this sort.

III. Variety.
Jade and Shoerl.

The shoerl is interspersed through the jade; in a strong fire it melts, but the jade only whitens. *Saussure Voyage dans les Alpes*, p. 84. Its specific gravity is from 3,318 to 3,389. The jade is yellowish, the shoerl green or black.

IV. Variety.

IV. Variety.

Jade, Shoerl, and Garnet.

Of confiderable hardnefs and weight, with large fpots of red, green, and yellow; the garnet red, the fhoerl green, and the jade yellow. *Sauffure*, p. 107.

V. Variety.

Quartz, Felt-fpar, and Shoerl,

Granite.

Thefe are fo well adapted to each other, that, as Mr. *Sauffure* well remarks, they could not have been fo compacted by an accidental mixture of maffes previoufly formed, but muft have cryftalized together. It may be feen among the paving ftones of *London*. The quartz is white, the fhoerl black or violet, and the felt-fpar reddifh.

VI. Variety.

Puddingftone, Breccias.

Stones which confift of a filiceous ground or cement, (commonly petro-filex, jafper, or filiceous grit) in which pebbles of filex or agate are interfperfed; if thefe be round or oval, are called *puddingftones*; if angular, *breccias*. Of the coarfer forts mill-ftones are often made. *Mem. Par.* 1758.

VII. Variety.

VII. Variety.
Coral Stone.

This is an aggregate of onyx, fardonyx, rnelian amethyft, and quartz.

Species II.
Compounds of the Siliceous with the Calcareous Species.

I. Variety.
Quartz and Spar.

Diftinct grains of each compacted together; the quartz generally white and femi-tranfparent; the fpar of a brownifh yellow. *Sauffure*, 104.

Species III.
Compounds of the Siliceous and Barytic Species.

Species IV.
Compound of the Siliceous and Muriatic Species.

I. Variety.
Quartz, Felt-fpar, and Serpentine.

II. Variety.
Shoerl and Soap-rock.

Compacted of diftinct maffes of each, *Sauffure* 104. The foap-rock is green, and the

the shoerl black. It gives fire with steel, when the shoerl is struck.

III. Variety.

Quartz and Steatites.

Observed also by Mr. *Sauſſure*, the quartz white, and the steatites green.

IV. Variety.

Qtartz, Shoerl, and Steatites.

The steatites inclosed in the quartz in the form of black kernels.

Species V.

Compounds of the Siliceous, and Argillaceous Species.

I. Variety.

Quartz and Mica. Stellſten of the Swedes. Granitello.

It strikes fire with steel, and does not easily melt; and hence used for furnaces, &c. When the mica abounds it is of a lamellar texture, its colour is generally grey, or green; the mixture of mica prevents the silex or quartz

Siliceous Genus.

quartz from cracking or fpliting; and hence its infufibility and ufe in furnaces.

II. Variety.

Feltſpar and Mica,
Granitone.

This ſtone is mentioned by *Ferber*, in his letters from *Italy*, p, 118. A ſtone of this ſort which moulders by expoſures to the air, is found in *Finland*, and is ſaid to contain ſometimes ſaltpetre, and ſometimes common ſalt, it is there called *Rapakivi*, 1 Linné von Gmelin, 621.

III. Variety.

Quartz and Horn-ſtone.

In ſmall diſtinct grains compacted together, this is found plentifully in the mountain of *Penmaumaure* in *Wales*. It exhales an earthy ſmell, gives fire with ſteel, and is of a thick lamellar texture: its ſpecific gravity is 2,811. the quartz is white, and the horn-ſtone black, which gives the ſtone a bluiſh appearance.

IV. Variety.

Quartz, Feltſpar, and Mica, or Quartz, Shoerl and Mica.
Granite, Moor-ſtone.

This ſtone conſiſts of diſtinct maſſes of each, firmly compacted together, their proportion and size are extremely variable, as well as their colour. The three firſt conſtitute the hardeſt ſort of the granite, and moſt anciently known; that into which the ſhoerl enters, is more ſubject to decompoſition; it never has any particular texture, but conſiſts of enormous ſhapeleſs maſſes, of great hardneſs.

In the finer granites, the quartz is tranſparent, in others generally white or grey, violet or brown; the feltſpar, white, yellow, red, green, or black, it is generally the moſt copious ingredient. The mica is alſo grey, brown, yellow, green, red, violet or black, and is commonly leaſt copious. The ſhoerl is generally black, and abounds in the granites that contain it. Hence the colour of granites chiefly depends of the feltſpar or ſhoerl. The *red* granites conſiſt commonly of white quartz, red feltſpar, and grey mica. The *grey* of white quartz, grey or violet feltſpar, and black mica. The *black* commonly contain ſhoerl, inſtead of feltſpar. The *green* commonly contain greeniſh quartz.

If granite be expoſed to a blow-pipe, its different concretions ſeparate from each other. In a crucible, Mr. *Gerhard* found the feltſpar melted into a tranſparent glaſs; under it the mica lay in the form of a black ſlagg, and the

the quartz remained unaltered; but when all three are powdered and mixed, it melts fomewhat better, yet ftill the quartz may be diftinguifhed by the help of a lens *Gerh. Gefch.* § 51. This well explains why fmall white grains are frequently found in lavas. Mr. *D'Arcet's* experiments coincide with this, and alfo thofe of Mr. *Sauffure,* p. 124.

V. VARIETY.

Quartz, Feltfpar, Shoerl and Mica.

This is alfo a fort of granite obferved by Mr. *Sauffure* in the Alps.

VI. VARIETY.

Jade, Shoerl, and Mica.

A fort of granite obferved by Mr. *Sauffure.*

VII. VARIETY.

Quartz, Garnet, and Mica, Norka, Murkftein.

This is either grey or reddifh, and ufed for mill-ftones, the mica is foon wore off.

VIII. VARIETY.

Porphyry.

Under this name I comprehend with Mr. *Sauffure,* all thofe ftones which in a compact filiceous siliceous ground (generally jasper, chert, shoerl, or lava) contain either feltspar, quartz, shoerl, mica, serpentine, or other species of stone in a *cryſtaline* form. When its ground is jasper it is hard. It is commonly either red, purple, grey, green, or black, according to the ground. The *red* commonly contains feltspar in small white dots or specks, and often together with these black spots of shoerl. The *green* is either a jasper or shoerl, with spots of quartz or shoerl. Sometimes a porphyry of one colour contains a fragment of a porphyry of another colour; the green are often magnetic. Those that have chert for their ground, are fusible *per se.*

SPECIES VI.

Compounds of the Siliceous, and various Genera.

I. VARIETY.

1. *Quartz, Mica, and Serpentine.*

2. *Quartz, Mica, and Steatites.*

3. *Quartz, Mica, and Shoerl, together with Serpentine or Steatites, or Soap-rock.*

4. *Quartz, Felt-spar, Mica, and Serpentine.*

All

All thefe ftones are called *Gneifs,* and are generally of a lamellar texture.

II. VARIETY.

Amygdaloides, Mandelftein of fome.

This confifts of a chert or jafper ground, in which fragments of calcareous fpar, and ferpentine, of an oval form, are contained.

III. VARIETY.

Variolite.

This is faid to be a compound of all forts of ftones, included in a ground of ferpentine. *Ferber. Italy,* p. 120.

IV. VARIETY.

Metallic Stone of Linnæus and Born.

It confifts of Quartz, clay, and fteatites, and is of different degrees of hardnefs, fometimes the fteatites is wanting, fometimes feltfpar is found in it.

V. VARIETY.

Quartz, Spar, and Mica. Saxum Angermannicum of Linnæus.

CHAP.

CHAP. IX.
Of Vegetable and Animal Earths.

Vegetable Earth has been thought by many to be of a peculiar nature, specifically different from every other; but late experiments have fully shewn.

1$^{ft.}$ That vegetables contain but a very small proportion of Earth of any sort, and that far the greater part of their substance consists of water, fixed air, and inflammable air in a concrete state, as remote principles, a small proportion of fixed alkali which probably is neutralized by vegetable acids, and a few other neutral salts. Thus according to the latest experiments, 33 pound of oak afford only 3 drachms of ashes. *Memoirs of Stockholm*, 1781.

2$^{dly.}$ That the Earth of vegetables is for the greater part, either calcareous, or a mixture of all sorts of Earths, and sometimes of the calces of iron and manganese, in various proportions, according to the species of the vegetable. Thus Mr. *Bergman* found the ashes of some vegetables to contain calcareous, ponderous, muriatic, argillaceous, and even siliceous Earth; and hence ashes effervesce with acids, and are fusible *per se*, even after perfect

Vegetable and Animal Earths. 155

perfect lixiviation. He alfo found fometimes animal Earth, (that is phofphoric felenite,) in afhes. The Earth remaining after the putrefaction of vegetables, is exactly of the fame nature. *Schæffer*, § 172. Mr. *Morveau* found the afhes of fome vegetables to contain 97,5 per cent, of calcareous Earth, the remainder magnefia. Mr. *Berniard*, Mr. *D'Arcet*, and Mr. *Achard*, have had nearly the fame refults. 19 *Roz.* 52.

The neutral falts moft ufually found in afhes, are tartar vitriolate, glauber's falt, common falt, digeftive falt, and felenite, alfo hepar fulphuris; according to *Model* a pound of rhubarb contains an ounce and a half of felenite.

Hence we fee why clay is fo unfavourable to vegetation, and how calcareous Earth is introduced into the bodies of animals.

Animal Earth, is obtained either from the fhells of fifh, or from thofe of eggs, or from pearls, or from the bones, horns, claws of land animals, or from the fkins of infects.

That obtained from the fhells of fifh and from thofe of eggs, is found by repeated experiments to be purely calcareous; only oyfter fhells difcover fome feeble veftiges of felenite. *Bergm.* on *Scheffer*, § 173, that obtained
from

from bones, horns, claws, teeth, &c. was found by Mr. *Gahn*, to be a calcareous Earth united to the phofphoric acid; hence the folution of bones in the mineral acids can never be neutralized, a circumftance which puzzled all preceeding chymifts, but which is now perfectly underftood, as fuch folution is in fact only the folution of a neutral falt if the bones be diffolved in the nitrous or marine acids, or a decompofition of a neutral falt, if the vitriolic acid be ufed as a folvent; in either cafe a free unfaturated acid muft be found. However fome bones contain an excefs of phofphoric acid, and fome an excefs of Earth, as ivory, whence fome have imagined this latter to contain a peculiar Earth. Some late and accurate experiments relating to the proportion of phofphoric acid in bones by Mr. *Berniard*, may be feen in *Rozier's* journal, for 1781, p. 280, 1782, p. 43.

The phofphoric acid is feparated from this Earth by calcining the bones to whitenefs then diffolving them in nitrous acid, and precipitating the calcareous Earth by the concentrated acid of vitriol. A felenite is thus obtained (decompofable either by calcination with charcoal, or by boiling in a folution of mild fixed alkali,) and the phofphoric acid remains in the liquor.

APPENDIX

APPENDIX I.

Of Diamond and Plumbaga.

These substances cannot well be arranged under any of the classes of minerals; not under that of Earths as they contain no Earth, nor under that of inflammables, as their inflammability commences in such high degrees of heat, and is so gradual that it can scarcely be remarked but by its effect in diminishing the weight of these substances after a long exposure to fire; so that they differ intirely from all other inflammables, whence I think it convenient to treat of them a part.

Diamond.

Diamond is always transparent, and mostly colourless, but sometimes tinged, yellow, reddish, green, blue, or brown; it is sometimes externally, but always internally bright; it is generally crystalized in octohedral crystals, but sometimes found in round masses: its texture is lamellar.

It strikes fire with steel, cuts the hardest crystals, and even rubies, being the hardest of all bodies: its specific gravity is from 3,5 to 3,66.

No acid has any effect on it, except the vitriolic; if diamond powder be triturated with this acid, and evaporated nearly to dryneſs, the acid grows black and depoſits pellicles, which burn, and are almoſt entirely conſumed.

In a heat ſomewhat greater than that in which ſilver melts, diamond is intirely volatilized and conſumed; it even produces a ſlight flame and diminiſhes common air, juſt as phlogiſtic ſubſtances do, and leaves a ſoot, ſo that the extraordinary conjecture of Sir *Iſaac Newton*, of its being an inflammable ſubſtance coagulated is fully confirmed. Of the uſual fluxes, only borax and microcoſmic ſalt have any effect on it.

It is found in *Golconda, Viſapour, Bengal*, the iſland of *Borneo, and Brazil.*

The nature of cubic diamonds has notyet been examined.

Plumbago, Reiſsbley, of the German's, Blyertz, of the Swedes.

This ſubſtance is externally black, but bluiſh white and ſhining like a metal when freſh cut: its texture is micaceous and ſcaly, yet granular. It is uſed for pencils.

It

Of Plumbago. 159

It is too soft to strike fire with steel: its specific gravity is from 1,987, to 2,267.

It is insoluble in the mineral acids.

In a strong heat and open fire it is wholly volatile, leaving only a little iron, which seems to be only accidentally found in it, and a few grains of silex.

The usual fluxes do not effect its fusion.

It is decomposed by detonnation with nitre, in a red hot crucible.

According to Mr. *Scheele*, who first discovered the nature of this mineral, 1 part plumbago requires 10 of nitre to decompose it, whereas 1 part charcoal requires but 5 of nitre: hence it contains twice as much phlogiston as charcoal does. By receiving the air arising from its decomposition in a bladder, he found $\frac{1}{3}$ of that air to be absorbable by lime water, and consequently to be fixed air, and in the remainder a candle would burn: but as nitre itself might afford fixed air by combustion, to get rid of all objections, he decomposed plumbago by subliming and reducing the arsenical acid, after mixing it with plumbago; and thus also he obtained fixed air. It is probable that 100 grains of it contain

tain 33 of aerial acid, and 67 of phlogiston; for 100 grains of nitre contain about 33 of real nitrous acid. This is decomposed when it receives as much acid as is necessary to convert it into nitrous air, or a little more. Now 33 grains of nitrous acid are converted into nitrous air by about 6,7 grains of phlogiston: then 1000 grains of nitre require for their decomposition 67 of phlogiston: and since 100 grains of plumbago decompose 1000 of nitre, they must contain 67 of phlogiston.

APPENDIX II.

Of the general Examination and Analysis of Earths and Stones.

Section I.

Of the Examination of Earths.

When Earths are well dried and separated from every visible heterogeneity, a portion of them should be weighed and distilled in a glass retort, until the bottom begins to grow red hot. In some cases it may be proper to receive the air that arises, in a pneumatic apparatus; in all it will be proper to examine what distills over, or sublimes, whether it be acid or alkaline, with paper tinged blue by litmus, and partly reddened by distilled vinegar: if the blue

Analysis of Earths and Stones:

blue be reddened, an acid exists in the distilled liquid; if the red be effaced, and the blue restored, a volatile alkali is the cause of it: if the liquor precipitates lime water, but does not precipitate nitrous selenite, then it contains fixed air: if it precipitates also nitrous selenite, it contains the vitriolic acid: if it contains the marine acid, it will not precipitate nitrous selenite, but it will the nitrous solution of silver. The loss of weight of the residuum in the retort, and the weight of the water in the receiver, will shew the proportion of the volatile ingredients.

Another portion should be digested in about 6 or 8 times its weight of pure water, and the properties of that water examined, to find whether the Earth contains neutral salts. Here the method given by Mr. *Bergman* in his analysis of mineral waters, should be followed.

Section II.

Of the general Examination of Stones.

Their specific gravity should first be examined; also their hardness; whether they will strike fire with steel, or can be scratched by the nail, or only by crystal or stones of still greater hardness; also their texture, perviousness nefs to light, and whether they be manifeftly homogenous or compound fpecies, &c.

$2^{d.}$ In fome cafes one fhould try whether they imbibe water, or whether water can extract any thing from them by ebullition or digeftion.

$3^{d.}$ Whether they are foluble in, or effervefce with acids, before or after pulverization; or whether decompofable by boiling in oil of tartar, &c. as gypfums and ponderous fpars are.

$4^{th.}$ Whether they detonnate with nitre.

$5^{th.}$ Whether they yield the fparry acid by diftillation with oil of vitriol, or a volatile alkali, by diftilling them with falt of tartar.

$6^{th.}$ Whether they are fufible *per fe* with a blow-pipe, and how they are affected by mineral alkali, borax, and microcofmic falt; and whether they decrepitate, when gradually heated.

$7^{th.}$ Stones that melt *per fe* with the blow-pipe are certainly compound, and contain at leaft 3 fpecies of Earth, of which the calcareous is probably one; and if they give fire with steel, the filiceous is probably another.

SECTION III.

Section III.
Of the Analysis of Earths and Stones.

The best general solvent for Stones or Earths seems to me to be *Aqua Regia*, composed of two parts nitrous, and one of marine acid: if the stone or Earth effervesces strongly with acids, no other preparation is requisite than a separation of such parts as are visibly heterogenous, and pulverization; the solution is then easily performed in a digesting heat, if requisite. The undissolved residuum, if purely siliceous, will melt into a transparent glass with about $\frac{1}{2}$ its weight of mineral alkali; if not, it is still compounded, and its soluble parts will yield to a reiterated digestion.

If the stone does not effervesce, or easily dissolve in acids, after pulverization and digestion, but leaves an insoluble residuum evidently compound, or but slightly altered, it will require to be pulverized and mixed with twice or thrice its weight of mineral alkali, and to be exposed to a low red heat for one or two hours. I found mica to require a mixture of 4 times its weight of mineral alkali; after which it is to be separated from the alkali by lixiviation and filtration, washing it with distilled water until the water is absolutely tastelefs and precipitates no metallic solution.

The powdered stone, thus edulcorated, is to be dried by heating it to rednefs, and then weighed, and 100 grains taken for subsequent experiments: it were better if still more were used, but the analysis would be more expensive.

The powder is next to be digested in 8 or 10 times its weight of *aqua regia*, in a boiling heat in a retort to which a receiver is luted, and the digestion reiterated as long as any thing appears to be dissolved by fresh portions of the acid. I found mica to require 50 times its weight of *aqua regia* before it was entirely decomposed, as the acid is so volatile as very soon to distill over. Oil of vitriol has the advantage of bearing a greater heat, dissolving baroselenite, and of acting more powerfully on argill than *aqua regia*; but a large retort must be used, for, often towards the end it puffs and throws up the Earth or stone, and carries it into the receiver; and it does not sufficiently act on calces of iron, if these be much dephlogisticated. Spirit of nitre affects them still less: hence I often use oil of vitriol first, then precipitate by a mild alkali what it has dissolved, and redissolve the precipitate in *aqua regia*. A perfect solution

Analysis of Earths and Stones.

tion being thus effected, the residuum is to be well washed, and the washings added to the solution: the residuum, well dried and weighed, gives the weight of siliceous Earth in the compound.

The solution is next to be examined; which I will suppose to contain the 4 soluble Earths, calcareous, ponderous, magnesia, and argill, and also a calx of iron: it always contains an excess of acid, of which it is in great measure deprived by boiling for a considerable time, as both acids are very volatile, and indeed, of the marine none remains but what is combined with the calx of iron, as the nitrous chases it from the Earths. By getting rid of this excess of acid, less alkali will be required for the succeding precipitation, and less aerial acid set loose which would retain much of the precipitate by re-dissolving it: the solution should then be evaporated to about ½ a pint.

The solution being thus prepared, it is usual to precipitate the calx of iron from it by the Prussian alkali; but to this method I have two objections; 1$^{ft.}$ that the ponderous Earth, if any, would also be precipitated and confounded in the Prussian blue; and 2$^{d.}$ that this precipitation, besides being exceeding slow, seldom fails of leaving some iron still in the solution, as the excefs of the Pruffian alkali, which muft neceffarily be added, to be certain that all the iron is precipitated, never fails to re-diffolve a portion of the Pruffian blue which thus remains in the liquor, and cannot be got rid off. Hence the method I ufe is as follows: firft, I prepare the Pruffian alkali after the manner of Mr. *Bergman*, by digefting and boiling a pure alkaline folution over Pruffian blue, until the alkali no longer effervefces with acids, nor precipitates a folution of nitrous felenite, or any other Earth, except the barytes: I even make it a little ftronger; for if it be barely faturated with the tinging matter, it foon fpoils and precipitates other Earths, the tinging matter evaporating. I next examine how much of this alkali is neceffary to precipitate 1 gr. of iron from its folution in dilute vitriolic or marine acid, and I mark this on the label of the bottle that contains the alkali. I now come to the application.

The folution of the earths being weighed I take 100 grains of it, and on thefe I gradually pour the Pruffian alkali (a portion of which is alfo previoufly weighed) until all the iron, or ponderous Earth and iron, is precipitated; the weight of the alkali ufed, gives that of the iron contained in 100 grains of the folution, and the quantity contained in

Analysis of Earths and Stones. 167

100 gr. of the solution, gives that contained in the whole solution, by the rule of proportion, from which the ponderous Earth, if any be found in subsequent experiments, is to be deducted.

The quantity of iron being thus found, the remainder of the solution is to be precipitated by aerated mineral alkali, and then boiled for half an hour to expel as much as possible of the fixed air; by this means the whole of its contents are precipitated, and nothing remains in solution, but cubic nitre and a little common salt; when the precipitate has settled after one or two days rest, the liquor is to be poured off, and the last portions taken up with a glass syringe. Distilled water is then to be added to the precipitate and boiled over it, and afterwards poured off and taken up until it comes of tastless.

The precipitate being sufficiently dried, is to be re-dissolved in nitrous acid twice, and evaporated to dryness, then calcined for one hour in a white heat, and lastly treated with about six or eight times its weight of distilled vinegar, in a heat of about 60 degrees, for one or two hours; by this means the ponderous, calcareous, and magnesia Earths will be extracted and separated from the argill and calx of iron, which will remain undiffolved.

Of this acetous folution 100 grains fhould be taken and examined with the Pruffian alkali, if any part be precipitated it is ponderous Earth, and by heating this to rednefs its weight may be known, or ftill better by a previous experiment, determining the quantity requifite to precipitate 1 gr. of acetous barofelenites, and by the rule of proportion, the quantity of it in the whole folution may be found.

The remainder of the acetous folution, is to be evaporated to drynefs, and heated white in a clean polifhed iron crucible for two hours, then weighed and thrown into hot diftilled water, the calcareous Earth, (if any,) will be diffolved in a fufficient quantity of this water, of which an ounce can fcarcely diffolve 1 gr. fo that frequent affufions of hot water may be requifite; the magnefia will remain undiffolved, and is to be dried and weighed, its weight gives that of the pure calcareous Earth, from which that of the ponderous (if any) is to be deducted; the lime-water may alfo be precipitated by an aerated alkali.

Laftly, the argill and calx of iron, which remained undiffolved by the acetous acid, are

Analysis of Earths and Stones. 169

are to be heated flightly, to prevent their cohering and reiteratedly boiled in dephlogisticated nitrous acid to dryness, and finally diffolved in that acid, which will then take up only the argill, which may be precipitated, dried and weighed; though indeed this troublesome operation may be unnecessary, as the weight of the martial part being known by the experiment, with the Prussian alkali; that of the argill is known of course, when only the two remain. This is even better, as the calx always increases in weight by these operations.

Besides this general method some others may be used in particular cases.

Thus *to discover a small proportion of argill, or magnesia, in a solution of a large quantity of calcareous Earth,* caustic volatile alkali may be applied, which will precipitate the argill or magnesia, if any be, but not the calcareous Earth. Distilled vinegar applied to the precipitate, will discover whether it be argill or magnesia.

2dly. *A minute portion of calcareous or ponderous Earth, in a solution of argill or magnesia,* may be discovered by the vitriolic acid, which precipitates the calcareous and ponderous, the solution should be dilute else the argill
also

also would be precipitated. If there be not an excess of acid, the saccharine acid is still a nicer test of calcareous Earth. 100 gr. of gypsum contains about 32 of calcareous Earth. 100 gr. of baroselenite contains 84 of ponderous Earth. 100 gr. of saccharine selenite contains 45 of calcareous Earth: the insolubility of baroselenite in 500 times its weight of boiling water sufficiently distinguishes it. From these *data* the quantities are easily investigated.

3dly. *A minute proportion of argill in a large quantity of magnesia*, may be discovered either by precipitating the whole and treating it with distilled vinegar, or by heating the solution nearly to ebullition, and adding more aerated magnesia untill the solution is perfectly neutral, which it never is when argill is contained in it, as this requires an excess of acid, to keep it in solution. ' By this means the argill is precipitated in the state of embryon alum which contains about ½ its weight of argill, (or for greater exactness it may be decomposed by boiling it in volatil alkali.) After the precipitation the solution should be largely diluted, as the Epsom salt, which remained in solution while hot, would precipitate when cold and mix with the embryon alum.

4^{thly}.

Analysis of Earths and Stones. 171

4^{thly.} A *minute portion of magnesia in a large quantity of argill* is best separated by precipitating the whole and treating the precipitate with distilled vinegar.

Lastly, *Calcareous Earth and Barytes* are separated either by precipitating the barytes by the Prussian alkali, or the calcareous by a caustic fixed alkali, or by precipitating both with the vitriolic acid, and evaporating the solution to a small compass, pouring off the liquor and treating the dried precipitate with 500 times its weight of boiling water; what remains undissolved is baroselenite.

Table of the comparative hardness of different Species of Stones, extracted chiefly from the Memoirs of Stockholm, for 1768.

Mr. *Quist*, the author of this Memoir determined the hardness of most of the following stones, by observing the order in which they were able to cut and make an impression on each other. The first are able to cut or scratch the succeeding, but not *vice versa*. He added also the specific gravity of the specimens he used; the first column shews the hardness; the second, the specific gravity. The four last species I have added from my own observation.

Diamond

Diamond from *Ormos*,	20	
Pink Diamond,	19	3,4
Bluish Diamond,	19	3,3
Yellowish Diamond,	19	3,3
Cubic Diamond,	18	3,2
Ruby,	17	4,2
Pale Ruby from *Brazil*,	16	3,5
Spinel,	13	3,4
Deep blue Sapphire,	16	3,8
Ditto paler,	17	3,8
Topaz,	15	4,2
Whitish ditto,	14	3,5
Bohemian,	11	2,8
Emerald,	12	2,8
Garnet,	12	4,4
Agate,	12	2,6
Onyx,	12	2,6
Sardonyx,	12	2,6
Amethyst,	11	2,7
Crystal,	11	2,6
Carnelian,	11	2,7
Green Jasper,	11	2,7
Reddish yellow ditto,	9	2,6
Shoerl,	10	
Tourmaline,	10	
Quartz,	10	2,7
Opal,	10	2,6
Chrysolite,	10	3,7
Zeolyte,	8	2,1
Fluor,	7	
Calcareous Spar,	6	

Gypsum

Table of Hardness.

Gypsum, - - - 5 -
Chalk, - - - 3 -

Remarks.

1$^{ft.}$ Artificial gems are easily distinguished from the natural, by their softness, fusibility, solubility in acids, and in many cases by their specific gravity.

2$^{dly.}$ Stones whose hardness does not exceed 11 may be scratched by steel.

3$^{dly.}$ It is remarkable that opal whose hardness is equal to that of quartz, does not strike fire with steel, as Mr. *Bergman* attests, is this owing to its brittleness? but it seems that opals are of different degrees of hardness, for Mr. *Quist* in a letter to Mr. *Rinman,* mentions his having seen opals nearly as hard as diamond. *Mem. Stock.* 1766.

PART

PART II.

Saline Substances.

ALL those substances which are known *only* by this denomination, require less than two hundred times their weight of boiling water to dissolve them.

They have mostly a peculiar taste, and those of the mineral kind are uninflammable.

CHAP. I.

Of Acids.

The *Acids* to be met with in the mineral kingdom, are the *aerial,* the *vitriolic,* the *marine,* the *sparry,* the *succinous, phosphoric, molybdenous, arsenical,* and *tungstenic.*

The *Aerial Acid* is found either in an aerial state, as in mines, caverns, wells, or combined with water in mineral or common springs, or combined with absorbent earths, or in ores, &c. it is easily known by its property of extinguishing lights, uniting to water, and then precipitating lime water, but not a solution of nitrous selenite.

The

Salts. 175

The *Vitriolic* when dephlogisticated, is always united to water, and as in the Earth, it must meet with bodies with which it is capable of combining, I believe it has never been found free from all combination, though it may unite to some bodies beyond the point of saturation. It is true Mr. *Baltaffari* says, he found some dry concentrated acid, adhering to selenite in a grotto in *Monte Zaccolino* near *Sienna*. 7 *Roz.* but this has been fully disproved by the subsequent observations of Mr. *Murray*, in the 37th vol. of the Memoirs of *Stockholm*. In a combined state it is found in various neutral salts.

The *phlogistigated* or sulphurous vitriolic acid, frequently occurs in a free aerial state, bursting from volcanic mountains, and also in some caverns and mineral waters.

Of the other acids, none has hitherto been found in an uncombined state, except the *sedative*, which has lately been found by Mr. *Hœffer*, dissolved in the *Laguni*, or lakes of hot mineral water near *Monte Rotundo*, *Berchiaio*, and *Castelnuovo* in *Tuscany*, in the proportion of nearly 9 grains in 100 of water. Mr. *Mascagni* has likewise found it adhering to shistus on the borders of the lakes, of a dirty white, yellow or greenish colour, and crystalized in the form of needles, 16 *Roz.* 364.

This

176 *Elements of Mineralogy.*

This Salt requires at leaſt 20 times its own weight of boiling water to diſſolve it, and 50 times its weight to keep it in ſolution. It is alſo ſoluble in hot ſpirit of wine, and this ſolution burns with a greeniſh flame. Its ſolution in water, when heated, turns that of litmus red. It vitrifies in a moderate heat, but the glaſs ſo formed is again ſoluble in water. Its ſpecific gravity is 1,479.

The *Nitrous Acid*, though generally ranked among the mineral acids, can ſcarce be called ſo, as it always requires for its formation, the putrefaction of animal or vegetable ſubſtances. It is never found diſengaged from all baſes (except perhaps in charnels and privys), but always united either to alkalis or Earths.

The Marine Acid is found only in a ſtate of combination with alkalis, earths and ſome metals.

The *Sparry* is found in fluor ſpars, lapis lazuli, chryſopraſium, and phoſphoric blende.

The *Succinous,* found only in amber.

The

Salts. 177

The *Phosphoric* has as yet been discovered only in fossile bones, and in one species of lead ore. It probably owes its origin to the decomposition of bones.

The *Molybdenous* acid being very lately known, has been found only in molybdena.

The *Arsenical* acid has been traced in the ores of other metallic substances, particularly of cobalt.

The *Tungsten* acid has hitherto been found only in the calcareous stone, called Tungsten.

CHAP. II.

Of Alkalis.

These are of two sorts, fixed and volatile; the fixed are either of vegetable or mineral origin, which differ in a few properties, but it is to be observed, that some vegetables afford also an alkali intirely similar to that of mineral origin, particularly marine plants, or those that grow near the sea; neither of them is ever found in a caustic state, but all are combined at least with the aerial acid. They then effervesce with most other acids, turn infusions of blue flowers of certain vegetables green,

green, cryftalife with the three ancient mineral acids, &c.

The *Vegetable Alkali* is feldom found in the earth, except in wells in towns, as at *Doway*, &c. 4 *Mem. Scav. Etr.* alfo in the argillaceous allum ore of *la Tolfa*, and united to the nitrous acid near the furface of the earth in *Spain* and the *Eaft Indies*, probably from the putrefaction of vegetables.

The *Mineral Alkali* is not only found in a ftate of combination with the vitriolic and marine acids, but alfo very commonly with the aerial, with which it retains, not only the name, but many of the properties of a free alkali, as the aerial acid is eafily expelled. In this mild ftate it is eafily known by its cryftalization, folubility in 2,5 times its weight of water, in the temperature of 60, efflorefcence by expofure to the air, effervefcence with acids, and the properties of the different neutral Salts, refulting from its union with the different acids, decompofing *terreno*-neutral and ammoniacal Salts, &c.

100 Parts of this alkali, when perfectly pure and recently cryftalized, contain according to Mr. *Bergman*, 20 of mere alkali, 16 of aerial acid, and 64 of water ; my determination

termination was something different from this, but then the Salt had lost some of its water by exposure to the air.

This alkali is found in *Hungary* in marshy grounds of an argillaceous or marly nature, either mixed with earth, or crystalized and efflorescing. In *Egypt* it is found at the bottom of lakes, dried up by the summer's heat. Also in the province of *Suchena*, 28 days journey from *Tripoli*, where it is called *Trona*, 35 *Mem. Stock.* also in *Syria*, *Persia*, the *East Indies*, and *China*, where it is known under the name of *Kien*. It is frequently met with germinating on walls, and is by many called *Aphronitron*; also in many mineral waters. It is in its native state frequently mixed with muriatic Earth, common salt, and marine Epsom, or marine selenite.

Volatil Alkali, in a mild state, is easily known by its smell, its volatility and its action on copper, the solutions of which, in the mineral acids, are turned blue by it. It is frequently found, though in small quantity, in mould, marl, clay, shistus, and in some mineral waters according to *Malouin. Mem. Par.* 1746. *Phil. Transf.* 1767: 2 *Bergm. Erde Kugel.* 304. It probably derives its origin in the mineral kingdom from the putrefaction or combustion of animal or vegetable substances. In a caustic state it never occurs.

CHAP. III.

Of Neutral Salts.

These consist of an acid, united either to an alkali, Earth, or metal, of each of which combinations we shall treat in their order.

SPECIES I.

Tartar Vitriolate.

This is very seldom found native; Mr. *Bowles* says it is contained in some Earths in *Spain. Bowles Spain,* 68.

It requires about 16 times its weight of water to dissolve it in the temperature of 60, and only 5 of boiling water, it forms non deliquescent permanent crystals, decrepitates when heated, but loses but little of its weight, is of very difficult fusion, precipitates the nitrous solutions of silver, lead, mercury, and chalk, is not rendered turbid by the addition of any alkali, but the acid of tartar dropped into its solution, forms a precipitate.

100 Parts of tartar vitriolate, contain about 31 of real acid, 63 of alkali, and 6 of water.

Glauber's

Species II.

Glauber's Salts.

It is found native in some lakes in *Siberia*, in several mineral waters, and in the sea, as some say; also in several parts of *Dauphiné* and *Lorraine* in the Earth, and sometimes germinating on the surface. *Monnet Mineralogie*, 439.

Its characters are the same as those of tartar vitriolate, except that it requires but 3 times its weight of water to dissolve it in the temperature of 60; its crystals moulder by exposure to the air, and by heat lose half their weight. The acid of tartar causes no precipitation when instilled into its solution.

100 Parts of this Salt contain about 14 of real acid, 22 of alkali, and 64 of water.

Species III.

Vitriolic Ammoniac.

This is said to have been found in the neighbourhood of volcanos, particularly of *Mount Vesuvius*, where, indeed, it might well have been expected; yet its existence is rendered somewhat dubious, since Mr. *Bergman* could scarce find any trace of it among the various specimens of salts from *Vesuvius*, which

which he examined, 3 *Bergm.* 236. and the reason probably is because the vitriolic acid, disengaged by the combustion of sulphur, is in a phlogisticated state, and all its combinations in this state are easily decomposed by the marine acid which plentifully occurs in volcanos. It is also said to be found in the mineral lakes of *Tuscany,* 16 *Roz.* 363. which is much more probable, as the vitriolic acid when united to water easily parts with phlogiston, and recovers its superiority over other acids: also on the surface of the Earth in the neighbourhood of *Turin.*

Vitriolic Ammoniac is easily known: for if quick lime or fixed alkali be thrown into its solution, the smell of the volatil alkali is perceived; and if this solution be poured into that of chalk or ponderous Earth in the nitrous acid, a precipitate will appear. 100 parts of it contain about 42 of real acid, 40 of volatil alkali, and 18 of water.

Species IV.

Selenite.

I have already mentioned this substance among the calcareous Earths. It is frequently found in mineral and common springs, and also in sea water. Its taste is neither

neither bitter nor aftringent, but earthy. Its folution mixes uniformly with that of nitrous or marine Selenite, but is precipitable by fixed alkalis, mild or cauftic, and alfo by the faccharine acid, but not by volatile cauftic alkali, which diftinguifhes it from *Epfom* and alum.

SPECIES V.

Epfom.

Many mineral waters contain this falt, particularly thofe of *Epfom*, *Egra*, *Sedlitz*, and *Seydchutz* : it has alfo been found native, mixed with common falt and coaly matter germinating on fome free ftones in coal mines. 8 *Roz.* 137.

This falt, in the temperature of 60, requires about its own weight of water to diffolve it; its tafte is bitter; it efflorefces by expofure to the air, when heated it lofes nearly ¼ its weight by evaporation; its folution is rendered turbid by a mixture with that of nitrous or marine felenite, which diftinguifhes it from folutions of felenite, but preferves its limpidity when mixed with a folution of nitrous or marine *Epfom* ; its earth is precipitable by all alkalis in any ftate, and alfo by lime.

100 parts of it contain about 24 of real acid, 19 of earth, and 57 of water.

Species VI.

Alum.

Alum requires about 15 times its weight of water to diffolve it in the temperature of 60. Its tafte is well known; it fwells and blifters when heated, and lofes nearly $\frac{1}{2}$ its weight. It is precipitable by all alkalis, and even by magnefia, which diftinguifhes its bafis from that of *Epfom*: but the precipitate retains nearly $\frac{1}{2}$ the weight of the acid with which it was originally united, and is in reality *Embryon Alum*; but by digefting it in volatile alkalis (for its bafis would unite to fixed alkalis) it may be perfectly purified. Its folution, like that of *Epfom*, renders nitrous folutions of filver or chalk turbid, but mixes uniformly with thofe of nitrous or marine alum, or of the vitriols of any metal: thefe properties diftinguifh it sufficiently.

100 parts of it contain about 24 of acid, 18 of earth, and 58 of water.

This falt is found native in a few mineral fprings*, though rarely, 1 *Bergm.* 280. and

* *Margr.* 2 *Theile*, 193.

in the mineral lakes of *Tufcany*, 16 *Roz.* 362. alfo germinating on the furface of free ftone or fhiftus in coal mines, or on lavas near volcanos, and on feveral rocks in the *Archipelago*, and in feveral parts of *Hungary*, *Bohemia*, and *Swifferland*, though feldom pure; but far the greater part of it is factitious, being extracted from various ores, the principal of which are the following:

SPECIES VII.

Aluminous Ores.

1$^{ft.}$ *Sulphurated Clay.* This conftitutes the pureft of all aluminous ores, namely, that of *La Tolfa* near *Civita Vechia*; it is white, compact, and of the hardnefs of indurated clay; hence called *Petra Aluminaris*, yet mealy and taftelefs. Mr. *Monnet* firft difcovered the real nature of this ore. According to him 100 parts of it contain upwards of 40 of fulphur, and 50 of clay, befides a fmall quantity of fixed vegetable alkali, and a very minute portion of iron. 13 *Roz. Supplem.* p. 338. With this Mr. *Bergman*'s analyfis nearly agrees; 100 parts of this ore containing, according to him, 43 of fulphur, 35 of argill, and 22 of filex. 3 *Berg.* 271. He alfo found the vegetable alkali and iron, but probably he did not feparate them, but
reckoned

reckoned them among the argillaceous contents, which muft alfo have contained a quantity of vitriolic acid. To make this ore produce alum, it is neceffary that it fhould firft be torrefied to decompofe the fulphur, whofe acid then re-acts on the argill, and being moiftened, or expofed to the air, it foon fwells, efflorefces, and forms alum. This ore was probably at firft a clay, mixed with fulphur, and hardened by volcanic fire, and derives its alkali from vegetables incinerated by the volcano. Mr. *Monnet* found alfo a little magnefia in this ore. *Mineralog.* p. 160. The red colour of the alum proceeds from iron in a particular ftate. 3 *Bergm.* 250.

2$^{d.}$ *Pyritaceous Clay.* This is found at *Schwemfal* in *Saxony* at the depth of 10 or 12 feet; it is a black, hard, yet brittle fubftance, confifting of clay, pyrites and bitumen; after it is dug it is left expofed to the air for two years, by which means the pyrites are decompofed, and alum formed. 3 *Jars Voy. Metallurg.* p. 293. The alum ores of *Heffe* and *Liege* are alfo of this fpecies, yet they are torrefied; a practice which *Jars* condemns. According to *Monnet* this ore contains alfo magnefia. *Mineralog.* p. 164. 64 pounds of this ore yield from 5 to 7 of alum. An earth of this fpecies, of a foliated

foliated texture, is also found in *Burgundy,* and is by some called *Ampelytes.* 1 *Chym de Dijon.* p. 107.

3^d *Shistus Aluminaris.* This differs from roof shistus in this, that it contains a variable proportion of pyrites intimately mixed with it, and also *Petrol. Bergm. Sciagr.* and 1 *Bergm.* 292. Its colour is blue or black, but when the proportion of petrol is very small, grey. When the proportion of pyrites is so large as to form a visible mass, the ore is commonly rejected as containing too much iron, though it might be worked to advantage, by adding a proportion of clay; a valuable improvement suggested by Mr. *Bergman.* When the proportion of petrol is considerable, it does not effloresce by exposure to the air, and therefore must be torrefied to burn off the petrol, and extricate the acid from the sulphur of the pyrites; but when the proportion of petrol is small, the pyritical part is decomposed by long exposure to the air and moisture; and thus alum is formed. In *Sweden,* if 100 pounds of the ore yield 4 of alum, it is worth working; but it generally yields more. The mine of *Becket* in *Normandy,* and those of *Whitby* in *Yorkshire,* are of this species.

4$^{th.}$ *Volcanic Aluminous Ore.* This is found at *Solfatera* near *Naples,* and elsewhere,

where, in the form of a white saline earth. In this ore alum is formed by the action of the phlogisticated vitriolic acid on argillaceous lavas.——100 parts of it contain, according to Mr. *Bergman*'s analysis, 88 of siliceous earth, 4 of argillaceous, and 8 of alum; but this proportion is variable. Before efflorescence it is in a stony form.

5$^{th.}$ *Bituminous Alum Ore.* Shale. 2 *Watson*, 314. This is a shistus impregnated with so much coaly matter or bitumen as to be inflammable; it also contains sulphur. 120 parts of calcined shale afford 1 of alum; it is found in *Sweden*, and among the coal mines at *Whitehaven*, and elsewhere. 8 *Roz.* 141.

Alum might also be extracted from many species of pyrites, but so contaminated with iron as scarce to quit cost; so also from calamine and pyritaceous wood.

Native alum, mixed with vitriolic ammoniac, is found crystalized on the borders of the mineral lakes of *Tuscany*. 16 *Roz.* 363. it is also found in a capillary form near the lake of *St. Agnano*, in the grotto of *St. Germano*. 37 *Mem. Stock.*

SPECIES VIII.

Species VIII.

Vitriol of Iron.

It is of a greenish colour when perfectly and recently cryftalized, but efflorefces by expofure to the air, and becomes yellowifh: it requires 6 times its weight of water to diffolve it in the temperature of 60; its acid is known by this, that the folution of this falt mixes without turbidity with the folutions of other falts that contain the vitriolic acid, as Epfom, felenite, tartar vitriolate, &c. but renders the folutions of nitrous or marine felenite turbid; and its bafis, by the black colour which the folution of galls or vegetable aftringents immediately produce in its folution.

100 Parts of it recently cryftalized contain 20 of real acid, 25 of iron and 55 of water.

It is frequently found native, either in coal mines, or in the cavities of pyritaceous mines, or adhering to the fcaffolds in a ftalactitical form. Alfo in fmall round ftones called *Ink* ftones, of a white, red, grey, yellow or black colour, which are almoft intirely foluble in water, and contain a portion of copper and zinc. 2 *Schlutter*, 620. 2 *Jars*, 265. Alfo fometimes in fhiftus. But the greateft part

part of that in use is prepared from the martial pyrites or mundic.

Martial Pyrites is an iron ore containing from $\frac{1}{6}$ to $\frac{1}{3}$ of sulphur, from $\frac{1}{8}$ to $\frac{5}{8}$ of iron, the remainder argill and silex, the three first intimately combined with each other, and the iron in a semiphlogisticated state. *Monnet Eaux Miner.* 281. 2 *Gerh. Beytr.* 57. It strikes fire with steel, and thence derives its name; it is generally of a yellow or grey colour, of a globular or cubic shape, internally radiated and sometimes lamellar, commonly in part soluble in nitrous acid with effervescence, and slowly in the vitriolic, with which it forms alum; it detonnates slightly with nitre and is very infusible: its specific gravity is from 3,7 to 4,912. Some pyrites instead of argillaceous contain calcareous Earth, these are common in *France*, and in them the iron is in a dephlogisticated state. *Monnet Mineral.* 339. Pyrites are frequently found in a statactical shape, and often form the matter of petrifactions: they are also found mixed and intersperfed through almost every other species of stone except granite. According to Mr. *Monnet*, those of a filamentous or striated texture contain least sulphur, those of a lamellar, most; the last efflorefce difficultly if at all, and are said to contain from 25 to 35 per cent of sulphur.

Vitriol

Salts.

Vitriol is formed in thefe ftones by expofing them a long time to the action of the air and moifture, or by torrefaction in open air, and fubfequent expofition to its action, which operation in fome cafes muft be often repeated, according to the proportion of fulphur, and the nature of the Earth; the calcareous pyrites are thofe in which it is moft eafily formed, and they efflorefce the fooneft, good pyrites properly treated, yield about $\frac{1}{3}$ of their weight of vitriol.

Vitriol is alfo prepared from mineral waters that hold copper in folution, which is precipitated by iron; this folution of iron is afterwards cryftalized and always retains fome copper. In *Hungary* it is prepared from pyritaceous fhiftus, and in many places from a fpecies of calamine; the vitriol of goflaar commonly contains a portion of zinc, as that of *Hungary* and *Saxony* does of copper; the Englifh and French vitriols are purer, yet fometimes contain a fmall proportion of alum. Turf and peat are fometimes impregnated with vitriol; other earths alfo often contain vitriol and alum. *Mon. Mineral.* 460. This vitriol is fometimes found of a white colour on the borders of the mineral lakes of *Tufcany*. 16 *Roz*. 363.

SPECIES IX.

Species IX.

Vitriol of Copper.

Its colour is blue, which degenerates into a mixture of blue and rusty yellow after it has been long expofed to the air; it requires about four times its weight of water to diffolve it in the temperature of 60. Its fpecific gravity is about 2,23; if a piece of clean polifhed iron be dipped into the folution of this falt, it will almoft immediately be covered with a cupreous coat, this together with the deep blue colour arifing from mixing it with a volatile alkali, difcovers its bafis, as its uniform mixture with other vitriolic falts does its acid.

100 Parts of vitriol of copper contain 30 of real acid, 27 of copper, and 43 of water. 80 Parts of good iron precipitate 100 of copper, from a folution, that does not contain a notable excefs of acid.

This falt rarely occurs cryftalized, but is often found naturally diffolved in water, in *Hungary, Sweden and Ireland*: from this water blue vitriol is generally prepared. Mr. *Cronfted* fays it is feldom free from iron and zinc; it is alfo occafionally extracted from fulphurated copper ores after torrefaction.
Schlutt.

Schlutt. 638. According to Mr. *Cronsted,* the blue vitriol of *Goslaar* contains a mixture of zinc.

Species X.
Vitriol of Zinc.

Its colour is white, it requires little more than twice its weight of water to dissolve it in the temperature of 60; its specific gravity is about 2,000; it mixes uniformly with vitriolic neutral salts, but precipitates nitrous or marine selenites from their solutions, which ascertains its acid principle; it is itself precipitated whitish by alkalis and earths, but not by iron, copper, or zinc, which sufficiently indicates its basis; if it contains any other metallic principle, this may be precipitated by adding more zinc, except iron, which will of itself precipitate by exposure to the air, or boiling in open air.

100 parts of vitriol of zinc, contain 22 acid, 20 of zinc, and 58 of water.

This salt is sometimes found native, mixed with vitriol of iron, and in the form of white hairy crystals, 2 *Linné von Gmelin,* p. 316, or in a stalactitical form in the galleries of Mines in *Hungary, Goslaar,* &c. or as an efflorescence on ores of zinc; it is also found dissolved in mineral waters, and generally with some proportion of the vitriols of iron and copper, 2 *Bergm.* 318,

318, but that in common use is mostly prepared at *Goslaar* from an ore which contains zinc, copper, and lead, mineralized by sulphur and a little iron; the copper ore is first separated as much as possible, and the residuum after torrefaction and distillation is thrown red hot into water and lixiviated. *Schlutt*, 639, 3 *Jars*, 320, it is never free from iron.

The vitriols of copper, iron, and zinc, are according to Mr. *Cronsted*, frequently found mixed in the waters pumped out of mines, sometimes all three are found crystalized in lumps of a yellow colour; the vitriol of *Fahlun* in *Sweden*, contains all three, *Bergm. Sciagr.* § 82.

Species XI.

Vitriol of Cobalt.

It is difficultly soluble in water, and both it and its solution are red, which sufficiently distinguishes its basis; its acid is known by the same tests as that of the former vitriols.

It is said to be found native in small pieces, mixed with a greenish efflorescence in cobalt mines, *Born, Index, Foss.* 51.

Halotrichium

Halotrichium, Trichites, or native alum mixed with vitriol of cobalt, is found in a capillary form in mines of gold, silver, and mercury, in *Hungary* and *Germany.* 2 *Lin. von. Gmelin* 316. the phlogisticated alkali, precipitates the cobalt which with borax gives an azure glass. 2 *Bergm.* 455.

Species XII.

Vitriol of Nickel.

This is also difficultly soluble in water; both it and its solution are of a green colour; it is found native effloresceing on *Kupfernickel* and generally mixed with vitriol of iron; 1 *Mem. Sued.* 213. *Cronst.* § 123. zinc precipitates the nickel, but not the iron.

Species XIII.

Vitriol of Manganese.

I do not know that this has been as yet found; as its colour and also that of its precipitate by fixed alkalis, is white, it may be confounded with vitriol of zinc; but the precipitate of the vitriol of manganese soon grows black by exposure to the air, especially if heated, and is then insoluble in the dephlogisticated nitrous acid, unless sugar be added, properties which the precipitate of zinc does not possess.

Species XIV.
Vitriols of Silver, Mercury and Lead.

These I shall treat of among the ores of those metals.

Species XV.
Nitre, or Prismatic Nitre.

Nitre requires about 7 times its weight of water to dissolve it in the temperature of 60: its specific gravity is 1,92, vegetable alkalis do not render its solution turbid, but the acid of tartar does; it deflagrates with burning coals, or on a red hot iron, and mixed with marine acid it makes *aqua regia*.

100 Parts of nitre contain about 30 acid, 63 vegetable alkali, and 7 of water.

It is said to be found formed by nature in certain clays in the *East Indies, China, Spain,*[*] and in *Siberia,* in the cavities of rocks,[†] also on the surface of masses of chalk, in the neighbourhood of *Rocheguyon,* [‡] and in some wells in great towns, as London and Berlin; but more frequently in old mortar, [§] some-

---

[*] 1 Watson, 315, Bowls, *Spain,* 70, 78, Suensk. Handl. 1772. 2 Quart. [†] Phil. transf. 1763, p. 209. [‡] Macq. Dict. *Nitre.* [§] 1 Wats. 293.

times it shoots on the surface of damp walls, and is then called *salpetere de houssage*. *Mon. Mineral*, 446, but Mr. *Lavoisier* has shewn that old mortar often contains only nitrous selenite, which is converted into true nitre by mixture with ashes, though those ashes contain a large proportion of tartar vitriolate and glauber's salt, because these salts decompose the calcareous selenite, and form nitre by the way of double decomposition, *Mem. Par.* 1777.

Species XVI.
Cubic Nitre.

This salt requires but 3 times its weight of water to dissolve it, at the temperature of 60; its specific gravity is about 1,87; vegetable fixed alkali decomposes it without forming a visible precipitate in its solution, neither does the tartarous acid precipitate any thing from it; with vitriolic acid (the nitrous being expelled) it forms glauber's salt; it deflagrates like prismatic nitre, and also forms *aqua regia*, in the same circumstances.

100 Parts of cubic nitre contain about 29 of real acid, 50 of mineral alkali, and 21 of water.

According to Mr. Bowles, it is found native in *Spain*.

Species XVII.

Nitrous Ammoniac.

It generally deliquefces; when mixed with a fixed alkali, the volatile betrays itfelf by its fmell; it deflagrates when the containing veffel is heated nearly red; with fpirit of falt it makes *aqua regia*.

100 Parts of it contain 46 of nitrous acid, 40 of volatile alkali, and 14 of water, as I believe.

It is frequently found in the mother liquor of nitre, *Linné von Gmelin*, 332, *Weber Abhand, von den Salpetre*, 17.

Species XVIII.

Nitrous Selenite.

This alfo deliquefces, its tafte is bitter, fixed alkalis decompofe it, and form cubic or prifmatic nitre, but cauftic volatile alkali cannot decompofe it, it does not deflagrate, yet paper moiftened with a faturate folution of it, crackles on burning, it lofes its acid in a ftrong red heat, its folution will not trouble that of filver in the nitrous acid; vitriolic acid will precipitate its bafis, as will the acid of fugar.

Salts. 199

100 parts of it contain, when well dried, about 33 of acid, 32 of calcareous earth, and 35 of water.

It exifts in old mortar, and the mother liquor of nitre; alfo in chalk rocks near *Rocheguyon. Macquer's Dict. Nitre.*

Species XIX.

Nitrous Epfom

Deliquefces, does not deflagrate, does not render the nitrous folution of filver turbid, is precipitated by cauftic volatil alkali, and alfo by the acid of fugar, but the precipitation is fcarce apparent, unlefs fpirit of wine or evaporation be applied. If nitrous felenite and nitrous *Epfom* be mixed, and both folutions be faturated, a precipitate will alfo appear; neither vitriolic acid nor mild magnefia occafion any turbidity in its folution.

100 parts of it contain about 36 of real acid, 27 of magnefia, and 37 of water.

It exifts in old mortar, and is found in the mother liquor of nitre.

Species XX.

Salt of Sylvius

Requires about 3 times its weight of water to diffolve it; its fpecific gravity is 1,836; diffolved in nitrous acid it makes *aqua regia*; it forms a cloud in the nitrous folution of filver; fixed alkali precipitate nothing from its folution, nor does a mixture of marine felentine, but the acid of tartar caufes a precipitate.

100 parts of it contain about 30 of real acid, 63 of vegetable alkali, and 7 of water.

It is found in fome boggs in *Picardy*, and fome mineral waters in *Normandy*. Monnet *Hydrolog*. 263.

Species XXI.

Common Salt

Requires about 2,5 its weight of water to diffolve it in the temperature of 60; its fpecific gravity is 2,12; the acid of tartar precipitates nothing from it; in other refpects it agrees with the above.

100 parts of it contain 33 real acid, 50 of mineral alkali, and 17 of water.

It

Salts.

It is not only found in the sea, salt lakes, and many salt springs in the proportion of even 36 per cent. but also in large masses under the earth in many countries, as *Poland, England, Tyrole,* &c. also in coal and beds of gypsum. *Born's Index.* Its colour is either grey, red, blue, yellow or black. *Cronsted* §. 129. *Born.*

Section XXII.

Sal Ammoniac

Requires about 3,5 times its weight of water to dissolve it in the temperature of 60; its specific gravity about 1,42 ; it makes *aqua regia* when mixed with nitrous acid ; it dissolves copper ; it wholly evaporates when laid on a hot iron.

100 parts of it contain 52 of real acid, 40 of volatil alkali, and 8 of water.

It is found native and of different colours, grey, black, green, red, in the neighbourhood of volcanos, and in the mineral lakes of *Tuscany.* 16 *Roz.* 362. Also in some mountains of *Tartary* and *Thibet.* 2 *Linné von Gmelin.* 335. and in the caverns or grottos of *Pouzzoli. Mem. Sued.* 243. also in various clays, though in small quantity. *Ibid.*

Species XXIII.

Species XXIII.

Marine Barofelenite.

This confifts of marine acid united to barytes; it is faid to have been found in fome mineral waters in *Sweden. Bergm. Sciagr.* §. 58. It is known by its eafy precipitability by the vitriolic acid, and the great infolubility and weight of the refulting compound.

Species XXIV.

Marine Selenite

Deliquefces; its bafis is alfo precipitable by the vitriolic acid, and its folution renders that of filver in the nitrous acid turbid, at the fame time that it makes no change in that of nitrous felenite; it obftinately retains its acid in a red heat.

100 parts of it contain, when well dried, about 42 of acid, 38 of earth, and 20 of water.

It is frequently found in mineral waters, *Monnet*, 457, and fometimes in fea water, *Cronft.* §. 128. *Mon. Hydrol*, p. 206, 294, but not always, 1 *Bergm.* 192, probably only where the bottom of the fea is calcareous,

alfo

also in the salt works at *Salsburgh. Born. Index* 52.

Species XXV.

Marine Epsom

Also deliquesces; its solution does not trouble that of nitrous or marine selenite, but it causes a cloud in the nitrous solution of silver; vitriolic acid makes no visible precipitate in its solution; but all alkalis, even the caustic volatil alkali, precipitate its basis; it loses its acid in a red heat.

It is found in the sea in greater plenty than any other salt, exept sea salt. 1 *Bergm.* 182.

Species XXVI.

Marine Alum.

This salt has not yet been found; if it exists, it may be known by its deliquescence and precipitability by magnesia, pure or mild; the mild should preferably be used, as it is most soluble.

Species XXVII.

Species XXVII.

Marine Salt of Copper.

This has been found in *Saxony* in the mine of *Johngeorgenstadt*; it is of a greenish colour and foliated texture, moderately hard, and sometimes transparent and cryftalized; it has been taken for a fort of mica, but Mr. *Bergman* found it to confift of copper and marine acid, with a little argillaceous earth. 2 *Bergm.* 431. Another fpecimen of a purer fort, and bluifh green colour, was also depofited in the mufeum of *Upfal*. *Ibid*.

Species XXVIII.

Marine Salt of Manganefe.

Mr. *Hielm* is the only perfon who has as yet found this falt; he difcovered it in fome mineral waters in *Sweden*; it is precipitated of a whitifh yellow colour by the *Pruffian* alkali, and of a brownifh yellow by the mineral alkali; it does not cryftalize in any diftinct form, but attracts the moifture of the air; to obtain it free from iron, it fhould be precipitated by the mineral alkali, rediffolved in nitrous acid, then calcined until this acid is expelled, and the refiduum treated

with

Salts.

with diftilled vinegar, which will then take up only the manganefe.

Species XXIX.

Marine Salt of Mercury.

See mercurial ores, Species III.

Species XXX.

Borax.

In the ftate in which it is naturally found requires about 18 times its weight of water to diffolve it in the temperature of 60; its fpecific gravity is about 1,74; it does not effervefce with the mineral acids, except they be heated, and then but flightly; when heated, it fwells and lofes $\frac{4}{10}$ of its weight, and in a ftronger heat runs into a glafs, which is rediffoluble in water.

If to a faturate folution of borax, oil of vitriol be added until it becomes fenfibly acid, the fedative falt will feparate from the borax, and fwim on the furface in the form of white fcales, the filtered liquor will on evaporation yield *Glauber's* falt.

100 parts of purified borax contain 34 of real fedative acid, 17 of mineral alkali, and 47 of

of water, but of the mineral alkali only about 5 parts are really faturated, the reft is unfaturated; and hence in many cafes borax acts as an alkali.

Borax comes to Europe from the *Eaſt Indies* in a very impure ſtate in the form of large, flat hexangular or irregular cryſtals, of a dull white or greeniſh colour, greaſy to the touch, or in ſmall cryſtals, as it were cemented together by a rancid, yellowiſh, oily ſubſtance, intermixed with marl, gravel, and other impurities. In this ſtate it is called brute borax, *chryſocolla* or *tincal*.

It is purified by folution, filtration and cryſtaliſation; and the cryſtals thus obtained are calcined to free them ſtill further from greaſineſs, and then diſſolved, filtered, and cryſtalized a 2d time; ſometimes more mineral alkali is added, as it is ſaid that tincal contains an exceſs of ſedative ſalt.

It has been long thought that borax was a factitious ſubſtance, but it is now beyond all doubt that it is a natural production, ſince Mr. *Grill Abrahamſon* ſent ſome to *Sweden* in the year 1772 in a cryſtaline form as dug out of the earth in the kingdom of *Thebet*, where it is called *pounxa*, *my poun* and *houi poun*; as borax is purified alſo in the *Eaſt Indies*, Mr. *Engeſtrom*

Engeſtrom ſuſpects that the tincal is only the reſiduum of the mother liquor of borax evaporated to dryneſs, and that the greaſineſs ariſes from its being mixed with butter milk to prevent its effloreſcence. It is ſaid to have been found in *Saxony* in ſome coal pits. *Gerh. Beytr.* 144.

PART

PART III.

Inflammables.

UNDER this head I do not comprise *all* minerals that may be inflamed if expofed to a ftrong heat, for otherwife feveral fulphureous metallic ores, pyrites, and even fome metallic fubftances, diamonds and plumbago, fhould be arranged under this clafs, which would occafion that confufion which is meant to be avoided by fyftematic claffification, but merely thofe fubftances, which in fact are inflammable, and do not come under the denomination of Earths, Salts, or metallic ores, and have general characters perfectly diftinct from them. Of thefe fome are fluid, fome liquid, and fome folid; the fpecific gravity of the latter never exceeds 2,5, and the former are the lighteft of all bodies. The French beftow the name of *Bitumen* upon all liquid and folid mineral inflammables, except fulphur; the Germans by that name denote only the folid. Thefe are all, except coal, electrics, *per fe*, and infoluble in water and fpirit of wine, but foluble in fome fpecies of oil. Mr. *Bergman* fays he poffeffes a concrete rape-feed oil, which is hard and pellucid like copal, and infoluble in water and fpirit of wine. 2 *Erde. Befchr.* 267.

SPECIES I.

Species I.

Inflammable Air, Fire Damp.

This is eafily known by its property of inflaming, when mixed with twice or thrice its bulk of common atmofpheric air. When pure, it explodes all at once, but when mixed or combined with fixed air, it burns with a blue lambent flame. It frequently occurs in coal-pits and mines, and often on the furface of fprings in *Perfia*, *Italy*, and *France*, and feems to be nothing more than the exhalation of petrol.

Species II.

Hepatic Air.

This air feems to confift of fulphur, held in folution in vitriolic or marine air; it is inflammable when mixed with ¾ of its bulk of common air. Water will take up about ½ its bulk of this air, and when faturated with it will turn filver black, but if ftrong dephlogifticated nitrous acid be dropped into this water, the fulphur will be precipitated.

100 Cubic inches of this air, when united to water, may hold 8 grains of fulphur in folution,

solution, in the temperature of 60, and more if hotter. Pure air alfo decompofes hepatic air.

It is found in many mineral waters, and particularly in the hot baths of *Aix la Chapelle*. The caufe and manner of their containing fulphur, which was long a problem, has at laft been happily explained by Mr. *Bergman*. It plentifully occurs in the neighbourhood of volcanos, and in feveral mines.

Species III.

Naphtha.

A fine thin fragrant colourlefs oil, which iffues out of white, yellow, or black clays in *Perfia* and *Media*, is known by this name. It burns with a bluifh yellow flame, and is as inflammable as æther, and like it, extracts gold from *Aqua Regia*. It is not decompofed by diftillation, and yet if long expofed to the air, it changes colour, thickens, and degenerates into petrol. Its fmell is very different from that of vegetable oils; it diffolves refins and balfams, but not gum refins, nor elaftic gum. It diffolves the effential oils of thyme and lavender, but is infoluble in fpirit of wine and æther. Its fpecific gravity is 0,708.

Species

Species IV.

Petrol, Bergoel, Steinoel.

Doctor *Priestley* has shewn in the 3d volume of his Observations and Experiments on Air, that essential oils, long exposed to the atmosphere, absorb not only the pure part, but also the phlogisticated part of it. An absorption, which must, in time, produce considerable changes in them; by a process of this sort, naptha is converted into petrol, which is an oil of various degrees of density, according to the time during which it has been exposed to the atmosphere; its colour is reddish, or yellow, brown, greenish, or blackish, it is found trickling from rocks, or issuing from the earth in the Dutchy of *Modena*, and in various parts of *France*, *Swisserland*, *Germany*, and *Scotland*, as well as in *Asia*. Also on the surface of the water of different fountains, or mixed with earth and sand, from which it is separated by infusion in water; the thinnest sort possesses the properties of naphtha, though in a lesser degree. It is rendered finer by distillation with water, and leaves a resinous residuum, and if distilled with a volatil alkali, the alkali acquires the properties of succinated ammoniac, and hence contains the acid of amber. Some sorts of it, according to *Monet*, are nearly of the denfity of nut oil. It is infoluble in fpirit of wine.

Species V.

Barbadoes tar, Erdepech, Bergtheer, Kedria-terreftris, Maltha.

Petrol long expofed to the air, forms this fubftance. It is of a vifcid confiftence, of a brown, black, or reddifh black colour, fometimes inodorous, but generally of a more or lefs difagreeable fmell, particularly when burned. It eafily melts, and burns with much fmoke and foot, and leaves either afhes or a flag, proceeding from heterogeneities contained in it. Spirit of wine cannot diffolve it. It contains a portion of the fuccinous acid, for with mineral alkali it gives a bitter falt, more difficultly foluble than common falt, and which treated with charcoal, will not afford fulphur. *Mem. Berlin,* 1758.

It is found in *Perfia,* in the neighbourhood of *Petrol,* in ftrata of gypfum and limeftone, or floating on water, alfo in *Siberia, Germany, Switzerland,* and in coal-pits, alfo in *America.*

Species VI.

Asphaltum, Iudenpech, Berghartz, Steinpech, Erhartete Bergtheer.

This is a smooth, hard, brittle, inodorous black or brown substance; it breaks with a smooth shining surface, melts easily when heated, and when pure, burns without leaving any ashes, but if impure, leaves ashes or a slag. According to Mr. *Monnet*, it contains sulphur, or at least the vitriolic acid, which seems confirmed by the experiments of Messrs. *Gerhard** and *Thory*,† it is slightly and partially acted on by Alcohol and æther.

It is found on the shores of the Red Sea, also in *Sweden, Germany,* and *France.*

Species VII.

Mineral tallow, Mumia, Belessoon.

This was found in the sea on the coasts of *Finland,* in the year 1736; it is perfectly white, and of the consistence of tallow, but more brittle, though as greasy. Its specific gravity is 0,770, whereas, that of tallow is 0,969; it burns with a blue flame, and a smell of grease, leaving a black viscid matter, which is more difficultly consumed, it is soluble in spirit of wine only when tartarised, and even

---

* 2 Beytrage. † 6 Crell Chemische Journal, p. 67.

then

then leaves an infoluble refiduum, but expreffed oils diffolve it when boiling. It is alfo found in fome rocky parts of *Perfia*, but feems mixed with petrol, and is there called *Schebennaad, Tfienpen, Kodreti.** Mr. *Herman*, a phyfician of *Strafburgh*, mentions a fpring in the neighbourhood of that city, which contains a fubftance of this fort diffufed through it, which feparates on ebullition, and may then be collected. 3 *Roz.* 346.

Species VIII.
Jet, Gagates, Lapis Obfidianus.

Jet is much harder than afphaltum, always black, fufceptible of a good polifh and glaffy in its fracture, which is conchoidal; it is highly electrical; its fpecific gravity is 1,744; it melts in a moderately ftrong heat with a difagreable fmell, when burnt it leaves a grey earthy ochrous refiduum; it is infoluble in fpirit of wine.

It is found in *England, Scotland, France, Italy, Germany, &c.*

Species IX.
Pitt or Stone Coal. Lithanthrax.

Coal is a black, folid, compact, brittle, inflammable fubftance, of a moderate hardnefs,

---

* *Mem. Sued.* 87. 2 *Lin. von Gmel.* 389. 2 *Gerh. Beytr.* 211.

laminated

Inflammables

laminated texture, more or lefs fhining, but rarely fufceptible of a good polifh, does not melt when heated, and always leaves fome afhes; it feems to confift of petrol or afphaltum intimately mixed with a fmall proportion of Earth, moftly argillaceous, feldom calcareous, and often with pyrites; according to Mr. *Gerhard*, fpirit of wine extracts a red colour from it, cauftic fixed alkali attacks the bituminous part, and fat oils act on and form a varnifh, at leaft with fome forts of it: a fixed alkali has never been found in it, nor any fulphur, except it contained pyrites. Four varieties of it deferve to be diftinctly confidered: none of them are electrics *per fe*.

I. *and* II. VARIETY.
Cannel Coal, and Killkenny Coal.

Cannel coal is of a dull black colour, breaks eafily in any direction, and in its fracture prefents a fmooth conchoidal furface, if broken tranfverfly: this fort contains moft petrol and in a lefs denfe ftate; hence it burns with a bright lively flame: its fpecific gravity is about 1,27; *Killkenny* coal contains the largeft proportion of denfe petrol or afphaltum: and hence burns with lefs flame and fmoke, and more flowly though intenfely, the quantity of Earth in this coal does not exceed $\frac{1}{12}$ of its weight: its fpecific gravity

gravity is about 1,4, it is frequently mixed with pyrites.

III. VARIETY.

Coal containing a moderate proportion of Petrol and Bitumen.

This burns with more or less flame according to the proportion of petrol; in its fracture, it presents a rougher surface than *Cannel* coal: its specific gravity is from 1,3 to 1,37; the best coal is of this sort, by distillation it affords first fixed air, then an acid liquor, afterwards inflammable air, and a light oil of the nature of petrol, then a volatil alkali, and lastly a dense pitchy oil; the residuum is nearly ¼ of the whole, and being slowly burnt, affords 13 per cent. of ashes, which is mostly argillaceous Earth, of which $\frac{3}{100}$ or thereabouts is magnetic. *Mem. Stock.* 1781.

100 Parts of this coal contain about 17 of Earth, of which 4 are martial; hence we see that coal does not consist of a shistus penetrated with petrol, as many have thought, for then a large proportion of silex, magnesia, and calcareous earth should be found in it.

IV. VARIETY,

IV. Variety.

Sulphureous Coal.

This confifts of the former mixed with a notable proportion of pyrites: hence it is apt to moulder and break when expofed to the air, and contains yellow fpots that look like metal; it burns with a fulphureous fmell, and leaves red afhes, or a flag; water acts upon it after it has mouldered: its fpecific gravity is 1,5, or more.

Befides thefe varieties, fhiftus, micaceous fhiftus, and gneifs are frequently found in the neighbourhood of coal-mines fo penetrated with petrol or bitumen as to conftitute an inferior fpecies of coal, but the bitumen being burnt, they preferve their form, and in fome meafure their hardnefs; I have alfo feen grey flates fo foft as to be fcraped with the nail, and which were greafy to the touch, that burned like coal.

All the different fpecies of coal arife from a mixture of the varieties here enumerated.

Note. That wherever coals exift, flates are found near them, and falt or mineral fprings often in their neighbourhood.

Species X.

Species X.

Bovey Coal, Taub Kohle. Xylanthrax.

This is of a brown, or brownish black colour, and lamellar texture, the laminæ are frequently flexible when first dug, though generally they harden when exposed to the air; it consists of wood penetrated with petrol or bitumen, and frequently contains pyrites, alum, and vitriol; its ashes afford a small quantity of fixed alkali, according to the German chymists;* but according to Mr. *Mills* they contain none;† by distillation it yields an ill smelling liquor, mixed with volatil alkali and oil, part of which is soluble in spirit of wine, and part insoluble being of a mineral nature.

It is found in *England, France, Italy, Swisserland, Germany, Iceland, &c.*

Species XI.

Peat Geanthrax.

There are two sorts of inflammable substances known by this name; the first and principal is of a brown, yellowish brown, or black colour, found in moory grounds, and

* 2 *Gerh. Beytr.* 271. † *Phil. Trans.* 1760.

and when fresh of a viscid consistence, but hardens by exposure to the air; it consists of clay, mixed with calcareous earth and pyrites, and sometimes contains common salt; while soft it is formed into oblong pieces, and the pyritaceous and stony matters are separated; when distilled it affords water, acid, oil and volatil alkali, and its ashes contain a small proportion of fixed alkali; they are either white or red according as it contains more or less ochre or pyrites. 2 *Ed. Essays*, 244. 2 *Gerh. Beytr.* 265. It is found in *Scotland*, *Holland*, and *Germany*. Another sort is found near *Newbury* in *Berkshire*; it contains but little earth, but consists chiefly of wood branches, twiggs, roots of trees, with leaves, grass, straw and weeds. *Phil. Transf.* 1757. p. 110.

Species XII.

Turf.

This consists of mould interwoven with the roots of vegetables; when these roots are of the bulbous kind, or in large proportion, they form the looser and worst kind of turf; but when mixed with a considerable proportion of peat, they form what is called *stone turf*; it at first hardens, but at last crumbles by long exposure to the air.

Species XIII.

Species XIII.

Amber, Bernstein, Agtstein, Succinum, Electrum, Carabé.

Amber is a hard, brittle, tastelefs substance, sometimes perfectly transparent, but mostly semi-transparent or opake, and of a glossy surface; it is found of all colours, but chiefly yellow or orange, and often contains leaves or insects; its specific gravity is from 1,065 to 1,100; its fracture is even, smooth and glossy; it is capable of a fine polish, and becomes electric by friction; when rubbed or heated, it gives a peculiar agreeable smell, particularly when it melts, that is, at 550 of *Fahrenheit,* but it then loses its transparency; projected on burning coals, it burns with a whitish flame, and a whitish yellow smoke, but gives very little soot, and leaves brownish ashes; it is insoluble in water and spirit of wine, though this latter when highly rectified extracts a reddish colour from it, but it is soluble in the vitriolic acid, which then acquires a reddish purple colour, and is precipitable from it by water; no other acid dissolves it; nor is it soluble in fixed alkalis, nor in essential oils, nor in expressed, without some decomposition, and long digestion; but balsams dissolve it readily; 75 gr. of it alkalise 100 of nitre,

nitre, and therefore 100 gr. of it contain nearly 90 of phlogifton; by diftillation it affords a fmall quantity of water, an oil of the nature of petrol, and a peculiar acid called the fuccinous acid. *Stockar*, p. 1, 11, 17, &c. According to *Baumer Reg. Men.* 22. 100 gr. of amber afford about 72 of petrol, and 4,5 of falt, that is, fuccinous acid; the remainder was fixed, or water.

It is found in maffes of different fizes in feveral pits in *Germany*, particularly in *Pruffia*, but the beft fort is that which is taken out of, or caft on fhore by the fea. According to Mr. *Scheele* amber yields by diftillation an aqueous acid, which poffeffes all the properties of vinegar; if fo, it is probably of vegetable origin. *Scheff. Forlef.* §. 68. 1 *Anmerk*.

Ambergris, Ambra.

This is a grey, brown, yellowifh, black or brown fubftance, of the confiftence of wax, and an agreeable fmell, lighter than water, and eafily inflammable, caft up by the fea on the coafts of *Madagafcar, Coromandel*, &c. but as Dr. *Swediar* has lately proved it to be of animal origin, I fhall take no further notice of it.

Copal.

Copal.

Mr. *Lehman* and many others rank this alſo among minerals; but Mr. *Bloch*, in a ſtill later diſſertation, has ſatisfactorily proved that it belongs to the vegetable kingdom. 2 *Beſchaft. Berl. Geſellſch.* p. 91.

Species XIV.

Sulphur, Brimſtone.

Sulphur is a taſteleſs, hard, brittle, idio-electric ſubſtance, of a yellow or greeniſh yellow colour, whoſe ſpecific gravity is from 1,9 to 2,35. According to Mr. *Bergman* it gently evaporates at 170, melts at 185, and flames at 302 of *Fahrenheit*. 3 *Bergm.* 242. It burns with a blue flame, and a diſagreeable ſuffocating ſmell; in cloſe veſſels it ſublimes without decompoſition, or only a decompoſition proportionable to the quantity of air they contain; when melted it becomes red, but recovers its colour on cooling.

It is inſoluble in water, though by long trituration it is ſaid water will take up ſome of it, but I believe it is rather diffuſed thro' than diſſolved in it; neither can ſpirit of wine unite to it, except when both are in a vaporous ſtate, and then 72 parts of ſpirit of wine

wine take up 1 of fulphur; it is foluble in hot oils, and alfo in fixed alkalis both in the dry and liquid way; it is decompofed by boiling in concentrated nitrous acid, partly decompofed and partly diffolved by the vitriolic, and dephlogifticated marine acid; it confifts of vitriolic acid and phlogifton united nearly in the proportion of 3 to 2; for 100 gr. of fulphur contain about 60 of acid, and 40 of phlogifton.

It is found native either in folid pieces of indeterminate fhape, running in veins thro' rocks, or in fmall lumps in gypfums and lime-ftones, and in confiderable quantity in *folfatera* and the neighbourhood of volcanos, or cryftalized in pale, tranfparent or femitranfparent, octagonal or rhomboidal cryftals, in the cavities of quartz, and particularly in the matrixes of ores, or in the form of fmall needles over hot fprings, or near volcanos, and fometimes in old privies.

$2^{dly.}$ *United with clay*, as in the aluminous ore of *la Tolfa*, and alfo at *Tarnowitz* in *Silefia*. The former has been already defcribed, the latter is a light grey earth, which when dry burfts in water like marl, poffeffes a ftrong peculiar fmell like camphor. If it be diftilled, fome fulphur fublimes.

100 gr. of this earth afford 8 of sulphur, besides gypsum, and a small quantity of iron. *Mem. Berl.* 1757.

3dly. *Mixed with clay, iron and selenite.* This compound is of a grey, brown or black colour, found near *Rome*, in *Auvergne*, Spain and *Iceland.* 2 *Lin. von. Gmelin.* 447.

4^{thly}. *United to lime-stone*, in the form of a calcareous hepar. This is found at *Tivoli* near *Rome*, and elsewhere in *Italy. Mem. Par.* 1770, p. 6. or dissolved in mineral waters; 3 pounds of which sometimes contain 25 gr. of sulphur. 2 *Gerh. Beytr.* 17. It often forms incrustations on the brinks of these springs.

5^{thly}. *In the form of an alkaline hepar.* This is said to be found in some waters in *Russia. Schab. Samm.* 4 *Theil.* p. 544. also at *Tivoli.*

6^{thly}. *United to iron and clay* in pyrites.

Lastly, United to various metallic substances, as shall be seen in the next part.

At *Ramelsberg* and the *Hartz* they extract sulphur from the sulphureous ores of silver, and lead mixed with pyrites, by sublimation during the torrefaction of those ores: this forms

forms *crude fulphur*, which is purified by a 2d fublimation; but in *Bohemia* and *Saxony* they obtain it by immediate diftillation from the pyrites, and this is again purified by fublimation in clofe veffels. - 2 *Schlut.* 222. Moft of that ufed here comes from *Italy*.

Sulphur is difcovered in earths or ftones either by its inflammation, or by diftillation, with or without white arfenic or mercury, or by folution of the matrix in marine, or dilute nitrous acid, or by digeftion in, or fufion with fixed alkalis.

PART IV.

Metallic Substances.

1. METALLIC substances are opake bodies, whose specific gravity exceeds 5,000, consisting of a heavy, dull, brittle earth combinable with phlogiston, and during that union possessing a peculiar shining appearance. They are all conductors of electricity, and more perfectly so than any other bodies during their union with phlogiston. They are all soluble either in the nitrous acid, or in aqua regia, and all precipitable in some degree by caustic alkalis, and (except platina) by the *Prussian* alkali; all when dephlogisticated communicate a tinge to borax or microcosmic salt when melted with these fluxes, or render them opake; all melt in some degree of heat, and most commonly assume a convex surface, or if in small quantity a globular form when in fusion, and in that state are miscible with each other for the most part, but refuse to unite with any other unmetallic substance, even their own calces*; but when calcined they are

---

* Iron is an exception to this rule, for even in its reguline state it is capable of uniting to its own calces slightly dephlogisticated, and to plumbago: some of them also may contain sulphur even in their reguline state as nickel, &c.

capable

Metallic Substances.

capable of union with other earths and salts. The phlogiston in all of them is in a pure state, that is, free from water and aerial acid, substances that invariably accompany it in all other compounds, except acid airs and sulphur. The more earthy part or calx of some metallic substances has been found to be of an acid nature.

2. There are 17 metallic substances now known; namely, gold, platina, silver, copper, iron, lead, tin, mercury, zinc, regulus of antimony, regulus of arsenic, bismuth, cobalt, nickel, regulus of manganese, syderites, and regulus of molybdena.

Of these gold, silver, platina and mercury are reckoned perfect or noble metals, because when calcined they recover their phlogiston without the addition of any phlogistic substance: whereas copper, iron, lead and tin cannot be entirely reduced without such addition, and hence are called ignoble or imperfect: however, all these (even mercury when solid) are malleable to a great degree, and hence called *intire* metals; whereas zinc, regulus of antimony, regulus of arsenic, &c. are scarce at all malleable, and hence are called *semi-metals*: however zinc and purified nickel are more malleable than any of the rest.

rest. Hence there are 4 perfect metals, 4 imperfect, 8 intire, and 9 semi-metals.

3. Metallic substances in their natural state are found either united to their full complement of phlogiston, and consequently possessing their respective and peculiar properties, and thence called *native*, or more or less deprived of their phlogiston, and the properties resulting from their union with it, most commonly, if not always, by combination with some other substance, and then they are said to be *mineralized*, because this is their most usual state in the mineral kingdom, and the substance so combined with them is called a *mineralizer*; the whole is called an *ore*; so also are earths and stones, in which metallic substances are contained in a notable proportion.

4. When the mineralizer is of a *saline* nature, and renders the metallic substance with which it is combined soluble in less than 20 times its weight of water, the compound is generally ranged among *salts*: thus the vitriols of iron, copper and zinc are rather classed with salts than with ores.

5. The commonest mineralizers are sulphur, arsenic, and fixed air: the least common are the vitriolic and marine acids; the phosphoric

phosphoric has been found only in one instance; metallic substances mineralized by fixed air are called *calciform* ores, from their resemblance to the calces formed by art.

6. It is true that some mineralogists of the first rank exclude arsenic from the number of mineralizers, as it is itself a metallic substance, saying, that with equal propriety other metallic substances that render metals brittle might be called mineralizers; they also add, that arsenic is never united to metals but in its reguline state, and therefore that the compound it forms should rather be called an *alloy* than an *ore*; and, indeed, if this last circumstance always took place, I should not hesitate to agree with them; but it seems clear to me that the calx of arsenic, and even its acid being capable of uniting with metals, (an union which the calx of no other metallic substance is capable of contracting) these metals cannot unite to that calx or acid without losing some part of their phlogiston, and consequently without being mineralized in the usual sense of that word; yet if regulus of arsenic be combined with metals without any loss of phlogiston (an union which art may produce by means of the black flux) I will allow the compound should rather be called an alloy; but such an union I believe seldom or ever takes place in the mineral kingdom.

Hence

Hence I chufe to follow the common language, which, without very cogent reafons, fhould never be departed from.

7. All metallic fubftances are therefore of neceffity flightly dephlogifticated when united to fulphur; but as metallic calces, in their moft dephlogifticated ftate, are alfo capable of uniting with fulphur, hence it happens that they are fometimes more and fometimes lefs dephlogifticated in various fulphurated ores, particularly the pyritous.

8. Metallic fubftances mineralized by fixed air are alfo fometimes more and fometimes lefs dephlogifticated.

9. Metallic calces always containing fome foreign ingredient afford a fmaller weight when reduced; and it is this laft that is moftly denoted, and when the proportion of metal in any ore is affigned.

CHAP. I.

Gold.

1. The diftinctive characters of gold are the following: 1°· A fpecific gravity reaching to 19,64. 2$^{dly.}$ Infolubility in all acids, except aqua regia, and the dephlogifticated

marine

marine acid, and precipitability from thefe acids in the form of a purple powder by folution of tin, or in a metallic form by the folution of vitriol of iron. $3^{dly.}$ A yellow, or reddifh yellow colour when in its metallic ftate.

Gold expofed to the utmoft heat of Mr. *Parker*'s lens for fome hours loft no fenfible part of its weight, yet when in contact with earthy matters, it communicated a blue or purplifh tinge to them, fo that I believe an exceeding minute portion of it was dephlogifticated.

Gold Ores.

2. Gold being incapable of uniting with fulphur, or even with arfenic, but very difficultly and while in fufion, or with fixed air, is for that reafon never found mineralized, but either native or invifibly mixed with other fubftances.

Species I.

Native.

3. Native gold is found either *feparate* from any matrix in lumps, or vifible grains mixed with fand, and in this ftate it is found in many rivers in *France*, *Africa*, and elfewhere, or invifibly difperfed through large maffes

masses of sand, particularly the yellowish red, or violet, and in this state it is so generally diffused through all species of Earths, though in exceeding small quantity, that Mr. *Bergman* thinks it is more universally found than any other metal, except iron. 2 *Erde. Beschr.* 313. If 100 pounds of sand contain 24 grains of gold, it is said the separation is worth attending to, but in *Africa*, 5 pounds of sand often contain 63 grains of gold, or even more; the heaviest sand, which is often black or red, yields most. In *Hungary*, 10,000 pounds of sand yield but 10 or 12 grains of gold; it was extracted, but with loss. *Born, letters from Hungary*. Or *visibly imbodied* in some matrix, and in this state it is found, either in a granular, foliated, or ramified form, in stones of the calcareous, but chiefly of the siliceous genus, as spar, gypsum, felt-spar, hornblend, jaspar, and most frequently quartz, in *Hungary, Tyrole, Siberia*, &c.

4. Gold interspersed through sand, is separated by mere mechanical means, as is amply described in the *Paris Memoirs* 1718, and 1736, and *Borns's Letters from Hungary*.

5. But when it is imbodied in Earths and stones, these may be essayed in the moist way by pounding them very fine, weighing a determinate portion, and attempting their solution,

lution, if calcareous, in nitrous acid, which will diffolve the matrix, and leave the gold at bottom untouched, or if gypfeous or filiceous by digefting them in aqua regia, as long as any metallic fubftance is taken up, which the folution of tin, or phlogifticated alkali will indicate, and then precipitating the gold by a folution of vitriol of iron.

6. Or by Amalgamation, with $\frac{1}{16}$ of their weight of mercury, in a copper or iron veffel, in which the mercury and pulverifed fand are put together with water, which is kept conftantly boiling, and the mercury after fome time, abforbes the gold, from which it is feperated by diftillation, *Lew. Com.* 194.— or by heating the fand red hot, and quenching it in water 3 or 4 times, then melting it with twice its weight of litharge, then reviving the litharge by charcoal, into lead, which then feparates from the fand, and laftly, freeing the gold from the lead by cuppellation. *Lewis, Ibid.*

7. Native gold is feldom found perfectly pure, being generaly alloyed with filver, or copper, or iron, or all three. If fuch alloy be diffolved in aqua regia, the filver will remain at the bottom in the form of horn filver. If then a folution of vitriol of iron be dropped into the folution of gold, this latter will be

234   *Elements of Mineralogy.*

be precipitated, and the copper and iron may be precipitated by the phlogisticated alkali, and separated as hereafter will be seen.

Species II.

Mixed with yellow or Martial Pyrites.

8. It is found thus mixed in the mine of *Adelfors* in *Sweden*. According to *Cronsted*, § 166, 100 pounds of this ore contains but one ounce of Gold, and it is said to be hardly worth extracting. The pyrites is of a bright yellow colour, close and compact. The gold in this ore is said to be mineralized by sulphur, by the medium of iron, because it cannot immediately be extracted by aqua regia or amalgamation, but Mr. *Bergman*, though he inclines to the opinion of the mineralization of gold, yet is candid enough to own, that the gold, when extracted from this ore, being of a granular or angular form, it is very doubtful whether it was not rather mixed than truly combined with the sulphur and iron, and its proportion being exceeding small, it is not wonderful that it should escape aqua regia, more especially as the nitrous acid becomes so phlogisticated by acting on the pyrites, as not to be able to dephlogisticate the marine, and mercury, from the nature of things, can have no access to it.

9. This

Gold. 235

9. This and such like ores, may be essayed by dissolving them in about 12 times their weight of dilute nitrous acid, gradually added, and a heat of about 120 degrees; this takes up the soluble part, and leaves the gold untouched with the insoluble matrix, from which it may be separated either by lotion, or by aqua regia, from which it is precipitable as above. The sulphur floats for the most part on the solution from which it should be separated by filtration. The solution may contain iron, copper, manganese, calcareous Earth, or argill; if it be evaporated to dryness, and the residuum heated to redness for half an hour, volatil alkali will extract the copper; the dephlogisticated nitrous acid, the Earths; the acetous, the manganese; and the marine, the calx of iron.

10. Gold may also be separated from pyrites after torrefaction, by aqua regia, *Mon. Mineral.* 277.

11. Pyrites containing gold, is also found in *Swisserland* and *Hungary*, that found in *Hungary*, contains 5 ounces of gold per quintal, *Mon. Expositions des Mines*, p. 47. the gold mines of *Norway*, are of the same nature as those of *Adelfors*, 2 *Jars*.

12. In

12. In the *dry way*, Mr. *Bergman* eſſays theſe ores, by mixing 2 parts of the ore, well pounded and waſhed, with one and a half of litharge, and 3 of glaſs, covering the whole with common ſalt, and melting it in a ſmith's forge, in a covered crucible ; he then opens the crucible, puts a nail into it, covers it, and heats it again, and continues to do ſo until the iron is no longer attacked. The lead is thus precipitated, and contains the gold which is ſeperated by cuppellation, *Scheff*. 239. 1 *Anmerk*.

Species III.

Mixed with Arſenical Pyrites.

13. Found at *Salzbergh* in *Tyrole*, in mountains of quartz and ſhiſtus; the quintal affords only about 25 grains. It is ſeparated by lotion, and affords a profit of between 4 and 500*l*. per an. 2 *Jars*. 78.

Species IV.

Mixed with a white, red, or Vitreous Silver Ore.

14. Near *Cremnitz* and *Schemnitz* in *Hungary*, 2 *Jars*. 165, 195.

Species V.

Mixed with a sulphurated Ore of Silver, Iron, Lead, and Manganese.

15. Lately found at *Nagaya* in *Transylvania*. This ore consists of small dark coloured plates of more or less brightness, inhering in quartz, and a soft whitish substance, which Mr. *Bergman* found to be manganese. Part of the gold may be extracted from it by eliquation in a cuppelling heat, its fusibility being promoted by the lead.

16. If the dark coloured plates be separated from the remaining mass, and treated with aqua regia, the gold and iron will be extracted, and may be separated as above mentioned, N.º 7. but none can be extracted by amalgamation, *Scopol. An. 3.* p. 90.

17. This ore is said to afford 10 ounces of gold per quintal, besides silver, its specific gravity according to *Gellert*, is 4,043.

Species VI.

Mixed with sulphurated Iron and Copper, with Manganese.

18. This is a yellow pyrites, found also at *Nagaya*, in which gold is contained; Mr. *Bindheim*

Bindheim lately effayed this ore in a particular manner. The pyrites being well pulverifed, were heated in an open crucible, until the fulphur was burnt off. The refiduum while hot, was thrown into water, a reddifh brown matter remained undiffolved. This, when dried, was digefted in 3 times its weight of aqua regia, then diluted and filtered, and æther poured on it and fhaken. The æther took up the gold, and being burnt off, left it in its metallic form, 4 *Berl. Schrift.* 393.

19. In *Peru* gold is found mixed with a ftony matter, not well known, and alfo with a red Earth, from both which it is there extracted by amalgamation, 2 *Jars.*

CHAP. II.

Platina.

1. Platina has as yet been found only among the gold mines of *Peru.* It comes to us in the form of large fmooth grains, of an irregular figure, fome of them hollow, whiter than iron, intermixed with quartz, and a ferruginous fand, and in the cavities, fometimes particles of gold, but more frequently quickfilver is found, which may be feparated by diftillation; whence it is conjectured, that it is not brought to us in its natural ftate, but that it has been feparated from gold with other matters,

matters, by amalgamation. Most of its particles are friable and magnetic, but some few are malleable to a considerable degree, and may be separated by a magnet, but according to the accurate experiments of Count *Sickingen*, even these contain about $\frac{1}{3}$ of their weight of iron. Before it is separated from quartz, its specific gravity is from 6,000 to 11,000, and after that separation from 16 to 18. It is soluble only in aqua regia, or dephlogisticated marine acid, and is nearly infusible in terrestrial fires, the great burning lens of *Paris* only agglutinated its particles in 20 minutes, Mr. *Parker's* perfectly melted them in less than two. It is precipitable from its solution by salammoniac, as our late excellent chymist Dr. *Lewis* has discovered, a property by which it is easily distinguished, and separated from all other metals. It is not precipitable by the Prussian alkali, as all other metals are.

2. Its ores, if it has any, are not yet known.

3. Platina is purified from iron by reiterated coction in spirit of salt, solution in aqua regia, and precipitation of the iron, by the Prussian alkali. When pure, its colour approaches to that of silver, its specific gravity is nearly 23,000, it is not in the least magnetic.

CHAP.

CHAP. III.

Silver.

1. Silver is the whiteſt of all metals; its ſpecific gravity when pure is 11,095; it is ſoluble in the concentrated vitriolic acid with the aſſiſtance of heat, and in the moderately dilute nitrous acid without that aſſiſtance; it is precipitable from both by the marine, and from the nitrous in great meaſure by the vitriolic; its calces are reducible without the addition of any phlogiſtic matter, and it is incapable of calcination by mere heat.

SPECIES I.

Native.

2. Native ſilver is found in a granular, lamellar, filamentous, capillary, arboreſcent, or cryſtalized form, inhering either in baroſelenite, lime-ſtone, ſelenite, quartz, chert, flint, ſerpentine, gneiſs, agate, mica, calcareous ſpar, pyrites, ſhiſtus, clay, &c. alſo in ſeparate maſſes of various ſizes, ſome of the weight of 60 pounds, in or near the veins of moſt metallic ſubſtances, particularly in *Peru*, and frequently in various parts of Europe, either of a white, brown, or yellowiſh colour.

3. It

Silver. 241

3. It is often diffused through sand and ochre, also in grey lime-stone in *Lower Austria*, and in a greenish clay near *Schemnitz*, or mixed with ochre, clay and calciform hickel.

4. It is seldom found pure; being generally alloyed with copper, and sometimes with a small proportion of gold, iron, or regulus of antimony*, and sometimes about 5 per cent. of arsenic †; it is separable from gold and regulus of antimony by solution in nitrous acid, and from copper and iron by precipitating it by the marine acid ‡, and from arsenic by torrefaction.

100 gr. of the horn silver contain 75 of real silver; it is reducible by triturating it with about its own weight of fixed alkali with a little water, then melting the whole in a crucible, whose bottom is covered with mineral alkali well pressed, and covering the mass of horn silver also with the mineral alkali.

5. The native silver found near *Konigsberg* contains so much gold as to acquire a yellow colour from it.

* *Bergm. Sciag.* §, 154. † 13 *Roz. Supplem.* p. 50.
‡ A more perfect manner of separating it from copper will be seen Nº. 21.

Species II.

Species II.

Mineralized by Sulphur.

Vitreous Silver Ore, Glafzertz.

6. It is found either in solid large lumps, or inhering in quartz, spar, gypsum, gneiss, pyrites, &c. of a lamellar, granular or capillary form, or cryftalized; it is generally of a lead colour firft, but grows black by exposure to the air, but sometimes grey or black, even when firft broken; its laminæ are flexible and ductil, and even malleable in some degree, and so soft, that they may be cut with a knife; its specific gravity is 7,200 *; it is one of the richeft of the silver ores.

100 parts of it contain from 72 to 77 of silver; it is rarely contaminated with any other metal besides a small proportion of iron.

7. It is found in *Hungary* near *Shemnitz*, and in *Saxony* near *Freyburgh*, particularly in the famous mine of *Himmelsfurft*.

8. It is analyfed by boiling it in moderately dilute nitrous acid, ufing about 25 times its weight, until the sulphur is quite exhaufted.

* *Gellert Anfangs.* 234.

Silver. 243

The filver is precipitated by marine acid, or common falt, and eftimated as in N°· 4. The *Pruffian* alkali will fhew if any other metal is contained in the folution; the gold, if any, will remain undiffolved; fixed alkalis will precipitate any other earthy matters contained in the folution.

9. In the dry way it may be reduced by melting it with the blow-pipe on charcoal; for the fulphur is diffipated; and the filver remains; or by melting it with $\frac{1}{8}$ of its weight of filings of iron, as the iron will take up the fulphur and be fcorified.

Species III.
Mineralized by a fmall proportion of Arfenic.

10. This ore is of a yellowifh white colour, and of a ftriated texture, refembling bifmuth, but much harder; it melts very eafily, and if kept in fufion, it lofes its arfenic, and the filver remains almoft intirely pure, as it contains but very little iron; it contains about 90 per cent. of filver, and is found near *Quadanal-Canal* in *Spain*. *Mon. Mineral.* 281.

Species IV.
Mineralized by a large proportion of Arfenic.

11. The proportion of arfenic in this ore is fo great, that it would fcarce deferve to be called

called a silver ore, if the arsenic were not easily dissipated: the quintal contains but from 4 to 6 ounces of silver; it is very soft, and easily cut, and when cut has a brilliant metallic appearance; it consists of conchoidal laminæ; it is found also at *Quadanal-Canal. Mon. Ibid.*

12. It is reduced by evaporating the arsenic, which then leaves the silver slightly contaminated with iron.

Species V.

Mineralized by Sulphur and Arsenic.

Red Silver Ore, Rothgulden ertz.

13. This is a heavy, shining substance, either transparent or opake, mostly of a crimson or reddish colour, though sometimes grey or blackish, but when scraped or powdered always reddish; found either in shapeless masses, or crystalized in pyramids or polygons, or dendritritical, or plated or radiated incrustations, on or in matrixes of quartz, flint, spar, pyrites, sparry iron ore, lead ore, pyrites, cobalt ore, jasper, baroselenite, gneifs, &c. when radiated or striated, it is called *rothgulden bluth.* In fire it crackles and melts after it has acquired a red heat, with an arsenical smell; it detonnates with nitre; its specific

cific gravity is from 5,4 to 5,684. Mr. *Bergman* found 100 gr. of it to contain 60 of filver, 27 of arfenic, and 13 of fulphur. 2 *Bergm.* 303. but fometimes it contains even 70 per cent. of filver. The darkeft ores are the richeft, and thefe often contain a little iron; the yelloweft are the pooreft; the moft yellow does not belong to this fpecies, being in fact orpiment, containing 6 or 7 per cent. of filver.

14. To analyfe this ore in the moift way, Mr. *Bergman* advifes to boil it after it is reduced to a very fine powder in dilute nitrous acids, as in N° 8, and to edulcorate the refiduum very carefully which contains the fulphur and arfenic, which may be feparated by boiling in a fufficient quantity of aqua regia: if the fulphur ftill retains any luna cornua, it may be feparated by cauftic volatil alkali.

15. In the dry way it is reduced after torrefaction by a mixture of iron and lead; the iron takes up the fulphur, and the lead the filver, which is afterwards feparated by cuppellation.

Species VI.

Mineralized by Sulpur, and a very small Portion of Arsenic and Iron.

Black Silver Ore. Schwartz ertz, Schwartz gulden. Silber mulm.

16. This is either of a *solid and brittle* consistence, which distinguishes it from the vitreous ore, and of a glassy appearance in its fracture when recent, or of a *looser texture*, and sooty or deep black colour, like moss or thin leaves lying on the surface of other silver ores, or of those of lead or cobalt, or in clays, ponderous spar, gneiss, &c. it may contain about 25 per cent. of silver: the former is found in *Dauphiné*, *Hungary*, and *Saxony*, and contains at most 60 per cent. of silver. *Mon. Mineral.* 302. 3 *Lin. von. Gmel.* 406.

Species VII.

Mineralized by Arsenic, and containing a large Proportion of Iron.

Arsenicomartial Silver Ore, Weiss ertz, Pyrites Argenteus of Henckel.

17. Mineralogists do not well agree about the ore to which this denomination belongs. I follow Mr. *Monnet*, who seems to have attended

tended to the division of ores most exactly. According to him this ore is a hard substance, of a white, shining appearance, and of a compact, lamellar or fibrous texture; the brightest is the poorest in silver; the richest gives only 10 per cent. the poorest 6 or 8 ounces: it contains no sulphur; and hence Mr. *Monnet* calls it a metallic regulus, not considering that the iron is in a calcined state, which fully proves that arsenic is a true mineralizer: the iron and arsenic are in various proportions, but the arsenic always exceeds.

It is found in Saxony, the *Hartz*, at *Quadanal-Canal*, &c.

18. It is essayed in the moist way, as in N°· 4.

Species VIII.

Mineralized by Arsenic and Sulphur, with a small Proportion of Copper, and a still smaller of Iron.

White Silver Ore, Weissgulden.

19. It is a heavy, soft, opake substance, fine grained or scaly, bright and shining in its fractures, of a whitish, steely or lead colour, sometimes crystalized in pyramidical or cylindrical forms, but often in amorphous grains, or resembling mofs, or in the form of thin

thin laminæ incruſtating other bodies, found in quartz, ſpar, ſtellſtein, pyrites, blend, lead ore, cobalt ore, ſparry iron ore, fluors, &c. It is very fuſible; its ſpecific gravity 5,000 or 5,300; its proportion of ſilver from 10 to 30 per cent.

20. It is found, though not commonly, in *Saxony*, *Hungary*, the *Hartz*, and *St. Marie aux Mines*.

21. Mr. *Bergman* analyſes this ore in the following manner. Having pulverized and weighed a certain portion of it, he attempts its ſolution in about 12 times its weight of dilute nitrous acid: the copper and ſilver are diſſolved, and a white reſiduum remains. The ſilver he precipitates, not with marine acid, for this would unite alſo to the copper, and with the ſilver form a triple ſalt, which would alſo fall, but with a clean plate of copper previouſly weighed; the ſilver being in its metallic form, may immediately be weighed, and its contents known: the copper ſhould then be precipitated by aerated mineral alkali; 194 gr. of this precipitate well dried are equivalent to 100 of copper in its metallic form; but from this laſt, the weight, which the plate of copper loſt, muſt be ſubtracted.

22. The

22. The white residuum, containing the sulphur, arsenic and iron, is next to be examined: by boiling it in spirit of salt, the arsenic and iron are taken up; the arsenic is to be precipitated by the addition of water, and then the iron by the *Prussian* alkali; the sulphur remains undissolved, and may be treated with volatil alkali to try whether it retains any copper or horn silver. 2 *Bergm.* 418.

Species IX.

Mineralized by Arsenic and Sulphur, with a large Proportion of Copper and some Iron.

Grey Silver Ore, Fahl erz.

23. This is a hard, grey, or dark grey substance, more or less brilliant, sometimes crystalized, but mostly amorphous, and is, in fact, the grey copper ore hereafter to be mentioned, Chap. 4. N°· 26, impregnated with silver, and varies much in its contents from about 1 to 12 per cent. of silver, and from 12 to 24 of copper, the remainder being sulphur and arsenic, with a little iron: the richer it is in copper, the poorer in silver, and reciprocally. Mr. *Monnet* remarks, that wherever copper is united to arsenic, silver is also found; it is the commonest of all the silver ores: the grey silver ore of *Dal* in *Sweden*

Sweden contains alſo regulus of antimony, and, according to Mr. *Bergman*, it contains 24 per cent. of copper, and 5 of ſilver; but this belongs to the next Species.

Species X.

Mineralized by Arſenic and Sulphur, with Copper, Iron, and Regulus of Antimony.

Brown Silver Ore, Leber erz.

24. Its colour is moſtly of a reddiſh brown, ſometimes dark grey, ſometimes it is found cryſtalized in pyramids, but moſtly amorphous; when ſcraped it appears red; it contains from 1 to 5 per cent. of ſilver; the greateſt part is copper, and the next in proportion is arſenic.

It is found in *Sweden*, *Germany* and *Spain*.

25. It is analyſed by boiling it in about 6 times its weight of dilute nitrous acid, which will take up the ſilver and copper, and leave the regulus of antimony and arſenic : theſe being boiled in ſtrong nitrous acid are dephlogiſticated, and the arſenic becomes ſoluble in water; the calx of antimony remains undiſſolved; the ſulphur may be found in a ſecond experiment, uſing aqua regia inſtead of

Silver.

of the concentrated nitrous acid; the silver and copper are separated as in N°· 21.

Species XI.

Mineralized by Sulphur and Arsenic, with Iron and Regulus of Antimony.

Plumose Silver Ore, Feder ertz.

26. In point of colour this ore varies from a dull white to grey, dark blue, brown or black; it is found in a capillary form, or, like wool, sometimes loose, at other times attached, its filaments are rigid and inflexible; the whiter it is, the richer; but it seldom contains even 1 per cent. of silver. It is found in *Saxony* and elsewhere. Some confound it with the foregoing.

Its analysis may be understood from N°· 21 and 25.

Species XII.

Mineralized by Sulphur and Arsenic, with Cobalt and Iron.

Cobaltic Silver Ore.

27. This ore is distinguished by rose-coloured particles, of cobalt dispersed through a dark brown, blackish, or grey, and somewhat shining solid mass. It is found in *Saxony,*

Saxony, and at *Allemont* in *Dauphiné*, and contains about 40 or 50 per cent. of filver, and very little cobalt; the arfenic is in an acid ftate, and united to the cobalt.

28. To analyfe it, let it be diffolved in nitrous acid; the filver and cobalt will be taken up, and moft of the iron will remain calcined, together with the arfenic; the filver may be precipitated by the marine acid, and the cobalt by an aerated fixed alkali, and its weight determined, as will be fhewn in Chap. 13.

Species XIII.

Mineralized by Sulphur, with Regulus of Antimony and Barytes.

Butter-milk Ore.

29. It appears in the form of thin pellicles, on granular fpar.

Species XIV.

Combuftile Silver Ore.

30. This is black and brittle, and leaves about 6 per cent of filver in its afhes, it is a coal in which filver is found. The filver is extracted as ufual by nitrous acid.

Species XV.

Species XV.

Mineralized by the Vitriolic and Marine Acids, with a little Iron, and sometimes with a mixture of the Vitreous Ore.

Corneous Silver Ore, Horn ertz.

31. This scarce and valuable ore is of a white, grey, pearly, or yellow, green, brown, purple, or black colour, frequently cryftalized in a cubic form, fometimes refembling an Earth, eafily fufible without any fmoke. The black fort is friable, and eafily pulverifed, but the other fort is in fome degree malleable, may be cut with a knife, and takes a fort of polifh when rubbed. The vitreous ore mixed with the black, is foluble in nitrous acid, and may by that means be feparated, the faline ores being infoluble in that acid; if pure from iron, thefe ores fhould contain 70 per cent of filver at leaft, but they moftly contain fome portion of iron, of which fome is even united to the marine acid according to *Monnet*. It is found in *Saxony, Bohemia, St. Marie aux Mines, Siberia,* and *Peru.* It was firft effayed by Mr. *Wolfe, Phil. Trans.* 1776, and afterwards, though lefs exactly, by Mr. *Monnet,* in 1777, fee 9 *Mem. Etr.* p. 717.

32. Mr.

254   *Elements of Mineralogy.*

32. Mr. *Bergman* gives the following most ingenious method of analysing these ores in the moist way.

1°· He digests this compound ore in the marine acid for 24 hours, by which means the vitriol of silver is decomposed, and the whole is converted into horn silver. He then judges of the quantity of the vitriol of silver, by the quantity of vitriolic acid let loose in the liquor, and to find how much this is, he decants the clear liquor, and drops into it a solution of nitrous baroselenite, which is immediately decomposed by the vitriolic acid, and forms true vitriolic baroselenite, of which 100 grains contain 15 of dephlegmated vitriolic acid, and so in proportion. Now 100 grains of vitriol of silver, contain 25,37 of the same dephlegmated acid, so that 25,37 grains of this acid, indicate 100 of vitriol of silver, and so in proportion, and thus the quantity of silver in the vitriol of silver is also found, as 100 grains of it contain 74,62 of silver,* and the proportion of vitrol of silver being known, that of horn silver of course, is known; but if the ore be of the black kind, after the whole is turned into horn silver, it should be digested in caustic volatil

---

* According to Mr. *Bergman*, 100 parts of vitriol of silver, contain but 68,75 of silver.

alkali,

alkali, which will take up the horn filver, and leave the vitreous ore. The iron, if any, fhould be precipitated from the firft folution, by the *Pruffian* alkali, after the precipitation of the barofelenite.

Uncertain Mineralizations.

Species XVI.

Goofe-dung Ore.

33. This is of a greenifh colour, mixed with yellow and red; it is faid to contain about 6 per cent of filver. Some think it a mixture of red filver ore, and calx of nickel.

Species XVII.

Foliaceous Silver Ore. Silberartiges, Bergzunder, Blatter erz.

34. Its colour is *mortdoré*. It is thought by fome to be native filver, by others a mixture of galena, ochre, and filver, it is found in mountain cork, it is fo light, that it fwims on water. It contains but one ounce of filver per quintal. See *Lehman's Experiments, Mem. Berl.* 1758.

Species XVIII.

Species XVIII.

Mineralized by Sulphur, Arsenic and Bismuth.

35. Such ores have been talked of, but their existence has not as yet been proved.

36. Silver has also been found in the sulphurated ore of zinc called pech blend, and in that of lead called galena, particularly the latter; also in the copper pyrites, but in small quantity, as shall be mentioned in their proper places.

37. If an ore yields ½ per cent of silver, it is generally worth extracting.

CHAP. IV.

Copper.

1. Its colour is pale red as is well known. Its specific gravity from 8,7 to 9,300, depending not only on its purity, but also on its condensation, by hammering. It is soluble not only in acids, but also in alkalis and neutral salts. It is precipitable from most acids, in its metallic form, by a clean plate of iron, and most of its acid solutions are convertible into a deep blue, by volatil alkalis. These characters are sufficient to distinguish it.

Species. I.

Species I.

Native.

2. Native copper, that is copper in a more or less malleable state, and either of its own peculiar, or of a grey or blackish colour, has been found either in grains, or in large shapeless solid lumps, or in a foliated, capillary, arborescent form, or cryſtalized in quadrangular pyramids, in or on clay, ſhiſtus, quartz, fluors, zeolytes, &c. in *Siberia, Sweden, Germany, Hungary, Tranſylvania,* &c.

3. It undoubtedly has sometimes been produced from precipitation by iron from waters in which it was held in solution, and this is the purest sort, but in many cases it could not have been produced in that manner, and then this sort is never very pure, but mixed either with gold, silver, or iron, or with sulphur; this last combination forms what is called *black copper*.

4. All these impurities are discoverable by solution, in nitrous acid; the gold remains undissolved in the form of a black powder, soluble in aqua regia; the silver may be precipitated by the marine acid, or still better by a clean polished plate of copper, the iron is separated

separated by boiling the whole as it is dephlogisticated, and rendered thereby insoluble.

Mineralized.

5. We may observe in general, that all copper ores after roasting, communicate a blue colour to volatil alkali, on digesting them in it. Before roasting, it is possible that arsenic may prevent that effect, or even sulphur, if in sufficient quantity.

SPECIES II.

Mineralized by the Aerial Acid.

Calciform Ores.

6. Of these there are three varieties, the red, the green, and the blue, all are soluble in acids, and blacken in a moderate heat.

I. VARIETY.

Red, Minera cupri calciformis Rubra, Minera hepatica, Leberertz.

7. We sometimes meet with this ore in a loose form, then called copper ochre, but generally it is moderately hard, yet brittle, sometimes crystalized and transparent, either in a capillary form, or in cubes, prisms, or pyramids,

pyramids: it is found in *England, Scotland, Germany*, &c. it effervesces with acids.

8. According to Mr. *Fontana*, 11 *Roz.* 511. 100 parts of it contain 73 of copper, 26 of fixed air, and 1 of water. Mr. *Bergman* also found it to contain fixed air, 2 *Bergm.* 430. The brown, or hepatic ore, contains a variable proportion of iron or pyrites, and sometimes sulphurated copper, and hence affords from 20 to 50 per cent. of copper. It is often iridescent.

II. VARIETY.

Green, Malachite, Mountain Green.

9. *Malachite* has the appearance of green jasper, but is not quite so hard, for it does not strike fire with steel; it is either of a radiated or equable texture, generally of an oval form, and the size of an egg, but sometimes it forms capillary filaments. Its specific gravity, according to *Muschenbroeck*, is from 3,5 to 3,994; it is sometimes mixed with calcareous Earth and gypsum. It is found in *Norway, Siberia*, &c.

10. According to Mr. *Fontana*, 100 Parts of the purest sort, contain 75 of copper, and 25 of aerial acid and water.

11. *Mountain Green,* is generally found in a loose and friable state, rarely crystalized and indurated, often mixed with calcareous Earth and iron, and some arsenic. 100 Parts of the purest contain 72 of copper, 22 of aerial acid, and 6 of water.

III. VARIETY.

Mountain Blue, Chrysocolla of some.

12. This also most frequently appears in a loose form, but sometimes indurated and even crystalized, but it is then mixed with quartz. 100 parts of it contain about 69 of copper, 29 of aerial acid, and 2 of water. Mr. *Morveau,* in the *Memoirs of Dijon,* for 1782, has shewn, that the calces of copper are determined rather to a blue than a green colour, by a greater proportion of phlogiston.

13. They are analysed in the moist way by solution in acids, and precipitation by the mineral aerated alkali, if they be pure, or by the *Prussian* alkali, if they contain earths. 194 grains of the precipitate formed by the mineral alkali are equivalent to 100 of copper in its metallic state: so also are 350 gr. of the precipitate formed by the *Prussian* alkali, as Mr. *Bergman* has determined: copper also may be precipitated in its metallic state

Copper. 261

state by means of iron, though it is not easy to get it pure, if the nitrous acid be the solvent.

14. I have found that 112 gr. of good iron, precipitate 100 of copper from a saturate and dilute solution of it in the nitrous acid, and 80 gr. of the same iron precipitate, 100 of copper from a saturate and dilute solution of it in the vitriolic acid; so that weighing the iron before and after, the quantity of copper may be estimated by the loss of weight of the iron; but care must be taken that the iron do not remain in the nitrous acid after the copper is precipitated. Experience will point out some other precautions too tedious to be inserted here.

15. If iron be mixed with the ore, it may be separated by long boiling in nitrous acid.

16. In the dry way, after torrefaction, they may be essayed by melting them with $\frac{1}{2}$ or $\frac{3}{4}$ of their weight of borax, and $\frac{1}{4}$ of their weight of pitch. Some loss always attends the black flux. Thus Mr. *Fontana* having essayed 576 gr. of a calciform ore by black flux, obtained but 376 or 380 of copper, yet by distillation he got 408. 11 *Roz.* p. 511.

SPECIES III.

Species III.

Cupreous Stones.

Analogous to the calciform ores are the cupreous stones, *Turquoise* and *Lapis Armenus*.

17. *Turquoise* is the tooth of an animal penetrated with the blue calx of copper; it loses its colour when heated; it is opake, and of a lamellar texture, and susceptible of a fine polish; its specific gravity is from 2,5 to 2,908; some are of a deep blue, some of a whitish blue, but become of a deeper when heated. This stone is found in *Persia* and *Languedoc*. The copper may be extracted from it by distilled vinegar. According to *Reaumur*, Mem. Par. 1715, nitrous acid will not dissolve that of *Persia*, though it will that of *France*, which shews a difference between them.

18. *Lapis Armenus* is another blue stone which does not admit of any polish, and consists of calcareous earth, or gypsum penetrated with the blue calx of copper: hence it sometimes effervesces with acids, and sometimes not, but never gives fire with steel; it loses its colour when heated.

Species IV.

Species IV.

Mineralized by Sulphur with scarce any Iron.
Vitreous Copper Ore, Kupfer glass ertz.

19. Its colour is red, brown, blue or violet; it is generally so soft as to be cut with a knife, and as to form, it is sometimes crystalized in regular figures, and sometimes amorphous; it is much more fusible than pure copper; its specific gravity is from 4,81 to 5,338. It is found in the mines of other copper ores, and in lime-stone, spar, quartz, mica and clay; it is the richest of all the copper ores, and affords from 80 to 90 per cent. of copper, 10 or 12 of sulphur, with a small proportion of iron; the red ores are the poorest, containing most iron.

20. To analyse this ore, Mr. *Bergman* advises a solution of it in 5 times its weight of concentrated vitriolic acid by ebullition to dryness and the subsequent addition of as much water as will dissolve the vitriol thus formed. This solution he precipitates by a clean bar of iron, and thus obtains the copper in its metallic form. If the solution be contaminated with iron, he re-dissolves thus the copper thus obtained, in the same manner, and so procures a richer solution, which he again precipitates with iron.

21. Dr.

21. Dr. *Fordyce,* in the *Philosophical Transactions* for 1780, suggests an improvement, by first dissolving the ore in nitrous acid, and precipitating it by a fixed alkali (if this solution be boiled, any iron it may contain will be precipitated) the precipitate he re-dissolves in vitriolic acid, and precipitates it with iron.

22. The proportion of sulphur may be found by dissolving the ore in dilute aqua regia, as the sulphur will remain undissolved.

Species V.

Mineralized by Sulphur, with 20 or 30 per cent. of iron.

Azure Copper Ore, Kupfer Lazur, Kupfer malm.

23. This differs from the foregoing only in containing more iron; its colour consists in various shades of blue, or reddish blue; it is as hard, and much more brittle; it contains from 40 to 60 per cent. of copper, from 20 to 30 of iron, and the remainder sulphur; the poorer it is in iron, the richer in copper; it has been by many confounded with indurated *mountain blue.*

Species VI.

Species VI.

Mineralized by Sulphur, with a large Proportion of Iron.

Yellow Copper Ore, yellow Pyrites.

24. Its colour is yellow, or yellow mixed with red or green, or variegated like a pigeon's neck; it is moderately hard, not readily giving fire with steel as other pyrites do; in its fracture it presents sharp fragments; it is sometimes found crystalized, and sometimes amorphous; its specific gravity is about 4,16; it occurs both in separate masses and imbodied in stones, and is the commonest of all the copper ores.

25. With respect to its contents, the crystalized sort is the poorest in copper, of which it contains only from 4 to 8 per cent, the remainder is chiefly iron; it is generally reddish, and is in fact a martial pyrites, with a small proportion of copper; the greenish yellow contains most sulphur, and from 15 to 20 per cent. of copper; the pure yellow contains most copper; namely, from 20 to 30 per cent. its texture is foliated; these pyritous ores always contain argill, and a little of siliceous earth.

Species VII.

Species VII.

Mineralized by Sulphur and Arsenic, with a little Iron.

Arsenical, or grey Copper Ore. Kupfer, fahl ertz, Weiss kupfer ertz.

26. This is of a white, grey, or brown colour; it is moderately hard, and very brittle, sometimes cryftalized, and often of an indeterminate figure; it is of very difficult fusion, and heavier than the preceding.

27. It contains from 35 to 60 per cent. of copper; the brown is the richeft in copper; the white or grey contains moft arfenic; it frequently contains filver, and if this exceeds 1 or 2 per cent. it is called *grey filver Ore*.

It is found imbodied in all forts of ftones, and mixed with other copper ores as well as with the ores of other metals.

28. The analyfis of thefe ores in the moift way may be underftood from what has been already faid. To effay them in the dry way, they fhould firft be pulverized and feparated as much as poffible from ftony and earthy particles, then roafted to feparate the fulphur and arfenic, then melted with a mixture of an equal weight of Mr. *Tillet's* flux, which
consists

consists of 2 parts pounded glass, 1 of calcined borax, and $\frac{1}{4}$ of charcoal: if the ore be poor more borax may be added; black flux is hurtful, as it forms an hepar which holds part of the copper in solution. *Mem. Par.* 1775.

29. Mr. *Margraaf*, in the Memoirs of *Berlin* for 1775, recommends a mixture of equal parts of clay well washed, fluor, and lime-stone, and $\frac{1}{2}$ part of charcoal, with an equal weight of the torrefied ore; the whole to be melted in a porcelain heat. The coal he uses is that left after the distillation of tartar.

Species VIII.

Mineralized by Sulphur and Arsenic, with Zinc and Iron.

Blendose Copper Ore.

30. Mr. *Monnet* says he has met with this ore only at *Catharineberg* in *Bohemia*; it is of a brown colour, of a hard, solid, and compact granular texture; it contains from 18 to 30 per cent. of copper.

31. It is analysed in the liquid way by solution in nitrous acid and precipitation of the copper by iron: the iron and zinc are precipitated

pitated then by the *Pruſſian* alkali; the precipitate calcined is re-diſſolved in nitrous acid, and the ſolution evaporated to dryneſs; the iron being thus deplogiſticated becomes inſoluble in nitrous acid; the calx of zinc is re-diſſolved in that acid, and again precipitated by the *Pruſſian* alkali. 100 gr. of that precipitate waſhed and dried are equivalent to 20 of zinc in its metallic ſtate, and 100 gr. of dephlogiſticated iron are equivalent to 73,5 of iron in its metallic ſtate.

Species IX.

Argillaceous, Shiſtoſe, or ſlaty Copper Ore, Kupfer Schiefer.

32. This ore ſeems to conſiſt of the vitreous copper ore, intimately combined with ſhiſtus, and not barely diſperſed through it in viſible particles; it is of a brown or black colour, lamellar texture, and very heavy; it affords from 6 to 10 per cent. of copper, and is of difficult fuſion, unleſs lime-ſtone be added; it contains a little bitumen, calcareous earth and iron, as *ſhiſti* do.

Species X.

Bituminous Copper Ore. Kupfer brand ertz.

33. This is ſaid to be found in *Sweden*; it is a ſpecies of coal which gives little or no flame,

flame, but confumes and leaves afhes, from which copper is extracted.

Species XI.

Copper in a foreign Form.

34. Animal and vegetable fubftances are fometimes found penetrated with copper.

Species XII.

Mineralized by the Vitriolic or Marine Acids.

35. Thefe are mentioned and defcribed in the fecond part: in the dry way they are reducible by Mr. *Tillet's* flux.

CHAP. V.

Iron.

1. Its fpecific gravity is from 7,6 to 8,00, that of the moft dephlogifticated calx of iron, only 6,7. It is foluble in all acids, and the faturate folution precipitable by vegetable aftringents of a *black* colour, and by *Pruffian* alkali of a *blue*; in its metallic or flightly dephlogifticated ftate it is attractable by the magnet; it is the moft difficultly fufible of all metallic fubftances, except platina and manganefe.

Species I.

Species I.
Native.

2. It is now known that native iron exists in many places, the moft remarkable mafs of this fort is, that difcovered in *Siberia*, which weighs 1600 pounds. It is of that fpecies called *redfhort* iron, being malleable while cold, but brittle when red hot. *Pallas Reifen*, 3 *Theil*. p. 411.

Mineralized.

Calciform Ores.

3. The bafis of the calciform ores, is either the black or blackifh brown calx of iron, which is in fome meafure phlogifticated and magnetic, or the red calx of iron, which is more dephlogifticated, and not magnetic before torrefaction.

Species II.

Brown Calx of Iron, mixed with Iron in its metallic State.

Steel Ore. Stahlerz. *Ferrum Chalybeatum, Lin. Minera Ferri nigra. Cronft.* §. 212.

4. Of a dark fteel colour, folid, compact, and fhining in its fracture; fcarcely gives fire
with

with steel, gives a black powder, is magnetic, and in some degree malleable when red hot. It affords from 60 to 80 per cent. of good iron. It is found at *Adelfors* and *Dannemora* in *Sweden*, also in the *Isle of Elbe*, and *North America*.

5. Chrystalized iron ore in an octohœdral or cubic form, *ferrum tessulare*, and *minera ferri crystalizata* of *Wallerius*, belongs to this species, it is somewhat less magnetic, probably because it contains less of metallized iron.

Species III.

Magnet.

6. This differs but little in its appearance from the preceding ore, but has less lustre; it is either coarse or fine grained, the coarse grained loses its power soonest. It seems to contain a small quantity of sulphur, as it smells of it when red hot. It is probable that it contains more particles of iron in its metallic form, than the preceding ore, but it is often contaminated with a mixture of quartz and argill. It is possible it may contain nickel, for this when purified to a certain degree, acquires the properties of a magnet, 2 *Bergm*. 242. Its constitution has not as yet been properly examined.

Species IV.

Brown Calx of Iron, combined with Plumbago.

Black Eisen Glimmer, Schwartz Eisen Rahm or Eisenman.

7. This confists of black shining scales, more or less magnetic; Mr. *Rinman* found it to confist of plumbago, and 26 per cent. of iron. *Historia Ferri.* §. 57.

Species V.

Brown Calx of Iron, united with the white Calx of Manganese, and mild Calcareous Earth in various proportions.

White or Sparry Iron Ore, Weifs Eisen Spath, Stahlstein.

8. Its colour when fresh dug is whitish, but by exposure to the air, it first becomes grey, then brown, at last reddish, yellowish, or black. Its shape, either amorphous or rhomboidal, it is frequently transparent, its texture lamellar, scaly, granular, or cellular. Sometimes it assumes a stalactitical form, and sometimes it is found in a powdery state, and is then of a brown blackish colour, is frequently intersperfed with quartz and pyrites,

rites, &c. and does not give fire with steel, unless these foreign substances be struck. Its specific gravity is from 3,6 to 3,895, or 4,000 it feebly effervesces with acids, particularly when pounded and heated, affords from 20 to 27 per cent of fixed air. It is scarce ever magnetic before calcination, but if heated, it decrepitates, grows black, becomes magnetic, and loses from 15 to 40 per cent of its weight.

9. 100 Parts of this ore from *Eisenärtz* in *Steria*, afford according to Mr. *Bergman*, 38 of the brown calx of iron, 24 of the white calx of manganese, and 38 of mild calcareous Earth. Another sort from *West Silvretberg* contains 22 of the brown calx of iron, 28 of the white calx of manganese, and 50 of mild calcareous Earth. What quantity of iron and manganese in a reguline state, these quantities of each calx would produce, may be seen by the table inserted at the end of this treatise; the aerial acid is united not only to the Earth, but also to the metallic calces, as appears by its proportion. Many other ores are poorer, and some to such a degree as not to deserve the name of an ore. It is frequently mixed not only with quartz and pyrites, as already mentioned, but also with shoerl, zeolyte, mica or asbestos.

10. When this ore bears a ftalactitical appearance, and is very white, it is called *flos ferri* and *eifen bluth*: this affords 27 per cent. of reguline iron according to Mr. Rinman, and confequently 35 of the brown calx.

Species VI.

Magnetic Sand.

11. That of *Virginia*, whofe colour is black, is of this fort; its fpecific gravity is 4,600, and it contains about ½ its weight of iron; but its compofition has not yet been difcovered.

Species VII.

Red Calx of Iron indurated, and combined with a little Argill, and frequently with Manganefe.

Hæmatites. Glafs kopf.

12. It is generally of a red, yellow, purple, or brown colour, of a metallic luftre, and very hard, though feldom fo hard as to give fire with fteel; when fcratched, it fhews a red trace; it is not magnetic before torrefaction, but by that heat it becomes black and magnetic; its ftructure is either folid, granular, fcaly, or fibrous; it occurs either in

fhapelefs

shapeless masses, or in a stalactitical form, or even crystalized in regular forms according to *Gmelin*, though Mr. *Delisle* denies it: in some places it forms whole mountains; it affords from 40 to 80 per cent. of iron. According to Mr. *Gerhard* it contains argill, for he extracted alum from it. Mr. *Hielm* found it also to contain manganese.

Species VIII.

Hæmatites in a loose form, mixed with a notable Proportion of Argill.

Hæmatitical yellow, red and brown Ochres.

13. Ochres are distinguished from clays by containing a larger proportion of martial particles; those that become brown by calcination, and also magnetic, belong to this species; sometimes the ferruginous particles are mixed with argill, and calcareous or muriatic earths, and then these ochres effervesce with acids.

Species IX.

Red Calx of Iron combined with Plumbago.

Red Eisen Glimmer, Eisenrahm and Eisenman.

14. This differs from the black in this, that it is not magnetic before torrefaction.

Species X.

Red Calx of Iron, mixed with a small Proportion of the brown, and indurated.

Torsten.

15. This is of a bright bluish black, or yellowish grey colour, and fibrous texture, shews a red trace when scratched, and is weakly magnetic before calcination. According to Mr. *Rinman* it is less dephlogisticated than hæmatites. *Historia Ferri.* §. 285.

Species XI.

Emery.

16. Emery seems to be a mixture of the red and white calces of iron, with some unknown stony substance, perhaps tripoli; it scarcely yields in hardness to any substance, except diamond; the best sort is of a dark grey colour, but becomes brown, and in great measure magnetic by calcination; other sorts are of a reddish rusty white, or yellowish colour; its specific gravity is from 3,000 to 4,000; it is never used as an iron ore, nor is its proportion of iron well known.

Species XII.

Red Calx of Iron united to Siderite.

Grey Iron Ore.

17. This has a shining metallic appearance, and commonly gives fire with steel; it is not in the least magnetic, and when scratched shews a red trace; it yields from 40 to 66 per cent. of *coldshort* iron.

18. The ore called by the Swedes *siu stierne malm*, or *minera pleiadum*, is a mixture of the grey iron ore, with rhombic nodules of that described in N.º 5.

Species XIII.

Argillaceous Iron Ores.

19. Of these we may distinguish two principal varieties, namely, those found in mountains and high lands, and those found in swampy grounds, or low lands overflown with water; both are destitute of metallic lustre, but very weighty, and some of them when dry absorb water like clays.

I. Variety.

I. VARIETY.

High land Argillaceous Ores.

Minera ferri Ochracea.

20. These are either yellow, red, brown, or greyish, indurated and friable, or loose and powdery, or in grains; they consist chiefly of the red or yellow calx of iron, or of the grey iron ore, or *torsten* in a loose form, mixed with argill or clay, and consequently often contain manganese, or siderite, and some, particularly in *France*, and the neighbourhood of *Liege*, are said to contain the calx of zinc. Hence there are many varities of them, and their yield of iron, as well as its qualities, are very different: they do not effervesce with acids, (unless calcareous or muriatic earth be casually mixed with them,) and are difficultly soluble in them; the most soluble are the best; they never obey the magnet before calcination, and rarely after it.

21. Horn-stone over-loaded with iron belongs to this species.

22. Mr. *Rinman* mentions a *white* iron ore found in *Kent*, mixed with clay or marl, which affords 47 per cent. of brittle iron, and

and is scarcely soluble in acids. *Histor. ferri,* p. 733.

II. VARIETY.

Swampey Argillaceous Ores.

Minera ferri Lacustris vel subaquosa. Mine de fer Limoneuse.

23. When dry, this ore is friable, and brown, or brownish black, and appears either in lumps of an irregular shape, or in round balls porous or solid, or in flat round pieces, or in grains, and sometimes in slender triangular prisms parallel to each other, and very brittle. It is mixed with argill and extractive matter, and becomes magnetic after calcination, by which operation it loses about ⅓ of its weight, and the greater part of what is thus volatilized is water, the remainder aerial acid and volatil alkali. The crude ore affords about 36 per cent. of regulus, and after calcination about 50 per cent. it is the chief matrix of siderite, and the iron procured from it is *coldshort,* at least in *Sweden.* The iron of *Husaby,* of which Mr. *Bergman* treats in his analysis of iron, is drawn from this ore. Mr. *Hielm* has found some sorts of it to contain 28 per cent. of manganese.

Species XIV.

Red Calcareous Iron Ore:

24. This is found in a loose form in many parts of *England*; it effervesces strongly with acids, and is used as a pigment.

Species XV.

Siliceous Iron Ore.

25. Besides jasper, garnet and trapp overloaded with iron, there is found, principally in *France*, a black, heavy, unmagnetic sand, of the siliceous kind, which is said to contain iron and zinc in great quantity.

26. Baron *Born*, in his letters from *Hungary*, mentions a blue crystalized iron ore, which he says is a shoerl overloaded with iron.

Species XVI.

Muriatic Iron Ore.

27. Serpentine overloaded with iron forms this species, but it is seldom worked.

Species XVII.

Martial Calamine.

28. Calamine is properly an ore of zinc, but sometimes it contains so large a proportion

tion of iron as to be worked with a view of obtaining this metal; it confifts of a mixture of quartz and argill, with the calces of iron and zinc; its colour is yellow, red, or brown, and it is moderately hard.

Species XVIII.

Mineralized by Sulphur.

Martial Pyrites.

29. Thefe are ftony concretions of fulphur, clay, and calx of iron, fo hard as to give fire with fteel. There are two principal varieties of them.

I. Variety.

Pale yellow Pyrites.

30. This has been already defcribed among the ores of alum.

II. Variety.

Brown or reddifh brown Pyrites. Minera ferri hepatica, Waffer kiefs.

31. It is generally of a fpherical fhape, or cryftalized in cubic, rhomboidal, or other polyhædral forms, and is devoid of metallic luftre; it difficultly gives fire with fteel, and contains very little fulphur, but much more iron

iron than the yellow pyrites, and not unfrequently a mixture of calcareous Earth. It is sometimes magnetic before, and always after calcination. It is incapable of vitriolization. The iron it affords is brittle.

Species XIX.

Mineralized by Sulphur and Arsenic.

White, Grey, or Bluish grey Pyrites, Marcassite, Raush gelb kiefs, Gift kiefs, Arsenic Stein.

32. It is found either in solid compact masses of a moderate size, or in grains, it gives fire with steel; when burnt, it affords a blue flame, and an arsenical smell, and by distillation, orpiment, or realgar, it is not magnetic, either before or after calcination, it contains much more of arsenic than of sulphur. It is analysed by digestion in marine acid, to which the nitrous is gradually added, otherwise the sulphur would be destroyed. See N° 34.

Species. XX.

Mineralized by Arsenic singly.

Mispickel. Speifs of the Bohemians.

33. Its colour is generally of a bright white, resembling a mixture of silver and tin, rarely variegated

variegated like a pidgeons neck, and is not eafily altered by expofure to the air. Its form either granular, cufpidated, cuneiform, prifmatic or rhomboidal. It is magnetic neither before nor after calcination, is foluble in acids, affords arfenic by diftillation, in the proportion of 30 or 40 per cent, and fometimes contains a fmall proportion of copper and filver. It is frequently mixed with other metallic ores, and often found in indurated clay, quartz, fpar, fhoerl, &c.

34. When iron contains lefs than $\frac{1}{18}$ of arfenic, it is magnetic, *Scheff.* §. 300, therefore if the calcination be pufhed fo far, the iron will remain magnetic. It may be analyfed by folution in the marine acid, which will take up the iron and leave the arfenic, or by folution in aqua regia, which will take up both, but water being added, will precipitate the arfenic and leave the iron. The filver will remain in the form of horn filver, and the copper may be feparated by the methods already mentioned.

Species XXI.

Combuftible Iron Ore.

35. Of this kind Mr. *Cronfted* mentions two varieties, one, of which the greater part
is

is volatil, in a ſtrong heat long continued, and ſeems to contain iron, plumbago, and coal intimately mixed. The other burns with a languid flame, loſes about $\frac{1}{4}$ of its weight, reſembles pit-coal, but is ſomewhat harder, and yields about 30 per cent of iron.

Species XXII.

Mineralized by the Vitriolic Acid.

36. This has been mentioned under the head of ſaline ſubſtances.

Uncertain Mineralizations.

Species XXIII.

Iron Blende.

37. This is ſaid by Mr. *Monnet* to be a ſtone of a grey iron colour, formed of diverging laminæ, of great hardneſs and a metallic appearance, but inſoluble in acids, and infuſible in the ſtrongeſt fire, *Mineral.* 356. Sometimes this ſtone contains arſenic, in this caſe it blackens by expoſure to the air.

Species XXIV.

Wolfram.

38. This ſtone which is generally found in tin mines, is of a black or brown ſhining colour,

colour, of a radiated or foliated texture, of a moderate hardnefs, and fometimes fo brittle, as to be eafily broken between the fingers, but very weighty fince its fpecific gravity is 7,119; when fcratched it fhews a red trace, which diftinguifhes it from tungften. It is fcarcely foluble in acids, and of very difficult fufion. According to *Lehman*, it confifts of filiceous Earth, calx of iron, and a fmall proportion of that of tin, *Chym. Schrift.* 356, and from his experiments, I am inclined to think it contains manganefe.

SPECIES XXV.

Native Pruffian Blue.

39. It confifts of clay mixed with iron, and fome unknown tinging fubftance, generally found in fwampy grounds or bogs. It is at firft white but when expofed to the air, it becomes either of a light or deep blue. When heated, it turns greenifh, and emits a flight flame, and then becomes red and magnetic, it is foluble both in acids and alkalis, but the latter precipitate it from the former, and the former from the latter; the precipitate is at firft greenifh, but gradually affumes a white hue, but recovers its blue tinge if it be fteeped in vegetable aftringents, *Bergm. Sciagr.* §. 206. *Phil. Tranf.* 1768

1768. The Earth of *Beuthnitz* in *Silesia*, mentioned in the *Memoirs* of *Berlin* for the year 1757, seems to belong to this species, it contains about $\frac{1}{4}$ of its weight of iron.

Species XXVI.

Green Earth of Verona and Normandy.

Terre Verte.

40. This is used as a pigment, and contains iron in some unknown state, mixed with clay, and sometimes with chalk and pyrites; allum and selenite are also accidentally found with it. It is difficultly soluble in acids, is not magnetic before calcination, and becomes of a coffee colour when heated. It is said to afford about 40 per cent of iron. If iron be precipitated from vinegar, by the arsenical acid, the precipitate will be green, 36 *Mem. Stock.* and it will preserve its colour though exposed to the air. Iron precipitated from the marine acid by lime water, is frequently green, and green fluors are known to derive their colour from this metal. The molybdenous acid gives also a green colour to iron, but this fades.

Of the Analysis and Essay of Iron Ores.

In the moist Way.

41. The general method of analysing in the moist way the *calciform ores*, which do not contain much earth or stony matter, is, after reducing them to a subtil powder, to dissolve them in the marine acid, and precipitate them by the *Prussian* alkali; the quantity of alkali used discovers that of iron in its metallic state, which the ore would afford, as already mentioned in the analysis of earths, or the precipitate washed and dried may be weighed; its weight divided by 6 (subtracting 4 per cent. for the iron already contained in the alkali) gives the quantity of iron in its metallic state which the ore contains.

But if the iron be united to any considerable proportion of zinc or manganese, its estimation by the above methods is not sufficiently accurate; therefore the *Prussian* blue must be calcined to redness, and the calx treated with dephlogisticated nitrous acid, which will then take up only the calx of zinc: when this is separated, the calx should be again treated either with nitrous acid, with the addition of sugar, or still better, with the acetous acid, either of which will separate the manganese, if any; the remaining calx
of

of iron may then be diffolved by the marine, and precipitated by the mineral alkali, or it may be further calcined, and then weighed. The annexed tables fhew the correfpondence betwixt the weight of the calx, or the precipitates with that of iron in its metallic ftate. See alfo Chap. 15. N°· 18.

42. To analyfe the *white calcareous iron ore*, it fhould be firft calcined to find the weight of the fixed air and water, then thrown into dephlogifticated nitrous acid, and fhaken for a few minutes until the menftruum begins to acquire a yellow colour; it will then contain the calcareous earth only, which may be precipitated by the mineral alkali, and weighed; the refiduum well calcined may be treated with the acetous acid as above.

43. According to Mr. *Rinman*, the contents of this ore may be conjectured very nearly from its fpecific gravity; for as 80 is to 100, fo is the fpecific gravity of this ore to its contents per cent.

44. The pyritous, argillaceous and ftony ores are analyfed by folution in marine acid, to which, if neceffary, a little of the nitrous may be added: this digeftion fhould be continued as long as the menftruum acquires a yellow

a yellow colour; coction may be requisite at the end.

45. Many ores, which are difficultly soluble before calcination, become easily soluble after they are calcined.

46. To discover siderite in an ore, it should be dissolved in dilute vitriolic acid; the solution, after standing some hours, will deposit a white calx, if siderite be contained in it.

In the dry Way.

47. Mr. *Morveau* recomménds the following flux for all iron ores: 8 parts pulverised glass, 1 of calcined borax, and $\frac{1}{2}$ of charcoal, well mixed; of this flux he takes two parts, or, if the ore be very poor, 3 parts, and 1 of the ore, and places them in a crucible, lined with a mixture of a little clay, and pounded charcoal $\frac{1}{8}$ of an inch thick, to which a cover is luted: this he places in a smith's forge, and urges it with a strong heat for half an hour; to find whether the ore requires calcination, he institutes this trial with equal weights of the ore calcined and uncalcined, and compares the results; the weight of the ore should not exeed 60 grains.

48. Mr. *Bergman* essays the white sparry iron ore by placing it in a crucible lined with charcoal

coal ½ an inch thick at bottom, and ⅛ on the sides, simply covering it with calcined borax, luting on this another crucible, which he also exposes to the heat of a smith's forge.

49. Argillaceous and siliceous iron ores may be essayed in the following manner: take of the ore 4 parts, quick lime 1,25, fluor spar 1,25, powdered charcoal 1, decrepitated common salt 4; the whole, being well mixed, place in a crucible lined with charcoal, to which a cover should be luted, and the lute being dry, commit it to a smith's forge, giving a moderate heat for ¼ of an hour, and the strongest for the remainder of the hour; if the lime be slacked, double the quantity must be used. 6 *Crell. Nov. Entdeck.*

50. Calcareous ores may be treated in the same manner, except that instead of quick lime double the quantity of fluor should be used.

51. Pyritous ores are also essayed nearly in the same manner; the proportions being 4 parts of the ore previously roasted, 2 of quick lime, 2 of fluor, 1½ of charcoal, and 4 of decrepitated common salt. *Ibid.*

52. Iron ores, which, though at first bright in their fracture, soon grow black by exposure to the air, contain much manganese.

53. To find whether iron or its ore contains manganese, let a small quantity of it be heated white in a crucible, and on this project 5 times its weight of purified nitre, taking care that no coal or ashes should get into the crucible: when all is cold, the upper part of the crucible will be covered with a greenish or bluish crust, if the iron contain manganese. 3 *Bergm.* 66. When the solution of iron in the marine acid is of a red colour, this also denotes the presence of manganese, though that colour soon changes to a yellow, by extracting phlogiston from the martial part.

54. Mr. *Bergman* gives also a method of finding whether the ore affords coldshort or redshort iron. He melts the regulus obtained from the ore with ¼ of its weight of good malleable iron in a crucible lined with charcoal, and well covered. If the regulus thus obtained be brittle when cold, the ore affords coldshort iron, or if it cracks under the hammer in a white heat, it is redshort. 3 *Bergm.* 46.

CHAP. VI.
Tin.

1. The colour of tin is too well known to need being described; its specific gravity is

from 7 to 7,45; the lighteſt is the pureſt; it melts the moſt readily of all metals; it is eaſily diſſolved in ſpirit of ſalt or aqua regia, and its ſolution is precipitated blue or purple by that of gold.

Species I.

Native.

2. The exiſtence of native tin has long been queſtioned, but it has undoubtedly been found ſome years ago in *Cornwall* in the form of thin flexible laminæ iſſuing out of a matrix of quartz, or regularly cryſtalized. *Phil. Tranſ.* 1766. p. 37. and Mr. *Quiſt*, a very competent judge, atteſts its purity in the *Memoirs* of *Stockholm* for the ſame year.

3. To aſcertain its purity, Mr. *Bergman* adviſes dephlogiſticating it by the nitrous acid. 140 gr. of this calx waſhed and dried are equivalent to 100 of tin in its metallic form; the ſolution will take up the copper, and a ſmall proportion of iron which the tin may contain, and theſe again may be ſeparated by boiling; if there be any arſenic, it will be found in the waſhings.

Species II.

Calciform Ores.

4. These ores are remarkable for their great weight, their specific gravity being from 5,955 to 6,75: they may be reduced to 4 Varieties.

I. Variety.

Tin Spar, white Tin Ore.

5. It is generally of a whitish or grey colour, sometimes greenish or yellowish, semi-transparent and crystalized in a pyramidical form, or irregularly: it was formerly thought to contain arsenic; but Mr. *Margraaf* found it the purest of all tin ores, 1 *Margr.* 188, 189, though it is said to contain sometimes a mixture of calcareous earth; its specific gravity is 6,007.

II. Variety.

Opake, brown or black Tin Ore.

6. This is also crystalized and imbodied in a stony matrix of quartz, fluor or mica, or mixed with white or yellow pyrites, or in ores of lead or zinc, cobalt, wismuth or iron; when these crystals are large, they are called by the Germans *zingraupen*, and when small

zin zwitter; the black are reckoned the richest, and afford about 80 per cent. of tin; they all contain a mixture of iron.

7. The ore called *weiſs zingraupen* is that which was mentioned under the calcareous genus by the name of *tungſten*; it contains no tin. When any arsenic is found in tin, it proceeds from the matrix, for tin itself is never mineralized by it; and for the same reason zinc is sometimes found in tin.

8. The specific gravity of this ore is 6,75. *Mem. Stock.* 1778, p. 321.

III. Variety.

Reddiſh or reddiſh yellow Tin Ore, Garnet Tin Ore.

9. This consists of small crystals semitransparent or opake, and sometimes it is found of a spherical form, striated, and resembling hæmatites or zeolyte; its specific gravity is from 5 to 5,8; it contains more of iron than of tin.

IV. Variety.

Tin Stone, Zinſtein of the Germans, Tinberg of the Swedes.

10. The preceding varieties consist for the most part of metallic particles; the present, chiefly

chiefly of stones or sands of different sorts, which contain calx of tin invisibly disseminated through them; their specific gravity, when the proportion of tin is of any importance, is considerable; they may be of any colour, blue, grey, black and brown are the commonest; they are called *Lodestones*.

12. Tin ores are very scarce, not being hitherto found in any considerable quantity, except in the *East Indies*, *Cornwall*, *Bohemia* and *Saxony*.

13. It is remarkable that tin has not as yet been found in any stones of the calcareous genus, except fluors, but only in those of the siliceous or agillaceous kind.

Species III.

Mineralized by Sulphur.

14. This was lately discovered by Mr. *Bergman* among some minerals which he received from *Siberia*. He observed two sorts of it analogous to the two artificial combinations of tin with sulphur; one nearly of the colour of zinc, and of a fibrous texture, which contained about twenty per cent. of sulphur, and the remainder tin; the other inveloped the former like a crust, resembled *aurum musivum*, and contained about 40 per cent. of sulphur

fulphur, a fmall proportion of copper, and the remainder tin. *Mem. Stock.* 1781, p. 328.

15. To effay tin ores in the *liquid way* has hitherto been thought impracticable; however, Mr. *Bergman* has devifed the following method, which is generally fuccefsful. Let the tin ore, well feparated from its ftony matrix by wafhing, and reduced to the moft fubtile powder, be digefted in concentrated oil of vitriol in a ftrong heat for feveral hours, then when cool add a fmall quantity of concentrated marine acid, and fuffer it to ftand for one or two hours; then add water, and when the folution is clear pour it off, and precipitate it by fixed mineral alkali. 131 gr. of this precipitate wafhed and dried are equivalent to 100 of tin in its reguline ftate, if the precipitate confifts of pure tin; but if it contains copper or iron, it fhould be calcined for one hour in a red heat, and then digefted in nitrous acid, which will take up the copper, and afterwards in marine acid, which will feparate the iron.

16. In the *dry way*, thefe ores, after pulverization and feparation of the ftony matter by wafhing, are to be melted with a mixture of double their weight of a flux, confifting of equal parts of pitch and calcined borax, in a crucible

crucible lined with charcoal, and to which a cover is luted; fusion should be speedily procured.

17. Mr. *Bergman* recommends a mixture of one part of the ore with two of tartar, 1 of black flux, and ¼ part of rosin: this is to be divided into three parts, and each successively projected into a crucible heated white, and immediately covered after the foregoing portion ceases to flame; the whole operation takes up but 7 minutes or less. *Sheff*. §. 304.

CHAP. VII.
Lead.

1. This metal is sufficiently distinguishable by its colour, which is well known, its specific gravity, which reaches from 11,3 to 11,479; its great softness and easy fusibility. It is more or less soluble in all acids, and particularly in the nitrous, and all its solutions have a sweetish taste, it is precipitable from the nitrous by the vitriolic or marine, and from the marine also, by the vitriolic.

SPECIES I.

Native Lead.

2. It is said to have been found in *Monmouthshire*

mouthshire in small pieces, *Phil. Tranf.* 1772, p. 20, also in the *Vivarais*, *Genfanne hift. Languedoc*, vol. 3. p. 208. *Henckel* also mentions it in his *Flora Saturnifans*. If it contains copper, this latter may be detected by a plate of iron immersed in its solution in nitrous acid, and the presence of silver, if any be contained in it, will be discovered by a plate of copper.

Species II.

Mineralized by the Aerial Acid.

Calciform Ores.

3. Of these we may distinguish 5 varieties, all easily soluble in nitrous acid, and with effervescence if heat be used, and also in expressed oils; all contain a little iron, but never silver.

I. Variety.

White, Lead Spar, Lead Ochre, Native Cerufs.

4. *Lead Spar* is sometimes transparent, but generally opake, and cryftalised in regular forms, of a laminar or striated texture. Lead ochre, or native cerufs is the same substance, but in a loose form, or indurated and shapeless; sometimes it is found in a silky form. Both contain a little iron, and sometimes calcareous

calcareous earth and argill. *Jacquin's Mifcell.*
-157. 3 *Roz.* 348. both grow red or yellowifh
when fufficiently heated. They effervefce
with acids, and afford from 60 to 80 or 90
per cent. of lead; both are found in *Brittany*,
Lorrain, *Germany*, and *England*.

II. VARIETY.

Red, Brown, or Yellow.

5. This is alfo found either regularly
cryftalized, or in fhapelefs maffes, or in powder.
It differs from the former only by containing
more iron. That in powder contains a mixture of clay. It affords about 70 or 80 per
cent. of lead.

III. VARIETY.

Green.

6. Either cryftalized in needles as in
Brittany, or in a loofe powder as in *Saxony*,
but moftly adhering to, or invefting quartz.
It owes its colour to iron, and feldom contains copper. 3 *Lin. Von Gmel.* 225. 10
Roz. 375.

IV. VARIETY.

Bluifh.

7. This is alfo fometimes cryftalized, fometimes

times amorphous. It owes its colour to a mixture of copper.

V. Variety.

Black.

8. The moſt uncommon of all, and occurs either cryſtalized, or of an indeterminate form.

9. Theſe ores, when freed as much as poſſible from earthy matter, are eſſayed in the moiſt way, by ſolution in ſpirit of nitre. The ſolution being boiled, depoſits the calx of iron. If the lead be then precipitated by an aerated mineral alkali, 132 gr. of the precipitate, will denote 100 of lead in its metallic ſtate. If the ore contains copper, it may be ſeparated by digeſting the calx in volatil alkali; if it be ſuſpected to contain ſilver and copper, then, after the ſeparation of the copper, the calx ſhould be rediſſolved in nitrous acid, and both the lead and ſilver precipitated by the marine acid; the marine ſalt of lead is rediſſoluble in 30 times its weight of boiling water, but that of ſilver will remain undiſſolved, or that of ſilver may be ſeparated by cauſtic volatile alkali.

10. In the dry way, theſe ores are reducible by the ſimple addition of phlogiſton and fuſion.

Species III.

Mineralized by the Vitriolic acid.

11. According to Mr. *Monnet*, this sometimes occurs in the form of a white ponderous calx, soluble in 16 or 18 times its weight of water. It does not effervese, nor is it soluble in other acids; it may be reduced by laying it on a burning coal. It originates from the spontaneous decomposition of sulphurated lead ores. *Mon. Mineral.* 371. According to Dr. *Withering*, it is found in great quantity in the island of *Anglesy*, but united to iron, and not reducible by the blow pipe or charcoal, he promises an exact analysis of it, this is of a yellow colour, and mixed with clay.

Species IV.

Mineralized by the Phosphoric acid.

12. This was lately discovered by Mr. *Gahn*; it is of a greenish colour, by reason of a mixture of iron; it does not effervesce with acids.

To essay it, a solution of it in nitrous acid must be had, with the assistance of heat. From this solution, the lead is to be precipitated by the acid of vitriol. 137 gr. of this precipitate, washed and dried, are equivalent
to

to 100 of lead in its metallic ſtate. The decanted liquor evaporated to dryneſs, affords the phoſphoric acid.

Species V.

Mineralized by Sulphur, with Silver and a little Iron.

Galena, Potter's Ore, Bley Glanz, Bley Schweif, of the Germans.

13. It is the commoneſt of all lead ores, of a bluiſh dark lead colour, formed of cubes of a moderate ſize, or in grains of a cubic figure, whoſe corners have been cut off; its texture is lamellar, and its hardneſs variable; the hardeſt ſort containing a greater mixture of iron or quartz; that in grains is thought to be the richeſt in ſilver; but the richeſt contains only about 1 or 1,5 per cent. that is, 12 or 18 ounces per quintal, the pooreſt about 60 gr. Ores that yield about ¼ an ounce of ſilver per quintal, are barely worth the coſt of extracting it; the proportion of ſulphur to lead in this ore is alſo variable within the limits of 15 and 25 per cent. that which contains leaſt is called *Bley Schweif*, and is in ſome degree malleable. The proportion of lead is from 85 to 60 per cent. by reaſon of an accidental mixture of quartz, that of iron

is

Lead.

is generally very small. Dr. *Watson* remarks, that the ores which are poorest in lead, are often the richest in silver. Mr *Monnet* asserted, that sulphurated lead ores are insoluble in nitrous acid, but Dr. *Watson* has shewn that dilute nitrous acid dissolves them compleatly. 3 *Wats.* 228. The specific gravity of Galena, is from 7,000 to 7,780; when melted it yields a yellow slag.

14. To analyse this ore in the moist way, let it be dissolved by boiling in the dilute nitrous acid, the sulphur and insoluble stony parts and calx of iron will remain undissolved; the iron may be afterwards separated by digestion in marine acid, and the sulphur by digestion in caustic fixed alkali, the residuum weighed before and after will shew the proportion of each.

15. The nitrous solution will contain the lead and silver; this solution should be precipitated by the mineral fixed alkali, and the precipitate washed in cold water, dried and weighed. After weighing it should again be digested in caustic volatil alkali, which will dissolve and take up only the calx of silver, the residuum being again dried and weighed, gives the proportion of the calx of lead, of which 132 gr. are equivalent to 100 of lead in its metallic state; and the difference between the weight

weight of the precipitate, before and after the application of the volatil alkali, gives the quantity of the calx of filver, of which 129 gr. are equivalent to 100 of filver in its metallic form.

16. If the ore contains any foluble matrix, which very feldom happens, it fhould firft be feparated by boiling in diftilled vinegar. 2 *Bergm.* 424.

17. In the dry way this ore may be effayed by melting it with $\frac{1}{3}$ of its weight of filings of iron.

Species VI.

Mineralized by Sulphur, with Silver and Regulus of Antimony.

Antimonial Lead Ore, Sproterz, Stripmalm.

18. Its colour is the fame as that of Galena, but its texture is different, being radiated, filamentous, or ftriated; when heated it yields a white fmoke; it affords from 40 to 50 per cent. of lead, and from ½ an ounce to 2 ounces of filver per quintal.

It is effayed in the *liquid way*, by folution in concentrated fpirit of nitre, which dephlogifticates the regulus, and leaves it in the form

form of a calx. 138 gr. of this calx are equivalent to 100 of the regulus. Or still better, by solution in spirit of salt which diffolves both the lead and regulus, and leaves the sulphur and stony matter which are separable, as shewn in N.° 14. If water be poured on the solution, the calx of antimony will be separated.

SPECIES VII.

Mineralized by Sulphur, with Silver and a large Proportion of Iron.

Pyritous Lead Ore.

20. This is of a brown or yellowish colour, of an oblong or stalactitical form, friable, and of a lamellar, striated or loose texture; it affords at most 18 or 20 per cent. of lead, which flows by barely heating it, as the iron detains the sulphur; it is no more than a mixture of galena with the brown pyrites, Chap. 5. N.° 31.

SPECIES VIII.

Mineralized by Sulphur and Arsenic, with Silver.

Red Lead Spar.

21. Lately discovered in *Siberia*; externally it is of a pale and internally of a deep red,

red, and for the moſt part cryſtalized in rhomboidal paralellipipeds, or irregular pyramids. According to *Lehman* it contains ſulphur, arſenic, and about 34 per cent. of lead, and according to Mr. *Pallas* alſo ſilver. *Pallas Reiſe.* 2 *Theil.* p. 274.

SPECIES IX.

Stony or ſandy Lead Ore.

22. This conſiſts either of the calciform lead ores, or galena, intimately mixed and diffuſed through ſtones or earths chiefly of the calcareous kind.

23. It is analyſed in the *moiſt way* in the manner already deſcribed, and in the *dry way*, if the matrix be calcareous, by adding the fluor ſpar, or if ſiliceous, the black flux with a little iron.

24. Ores of lead are moſt frequently found among ſtones of the calcareous or barytic genus.

CHAP. VIII.

Mercury.

1. It were ſuperfluous to mention its leſs obvious characters, as its liquidity alone ſufficiently

ficiently diftinguifhes it from all other metallic fubftances.

SPECIES I.

Native.

2. Native mercury has frequently been found in the mines of *Idria, Friuli, Lower Auftria, Deuxponts,* &c. flowing from a fhiftofe or quartzy matrix, and probably mixed with fome other metal, as its globules are not perfectly fpherical. In *Sweden* and *Germany* it has been found united to filver in the form of a fomewhat hard and brittle amalgam. *Mon. Mineral.* 387. 3 *Lin. von Gmel.* 41. It has alfo been obferved vifibly diffufed through maffes of clay, or ftone of a white, red, or blue colour and great weight, in *Spain* and *Idria,* and in *Sicily* in beds of chalk. *Borch Sicil. Mineral.* p. 508.

3. To examine its purity in the moift way, Mr. *Bergman* recommends folution in the nitrous acid; for, as he well remarks, the metals it is moft likely to be mixed with are gold, filver and bifmuth, as they are moft frequently found native: in this folution, gold, if any be contained in the mercury, will remain undiffolved; bifmuth may be feparated by the affufion of water, but the filver and

mercury will remain, and both should be precipitated by the marine acid; the precipitate washed in cold water and dried should be weighed, and then digested in hot water, the marine mercury will be dissolved; the residuum, containing only the marine silver, should again be washed, dried and weighed; the difference between the former and present weight gives the quantity of marine mercury, and the metallic contents of each may be deduced by the rule of proportion from the 2d table.

Species II.

Mineralized by the aerial Acid.

Native precipitate per se or *Calx of Mercury.*

4. This is said to have been lately found in *Idria* in hard compact masses of a brownish red colour, and granular texture, mixed with some globules of native mercury. By distillation it is recovered in its running form. 100 parts of it afford 91 of running mercury. *Roz. Jan.* 1784, p. 61.

Species III.

Mineralized by the Vitriolic and Marine Acids.

Vitriol and Marine Salt of Mercury.

5. Mr. *Woulfe* first discovered these salts at *Obermoschel,* in the dutchy of *Deuxponts:* they

Mercury. 309

they have a spar-like appearance, and are either bright and white, or yellow or black, mixed with cinnabar in a stony matrix; these well mixed with $\frac{1}{4}$ of their weight of vegetable alkali, afforded him cubic and octagonal cryſtals, that is, ſalt of ſilvius and tartar vitriol. *Phil. Tranſ.* 1776. The marine ſalt of mercury is in the ſtate of ſublimate corroſive.

6. Mr. *Bergman*'s ingenious and truly ſcientific method of diſcovering the proportion of theſe ſalts is nearly as follows: Firſt, by trituration and digeſtion in marine acid he expells the vitriolic, the mercury uniting preferably with the former of theſe acids; the whole is then diſſolved in a ſufficient quantity of hot water; into this ſolution he drops that of marine baroſelenite until no further precipitation is perceived; the true or vitriolic baroſelenite thus formed, being waſhed and dried, contains 13 per cent. of real vitriolic acid: now vitriol of mercury contains 19 per cent. of real acid. Hence the weight of the former being found, that of the latter will eaſily be known; for ſuppoſing the weight of the baroſelenite to be 100 gr. then it will contain 13 of vitriolic acid; and ſince 19 of vitriolic acid go to 100 gr. of vitriol of mercury, 13 will go to 68,4; then if the weight of the vitriol of mercury be

ſubtracted

subtracted from that of the whole of the ore, the remainder gives the weight of the marine salt of mercury, and this being sublimate corrosive, 100 gr. of it will contain 77 of mercury, and so in proportion.

Species IV.

Mineralized by Sulphur.

Native Cinnabar.

7. This is of different shades, from a yellowish to a deep red, and is found either pure in hard, friable masses, either shapeless or crystalized in cubes, and sometimes transparent, or intermixed with clay or stone, or intersperfed through the ores of other metals, particularly those of silver or copper, or martial pyrites; its texture is either radiated, striated, scaly or granular. 100 parts of cinnabar contain about 80 of mercury, and 20 of sulphur; artificial cinnabar contains a little more sulphur, and hence its colour is darker; its specific gravity is about 7,000; it sublimes in close vessels, and in open, it is decomposed and volatilized when sufficiently heated; it is insoluble in the nitrous and vitriolic acids; it is sometimes contained in very heavy red or brownish red stones or sand.

8. To analyse it in the moist way, its stony matrix

matrix should first be dissolved in nitrous acid, and the cinnabar being disengaged should be boiled in 8 or 10 times its weight of aqua regia, composed of 3 parts nitrous and 1 of marine acid; the mercury may then be precipitated from the solution in its running form by zinc.

9. In the dry way the mercury is obtained in its running form by distilling the cinnabar with $\frac{1}{3}$ of its weight of filings of iron, or even without iron, if the matrix of the cinnabar be calcareous.

SPECIES V.

Mineralized by Sulphur with Copper.

Black Ore of Mercury.

10. According to *Cronsted* and *Linneus* this ore is of a blackish grey colour, glassy texture, and decrepitates strongly when heated; the cinnabar is volatilized, and the copper remains, and may be distinguished by the usual tests.

SPECIES VI.

Pyritous Mercurial Ore.

11. Mr. *Monnet* relates, that he found in *Dauphiné* a grey or whitish friable substance,

100 parts of which afforded 1 of mercury, ⅓ of silver, and the remainder iron, cobalt, sulphur and arsenic. *Mineralog.* p. 392.

12. Cinnabar mixed with arsenic or realgar is said to be found in *Japan.* 3 *Lin. von Gmelin,* p. 65. At *Morsfeld,* cinnabar and the white calx of arsenic present themselves in the same rock. *Ibid.*

CHAP. IX.
Zinc.

1. Zinc is the most malleable of all the semi-metals; its colour is nearly the same as that of lead; its specific gravity is from 6,9 to 7,24; it is soluble in all acids, and its solution is colourless; it melts at a lower heat than silver or copper, but a higher than lead or tin, and at the same time inflames and sublimes, forming a light white calx, called flowers of zinc, which are very fixed in fire, and soluble in acids.

Species I.
Native.

2. This has not as yet been observed; that mentioned by *Bomare* appears to have been produced by art.

Mineralized,

Mineralized.

3. All the ores of zinc tinge plates of copper when ſtratified with them and charcoal, only the ſulphureous require previous torrefaction.

SPECIES II.

Mineralized by the aerial Acid.

Calciform Ores.

Of theſe there are 4 Varieties.

I. VARIETY.

Pure Calx of Zinc, Vitreous Zinc Ore, Zinc Spar.

4. Of a whitiſh, grey, bluiſh grey or yellowiſh colour, and of a hardneſs generally ſufficient to ſtrike fire with ſteel; in its fracture it reſembles quartz, amorphous, ſtalactitical or cryſtalized in groups, and weighty; by calcination it loſes ⅓ of its weight, without emitting a ſulphureous or arſenical ſmell, and is infuſible in the ſtrongeſt heat either ſingly or with mineral alkali, but eaſily fuſible with borax or microcoſmic ſalt. In the mineral acids it is ſoluble with efferveſcence, and with the vitriolic affords vitriol of zinc. 100 gr. of this ore contains about

65 of the calx of zinc, 28 of aerial acid, 6 of water, and 1 of iron, and sometimes a little of silex. 2 *Bergm. De Min. Zinci.*

5. *Note,* Mr. *Bergman* suspects the substance called zinc spar by Baron *Born* to be a different substance. Mr. *Bindheim* found it insoluble in acids before calcination, and in the dry way infusible with the three usual fluxes, but after calcination it becomes soluble in acids. 4 *Berlin Schrift.* 399.

II. Variety.

Mixed with a notable Proportion of Iron.

Tutenago.

6. Mr. *Engestrom,* in the Memoirs of *Stockholm* for the year 1775, has given us an analysis of an ore of this sort from *China* ; it was of a white colour, intersperfed with red streaks of calx of iron, and so brittle as to be easily broken betwixt the fingers; in the dry way it exhibited the same appearances as the former Variety, except that it lost no part of its weight ; it was soluble in the mineral acids, particularly with the assistance of heat, and with the vitriolic afforded vitriol both of zinc and iron ; the quantity of fixed air was so small as to be absorbed by the solution ; it contained in various specimens from 60 to 90 per

per cent. of zinc; the remainder was iron and a small proportion of argill. Mr. *Bindheim* also discovered this Variety in *Germany*, and found it to consist of zinc, a little iron and silex. 4 *Berl. Schrift.* 400.

III. VARIETY.

Mixed with Iron and Clay in various Proportions.

Calamine.

7. Its colour is white, grey, yellow, brown or red, not so brittle as the 2d Variety, and of various degrees of hardness, though scarce ever so hard as to strike fire with steel; its texture equable or cellular, and its form either amorphous, crystalized or stalactitical; when calcined it loses no part of its weight, except it be mixed with charcoal, and then flowers of zinc sublime; it is soluble in acids, and with the vitriolic affords vitriol of iron as well as of zinc, which shews the iron it contains is not much dephlogisticated. The specific gravity of the best sort, that is, the grey, is 5,000: 100 parts of this afforded Mr. *Bergman* 84 of calx of zinc, 3 of iron, 1 of argill, and 12 of silex; but in other specimens these proportions are very different; some ores are so poor as not to contain above 4 per

4 per cent. of calx of zinc; a good ore fhould afford at leaft 30 per cent. and its fpecific gravity be about 4,400 or 5,000.

8. Sometimes calamines contain a mixture of calcareous earth and lead. 3 *Lin. von Gmel.* 112. Moft of the Englifh calamines contain lead.

9. The firft and fecond Varieties are eafily analyfed in the moift way, by diffolving them in the dilute vitriolic acid; the filex, if any, will remain undiffolved, and the zinc and iron are taken up, and may be feparated by adding a piece of zinc previoufly weighed, and boiling the folution; the iron will be precipitated; the folution, which then contains only zinc, fhould be precipitated by aerated mineral alkali. 193 gr. of this precipitate are equivalent to 100 of zinc in its metallic form, from which the weight loft by the inferted zinc fhould be fubtracted; the weight of the fixed air and water may be collected by comparing the lofs of weight which the ore fuffers by calcination and folution in acids.

10. The analyfis of the 3d Variety, or calamine, is more complex. Mr. *Bergman* gives us two methods of performing it. The firft is to dephlogifticate it in the nitrous acid

with

Zinc.

with the assistance of heat and boil away the acid to dryness. Repeat this operation twice or thrice, using each time twice as much of the acid as the ore weighs; and, lastly, dissolve all that is soluble in a fresh portion of nitrous acid: by this means the zinc (and lead if any) with the argill, will be taken up, while the iron, being dephlogisticated, will with the silex remain undissolved; if the solution contains lead, the marine acid will precipitate it; after which the vitriolic may be used to precipitate the calcareous earth, if any be contained in the ore, or the lead and other metals may be precipitated by adding a piece of zinc as in N.° 9. The zinc may then be precipitated by the *Prussian* alkali, the weight of which divided by 5 gives that of zinc in its metallic form contained in the ore. The undissolved residuum should be treated with three times its weight of concentrated vitriolic acid, and evaporated to dryness, and all that is soluble extracted with warm water; the iron should be precipitated by the *Prussian* alkali, and the argill by the aerated mineral alkali, which should also be added to the nitrous solution after the zinc is precipitated.

11. The second method is shorter and more ingenious. He distills the vitriolic acid over calamine to dryness; the residuum he lixiviates

viates in hot water, what remains undiffolved is filex; to the folution he adds a cauftic volatil alkali, which precipitates the iron and argill, but keeps the zinc in folution, as it is foluble in vitriolic ammoniac; the precipitate he re-diffolves in vitriolic acid, and feparates the iron and argill as before.

IV. VARIETY.

Mixed with a notable proportion of Silex.

Zeolytiform.

12. The real contents of this fubftance were firft difcovered by Mr. *Pelletier*, a moft accurate Parifian chymift. It was long taken for a zeolyte, being of a pearl colour, cryftalized, femi-tranfparent, confifting of laminæ, diverging from different centers, and becoming gelatinous with acids. It was commonly called *zeolyte of Friburgh*, he found 100 gr. of it to contain from 48 to 52 of quartz, 36 of calx of zinc, and 8 or 12 of water.

SPECIES III.

Mineralized by the Vitriolic Acid.

13. This has already been mentioned in the fecond part.

SPECIES

Species IV.

Mineralized by Sulphur, by means of Iron.

Blende. Pseudo-galena. Black Jack.

14. Of this there are several varieties, generally of a lamellar or scaly texture, and frequently of a quadrangular form, resembling galena, they all lose much of their weight when heated, and burn with a blue flame; their specific gravity is inferior to that of galena. Almost all contain a mixture of lead ore, most of them exhale a sulphureous smell when scraped, or at least when vitriolic or marine acid is droped on them.

I. Variety.

Bluish Grey, and of a Metallic Appearance, Glanz Blende.

15. Its form is generally cubical or rhomboidal, its texture scaly or steel grained; by calcination it loses nearly $\frac{1}{6}$ of its weight; after calcination it is more easily soluble in the mineral acids. 100 Parts of it afforded Mr. *Bergman* about 52 of zinc, 8 of iron, 4 of copper, 26 of sulphur, 4 of water, and 6 of silex.

16. To analyse this ore in the moist way, Mr.

Mr. *Bergman* first expelled the water, and part of the fuphur by diftillation; the refiduum he treated with 3 times its weight of oil of vitriol evaporated to drynefs, this lixiviated with warm water, left only 6 parts undiffolved; in this folution a polifhed plate of iron was boiled, which precipitated the copper. He then by means of the phlogifticated alkali, precipitated the zinc and iron. This precipitate being calcined in an open fire, was feveral times treated with nitrous acid, evaporated to drynefs, until the iron was perfectly dephlogifticated; frefh nitrous acid being then added, diffolved the zinc only, which being precipitated by the *Pruffian* alkali, the proportion of zinc, in its metallic ftate, was found as in N.º 10. Neither metal, as contained in the ore, is much dephlogifticated.

II. Variety.

Black, Pecheblende.

17. Of moderate hardnefs, does not give fire with fteel, frequently cryftalized, and then fometimes tranfparent, or femi tranfparent; when pulverized, it gives a reddifh powder, when heated it decrepitates, and if laid on a burning coal it emits a fulfureous fmell, and depofes white and yellow flowers; it is not magnetic even after torrefaction, but lofes 25 per cent. of its weight. It is frequently

quently mixed with silver, arsenic, and other metals. 100 Parts of that of Danemora, examined by Mr. *Bergman*, exhibited 45 of zinc, 1 of regulus of arsenic, 9 of iron, 6 of lead, all slightly dephlogisticated, 29 of sulphur, 6 of water, and 4 of silex. 2 *Bergm.* 332.

18. This ore he analysed in the moist way after the following manner, first, by distillation he obtained the water, regulus of arsenic, and part of the sulphur; the residuum he boiled in marine acid, until all that was soluble was taken up. To the solution, after its filtration and some evaporation, he added vitriolic ammoniac, by whose decomposition vitriol of lead was precipitated in some measure, and the remainder of it by further evaporation. This being separated, the remainder was evaporated to dryness, and treated with nitrous acid, and at last, calcined to dephlogisticate the iron; the calx of zinc only, was then dissolved in the nitrous acid, and precipitated by the *Prussian* alkali.

III. Variety.

Red, or Reddish Brown. Röd Slag of the Swedes.

19. Its texture is generally scaly, sometimes crystalized, and semitransparent, it gives

gives fire with steel, it does not decrepitate nor smoke when heated, yet it loses about 13 per cent. of its weight by torrefaction.

100 Parts of that of Sahlberg, contained by Mr. *Bergman's* analysis, 44 of zinc, 5 of iron, 17 of sulphur, 5 of water, 5 of argill, and 24 of quartz.

20. In analysing this ore, the water and sulphur were obtained as before, nitrous acid was several times distilled to dryness over the residuum, which was at last calcined, and again treated with the nitrous acid, which then left the iron and quartz and a little argill undissolved; the *Prussian* alkali precipitated the zinc from this solution, and after that, the aerated volatil alkali precipitated the argill. The undissolved residuum was treated with oil of vitriol distilled to dryness, which took up the calx of iron, and a small proportion of argill. The *Prussian* alkali precipitated the iron, and the liquor being then evaporated, afforded a little alum and tartar vitriolate.

IV. Variety.

Phosphorescent Blende.

21. Its colour is generally greenish, yellowish green, or red, of different degrees of transparency,

transparency, or opake; when scraped with a knife in the dark, it emits light, even in water, and after undergoing a white heat, when distilled *per se*, a siliceous sublimate rises, which shews it contains the sparry acid, probably united to a metal since it sublimes. It is almost wholly soluble in the marine acid in a boiling heat.

Mr. *Bergman* found 100 parts of that of *Scharfenberg*, to contain 64 of zinc, 5 of iron, 20 of sulphur, 4 of fluor acid, 6 of water, and 1 of silex.

V. VARIETY.

Greyish yellow Blende.

22. This consists of a mixture of blende, galena, and petrol, it contains about 24 per cent. of zinc; it is probably the same as the grey blende of *Monnet Mineral.* p. 400.

VI. VARIETY.

White Blende.

23. Found at *Silverberget Cronst.* §. 230.

VII. VARIETY.

Yellow Blende.

24. Of the colour of wax, and semi-transparent, contains much sulphur, *Mon.* 400.

25.

25. In the dry way zinc is reduced by distilling its ore after torrefaction, with a mixture of its own weight of charcoal, in an earthen retort well luted, and a strong heat; but by this method, scarce half the zinc it contains is obtained.

CHAP. X.

Regulus of Antimony.

1. Its colour is of a silvery white, its texture micaceous; its specific gravity, when perfectly freed from iron, 6,860; it is remarkably brittle; the nitrous acid dephlogisticates it, but holds only a very minute portion of it in solution. The marine has very little effect on it, but it is in a considerable degree, soluble in aqua regia formed of 7 parts marine, and 1 of nitrous acid; or in a mixture of the vitriolic and marine acids, or even of the vitriolic and nitrous. It melts long after it becomes red hot, emits a white smoke, and evaporates, forming white flowers; in close vessels it sublimes without decomposition.

SPECIES I.

Native.

2. This was first discovered in the mine of *Sala* in *Sweden*, by that great metallurgist, Dr.

Dr. *Schwab*, in the year 1748; it was composed of shining white irregular planes or *facettes*, resembling *Mispickel*, for which it was long taken, and in effect contained a mixture of arsenic; it has also been lately found in the mines of *Allemond* in *France* by Mr. *Mongez* the younger, alloyed with about 3 per cent. of arsenic. 23 *Roz.* 66.

3. Its purity may be examined by boiling it in a large quantity of nitrous acid, which will hold only the arsenic in solution.

Species II.

Mineralized by the aerial Acid.

Native Calx of Antimony.

4. This was also lately discovered by Mr. *Mongez*; it consists of a group of white crystalized filaments diverging from a common center like zeolyte; urged with a blow pipe on charcoal it will dissipate, which, together with its insolubility in nitrous acid, is sufficient to distinguish it.

Species III.

Mineralized by Sulphur.

Antimony.

5. Its colour is dark, or bluish grey; its texture

texture fibrous, cuneiform, folid, or lamellar; this laſt is ſometimes called *antimonial galena*; its form generally indeterminate, but ſometimes cryſtalized; it is the moſt fuſible of all ores; its ſpecific gravity is from 4 to 4,2, and when melted 4,7 or 5,000; it ſullies the fingers, and is very brittle; when gradually heated in a crucible it loſes about 22 per cent. of its weight, and becomes a grey calx; it is perfectly ſoluble in the marine acid with the aſſiſtance of heat; the nitrous only calcines the reguline part, and the vitriolic has but little effect on it; 100 parts of it contain 74 of regulus ſlightly dephlogiſticated, and 26 of ſulphur. 3 *Bergm.* 167.

6. It is analyſed by ſolution in aqua regia, conſiſting of 1 part nitrous, and 4 of marine acid; the ſulphur is found on the filter.

7. In the dry way antimony is ſeparated from the ſtony parts of its ore by diſtillation *per deſcenſum*; it is afterwards reduced to a regulus by gently roaſting it untill it loſes 22,5 per cent. of its weight, and then mixing the grey calx thus formed with twice its weight of black flux, and briſkly fuſing it in a covered crucible.

SPECIES IV.

Species IV.

Mineralized by Sulphur and Arsenic,
Arsenicated Antimony.

8. This is the same as the plumose silver ore mentioned among those of silver, Species 11; besides the colours there mentioned, it is found red or green, and then contains but a small proportion of silver; its texture filamentous, very brittle and fusible.

9. It is analysed by solution in *aqua regia;* both the regulus and arsenic remain in the solution; the sulphur is separated by filtration; if the solution be then boiled with twice its weight of strong nitrous acid, the regulus of antimony will be precipitated by dephlogistication, and the arsenic converted into an acid, which will remain in the liquor, and may be procured by evaporation to dryness.

10. If silver or copper be suspected in this ore, it should be treated in as Chap. 3. N.º 25.

CHAP. XI.

Regulus of Arsenic.

1. Of a bright yellowish white colour, but soon loses its lustre, and grows black by exposure

sure to the air; it is of a loose structure, very brittle, and of a lamellar texture; its specific gravity is 8,310; if laid on a red hot iron it burns with a slight flame, white smoke, and garlick smell, is wholly volatilized, and tinges a plate of copper held over it white; it is easily soluble in the nitrous acid, more difficultly in the vitriolic, and scarce at all in the marine; boiling oils also dissolve it; it detonates with nitre.

Species I.

Native, Scherben Cobalt, Fliegenstein, Cobalt testacé.

2. Of a lead colour, of different degrees of hardness, friable, and of a scaly texture, seldom, if ever, crystalized; it possesses all the properties of the regulus above described.

3. It may be analysed by solution in aqua regia; the silver, if any, will remain precipitated; the iron, of which it commonly contains a small proportion, will remain in the solution; but if a small quantity of water be added to the solution, the calx of arsenic will be precipitated, and the iron remain.

4. *Mispickel*, which consists of arsenic nearly in a reguline state united with iron, has already

ready been mentioned among the iron ores, Species 20.

Species II.

Mineralized by the aerial Acid.

Calciform arsenical Ore, native Calx of Arsenic, flos arsenici.

5. It is found either indurated in the form of white opake, transparent, or semi-transparent crystals, or in a loose powdery state, frequently mixed with native arsenic; it is volatil when heated, though less so than the regulus; it does not detonate with nitre, though an effervescence arises.

Its specific gravity is from 3,706 to 5,000; it is soluble in about 70 or 80 times its weight of water in the temperature of 60, or in 15 or 20 times its weight of boiling water; the solution turns tincture of turnsole *red*, and syrup of violets *green*; it is scarcely soluble in the vitriolic acid, something more in the marine, and most perfectly in the nitrous diluted; when in a powdery form, it is called *flos arsenici*, and has been often taken for a calcareous earth.

6. *White pyrites*, which consists of the calx of arsenic, mixed with sulphurated iron, has been

been described among the iron ores. Species 19.

Species III.

Mineralized by Sulphur.

7. Of this there are two Varieties, the yellow and the red; both are sublimable in close vessels, detonate with nitre, with fixed alkalis form a hepar, and are soluble in oils.

I. Variety.

Yellow, Orpiment.

8. This is rarely found crystalized. Baron *Born* once found it in a polyhædral form in a blue clay in *Hungary*; it is generally composed of shining, flexible laminæ like mica, more or less solid; its specific gravity is about 3,315; it contains only about $\frac{1}{10}$ of its weight of sulphur; it burns with a blue flame.

II. Variety.

Red, Realgar, Rauschgelbe.

9. It is found either in shapeless or stalactitical masses, opake or semi-transparent, or transparent and regularly crystalized in octohædral pyramids or prisms, and then called *ruby of arsenic*; its specific gravity is 3,225.

Regulus of Arsenic.

100 parts of it contain 16 of sulphur; nitrous acid soon destroys its redness.

10. To analyse these ores, they should be digested in marine acid, adding the nitrous by degrees to help the solution; the sulphur will be found on the filter; the arsenic will remain in the solution, and may be precipitated in its metallic form by zinc, adding spirit of wine to the solution. 2 *Bergm.* 442.

SPECIES IV.

Calx of Arsenic diffused through Earths or Stones.

11. *Henckel* mentions a grey or bluish marl in which this calx was found; clay and calcareous stones are also sometimes impregnated with it; it is discovered either by the smell when laid on burning coals, or by lixiviation.

12. In the *dry way* calx of arsenic is separated from the ores which contain it by sublimation in a well luted retort, and a gradual heat, but some always remains, which cannot be expelled but by an open fire and the addition of charcoal.

13. White arsenic, that is, calx of arsenic, is reduced to a regulus, either by quickly melting it with a mixture of 2 parts soft soap,

soap, and two parts of mineral alkali, pouring it when in fusion into a hot iron cone, or by mixing it with oil to the consistence of a syrup, and then with a gradual heat distilling the whole to dryness; towards the end the regulus sublimes, and may be made more perfect by a second distillation with its own weight of oil; by reason of the offensive smell the distillation should be made in the open air.

CHAP. XII.

Bismuth.

1. Bismuth is of a reddish or yellowish white colour, of a lamellar texture moderately hard, and brittle; its specific gravity exceeds that of any of the semi-metals, or even most of the intire metals, yielding only to that of platina, gold, mercury, lead and silver, being from 9,600 to 9,700; its fusibility is nearly as that of lead; it is easily soluble in nitrous acid or aqua regia, but scarcely in the vitriolic, and still less in the marine; its solution is colourless, and is precipitable by the addition of pure water.

2. 113 grains of this precipitate from nitrous acid, well washed and dried, are equivalent to 100 of bismuth in its metallic form.

SPECIES. I.

Species I.

Native.

3. This is the commonest of all native metallic substances, and is generally found either in cubes or octagons, or of a dentritical form, or in that of thin laminæ investing the ores of other metals, particularly those of cobalt, from which it is easily distinguished and separated by its great fusibility; it is said to be sometimes alloyed with silver; if so, they are easily separated by solution in nitrous acid, and the addition of water, which precipitates only the bismuth, and leaves every other metal in the solution.

Species II.

Mineralized by the aerial Acid.

Native Calx of Bismuth.

4. When pure it is of a yellowish white colour, and either in a powdery form, or indurated like mortar; but it is frequently of a greenish yellow colour, being mixed with ores of other metals; the red and yellow part is most commonly cobalt ore, though it has often been mistaken for bismuth; it is frequently found in glittering particles interspersed through stones of various kinds; silver, iron, and other metals are also found in it; from all

all which it is feparable by folution in nitrous acid, as before explained.

Mineralized by the vitriolic Acid.

Wifmuth Bluth.

5. This is.faid to be of a yellowifh, reddifh, or variegated colour, and to be found mixed with the calx of bifmuth, incrufting other ores. Veltheim Grundrifs.

Mineralized by Sulphur.

6. It is chiefly found in *Sweden*, is of a bluifh grey colour, lamellar texture, and teffellar form like galena, but much heavier; it fometimes prefents parallel ftriæ like antimony, and its colour is variegated; it is faid to contain befides bifmuth alfo cobalt and arfenic. 3 *Lin. von Gmelin*, 133. This ore is very fufible, and the fulphur moftly feparates on fcorification; it is foluble in nitrous acid, and is analyfed like the foregoing ores.

Mineralized by Sulphur with Iron.

7. This is faid to be of a lamellar cuneiform texture, and to be found in *Norway*.

8. In the dry way bifmuth is extracted from its ftony ores by mixing 2 parts of the
pulverized

pulverized ore with 1 of pounded glafs, and 1 of calcined borax, melting the whole in a crucible lined with charcoal.

CHAP. XIII.

Cobalt.

1. Cobalt, or regulus of cobalt, as it is called by fome, is of a bluifh grey colour, very hard, brittle, and fteel grained; its fpecific gravity is about 7,700; its fufibility is nearly as that of copper; it is difficultly calcined, and its calx is of a blue, fo deep as to appear almoft black; and this calx melted with borax, or potafh and white filiceous fand, gives a blue glafs: this calx is not volatil; the regulus is eafily foluble in fpirit of nitre or aqua regia, and the colour of the folution is red, but difficultly in the vitriolic and fcare at all in the marine acid; the calx is more eafily diffolved by thefe acids; it yields even to the acetous.

SPECIES I.

Native.

2. This has not as yet been found; that which paffes for fuch is mineralized by arfenic.

Species II.

Mineralized by the aerial acid.

Black Ochre of Cobalt, Vitreous Ore of Cobalt, Kobalt mulm, Schlaken-Kobalt.

3. This appears either in a loose, powdery form, sometimes as fine as lamp black, either grey or blackish, and called cobalt oehre, or in black indurated scoriform masses, called *Schlaken Kobalt*, or vitreous cobaltic ore: they are both commonly free from sulphur and arsenic, and when there are any, they are only mechanically mixed with this ore; some small proportion of copper and iron is also sometimes found in it; it is frequently imbodied in stones or sands of a black colour; talc, chalk and gypsum impregnated with it have been called by the same name, and by some *Spiegel Cobalt*; it is also contained in some green and blue earths as already mentioned, p. 78, and 79.

4. To analyse this ore let it be dissolved in the nitrous acid; a plate of copper dipped in the solution will discover and precipitate the silver, if any, and a plate of iron will discover and precipitate copper, if the solution contains any; but it should speedily be withdrawn lest the cobalt also should be precipitated;

tated ; then the whole should be precipitated by a fixed alkali, and dephlogisticated by abstraction of the nitrous acid and calcination ; if the calx be then digested in distilled vinegar, the cobaltic part alone will be taken up, and may be precipitated by mild mineral alkali. 160 gr. of this precipitate denote 100 of cobalt in its metallic state.

Species III.

Mineralized by the Vitriolic or Arsenical Acids.

Red Cobalt Ochre, Kobalt bluth, Fleurs de Cobalt.

5. This also is found either *loose* and pure, or mixed with chalk or gypsum, or *indurated* and crystalized in tetrahædral crystals, or in a stalactitical form; it melts easily, and then becomes blue; it frequently invests other cobaltic ores, and is found sometimes in stones, or sand. Mr. *Bergman* has shewn that the arsenical acid, and not the calx of arsenic, enters into this combination, for cobalt is never red, but when united to an acid.

6. To analyse this ore, Mr. *Bergman* advises to dissolve it in water, acidulated with some acid (suppose the nitrous) and then to precipitate the cobaltic part with mild mineral alkali; the liquor will contain cubic nitre

nitre and Glauber's falt, if the vitriolic acid be the mineralizer, or arfenicated foda, if the arfenical acid exifts in the compound.

Species IV.

Mineralized by Arfenic, with fcarce any Iron.

Grey Cobalt Ore. Stahl derben Kobalt, *Glantz Cobalt.*

7. Solid, heavy, compact, fometimes of a dull, and fometimes of a bright appearance, frequently cryftalized in a teffelar, fometimes in a dendritical form, and generally fo hard as to give fire with fteel.

8. It is analyfed by folution in aqua regia, or nitrous acid and evaporation to drynefs; the refiduum treated with the acetous acid will yield to it the cobaltic part; the arfenic fhould at firft be precipitated by the addition of water.

9. Or elfe this ore may firft be roafted to expell the arfenic, and then treated with nitrous acid, the cobalt will be diffolved with very little of the iron, then by boiling the folution moft of the iron will be precipitated, and by adding a fixed alkali, the remainder of the iron will firft be precipitated yellowifh, and afterwards the cobalt reddifh. *Mem. Berl.* 1779.

1779. p. 16. So alfo the *Pruffian* alkali will firft precipitate the iron blue, and afterwards the cobalt reddifh, *(ibid.)* or rather grey.

Species V.

Mineralized by Sulphur and Arfenic with Iron.

White arfenicated Cobalt Ore, Kobalt Glantz.

10. This bears a great refemblance to the laft, but is fofter, for it never ftrikes fire with fteel, and fometimes it is fo foft that it may be fcraped with a knife; it moftly appears under fome polygon form; the moft fhining forts of this, and of the former Species, have been called *Cobalt Glantz.*

It is analyfable like the former Species; the fulphur may be caught on the filter.

Species VI.

Mineralized by a fmall Proportion of Sulphur, with a notable Proportion of Iron without any Arfenic.

White unarfenicated Cobalt Ore.

11. It is fometimes found in large maffes, and fometimes in grains cryftalized, of a dull white colour, and frequently bears the appearance

pearance of mifpickel; it becomes black, and not red by calcination, which diftinguifhes it from pyrites; it contains fo little fulphur, that none can be extracted from it; when diffolved in aqua regia, its folution is yellow while cold, but greenifh when boiling, which viciffitude of colour is peculiar to marine cobalt; it contains much more iron than it does cobalt.

12. In the dry way cobaltic ores, after freeing them from their matrix by wafhing, and from fulphur and arfenic by roafting, are reduced by melting them with three parts black flux in a lined and covered crucible, in a fmith's forge; the beft ores contain from 60 to 80 per cent. of regulus, the worft under 25 per cent. Smalt is reducible in the fame manner.

13. To effay the tinging power of cobaltic ores, the roafted ore is melted with three times its weight of pot-afh, and five times its weight of pounded glafs or flint, putting in the pot-afh firft, then the glafs or flint, and over all the ore. *Scheff.* 322.

14. If any bifmuth be contained in the cobalt ore, it will not mix with the regulus of cobalt, unlefs nickel alfo be contained in it, but will fimply adhere to it, and may be feparated

parated by the hammer, or by melting it, as it melts much easier than cobalt; when cobalt is by means of nickel united to bismuth, the compound is called *Speiss*; so also is a compound of cobalt, nickel, bismuth, sulphur and arsenic.

15. In general, cobaltic ores are known by their property of affording sympathetic ink when digested in aqua regia, after the bismuth is precipitated by the addition of water.

CHAP. XIV.
Nickel.

1. Nickel is a reddish white semi-metal of great hardness, so that it can scarce be filed, and of an equable texture; its specific gravity varies according to its purity from 7,421 to 9,000, the purest being the heaviest; when very pure it is in some degree malleable, and always magnetic, and hence it is deemed to retain iron. The fusibility of the common regulus is nearly as that of copper: it calcines more difficultly than cobalt; its calx is green, and rises in a tuberose fungous form; it is difficultly soluble in the vitriolic or marine acid, but easily in the nitrous; all these solutions are green, and volatil alkali turns them blue,

blue, but iron difcovers no copper in them, as it does in every combination of copper, fulphur, iron, arfenic and cobalt. Hence nickel muft be deemed a diftinct femi-metal: befides, Mr. *Bergman* has fhewn that fulphur, arfenic and cobalt may be perfectly feparated from it, though perhaps iron cannot; but it feems to me very probable that nickel itfelf may be magnetic: the pureft regulus is much more difficultly calcined or melted.

Species I.

Native.

2. This is mentioned by Mr. *Rinman* to have been lately found in a mine of cobalt in *Heffe*; it is very heavy, and of a liver colour, that is, dark red; when pulverized and roafted under a muffle, it forms green excrefcences, and fmokes, but its fmoke has no particular fmell, and no fublimate, whether fulphureous or arfenical, can be caught; it is foluble in acids, and the folution is green; but a polifhed iron plate difcovers no copper.

Species II.

Mineralized by the aerial Acid.

Native Calx of Nickel.

3. It is found in the form of a green calx, mixed

Nickel. 343

mixed with calx of iron, scattered over the ore of kupfernickel; also in some green clays. *Cronst.* §. 255.

Species III.

Mineralized by the Vitriolic Acid.

Vitriol of Nickel.

4. Already mentioned in the 2d Part, p. 195.

Species IV.

Mineralized by Sulphur and Arsenic, with Cobalt and Iron.

Kupfernickel.

5. This is of a reddish yellow bright colour; its texture either uniform, granular or scaly, bright in its fracture, very heavy, and generally covered with a greenish efflorescence; by calcination it loses much of its sulphur, and becomes green, forming fungous ramifications.

6. Its analysis in the moist way is as yet very imperfect; by solution in the nitrous acid it is freed from its sulphur, and by adding water to the solution, bismuth, if any, may be precipitated, as may silver if contained

tained in it by the marine acid, and copper when any by iron. To separate cobalt from nickel when the cobalt is in considerable quantity, Mr. *Gerhard* advises to drop a saturate solution of the roasted ore in nitrous acid, into liquid volatil alkali: the cobaltic part is instantly re-dissolved, and assumes a garnet colour; when filtered a grey powder remains on the filter, which is the nickel: the cobalt may be precipitated from the volatil alkali by any acid. *Mem. Berlin,* 1779, p. 17 and 18. cobalt may also, in some measure, be separated from nickel, by melting it with three times its weight of liver of sulphur; the cobalt will be taken up, and may be separated by lixiviation. 2 *Bergm.* 244.

7. In the dry way a regulus is obtained from the ores of nickel by long continued torrefaction, which expels much of the sulphur and arsenic, and then melting the green calx thus obtained, with twice or thrice its weight of black flux in an open crucible covered with common salt by the strongest fire of a smith's forge, a regulus is found, which amounts to from 30 to 50 per cent. of the weight of the green powder: this regulus still contains sulphur, arsenic, cobalt and iron; its further depuration is very laborious, and may be seen in the second volume of Mr. *Bergman*'s works.

8. It

8. It is highly probable that nickel exists in some species of roof slates, and in hornstones, whose solution in spirit of nitre is of a green colour.

CHAP. XV.

Regulus of Manganese.

1. This semi-metal was for the first time clearly described, and its properties admirably investigated and explained by Mr. *Scheele* in the *Memoirs of Stockholm*, for the year 1774. It was afterwards exhibited in its metallic form by Mr. *Gahn*, and its properties in that state, described by Mr. *Bergman* in the second volume of his works; since that publication it has frequently been produced in *France* by Messrs. *Morveau* and *Lapeirouse*, and lately here by Mr. *Woulfe*.

2. This regulus is of a dusky white colour, an irregular and uneven surface, arising from its imperfect fusion; in its fracture it is bright and shining, but soon tarnishes by exposure to the air; it is harder than iron, less fusible, and very brittle; its specific gravity is 6,850. When pulverized it is always magnetic, though larger pieces be not so; if it be exposed to the air, particularly in moist weather, it soon crumbles into a blackish brown powder,

der, which is something heavier than the regulus. It is soluble in acids, but most readily in the nitrous, and its solutions are mostly colourless, but that in the nitrous is generally brownish from a slight taint of iron, but there is always a spungy residuum of the nature of plumbago, left undissolved. These solutions give a white precipitate with aerated alkalis, which precipitate when heated grows black.

3. The regulus is obtained by mixing the calx or ore of Manganese with pitch, making it into a ball, and putting it into a crucible lined with powdered charcoal $\frac{1}{10}$ of an inch thick on the sides, and $\frac{1}{4}$ of an inch at bottom, then filling the empty space with powdered charcoal, covering the crucible with another inverted and luted on, and exposing it to the strongest heat of a forge for an hour or more.

Species I.

Native.

4. This has not as yet been found, nor can it be expected, (unless perhaps alloyed in native iron) as manganese loses the proportion of phlogiston necessary to its metallic form, more readily than any other metallic substance.

Species II.

Mineralized by the Aerial Acid.

Native Calces of Manganese.

5. The aerial acid is the only mineralizer of manganese in a dry state, yet known; and according to the different degrees of phlogistication of the manganese, it forms with it calces of different colours and different properties, to understand which it is necessary to remark, that when manganese is as much phlogisticated as it can be, without being in a reguline state, it forms a *white* calx, which contains a large portion of fixed air (about 40 per cent.) which enables it to retain phlogiston, as the compound of acid and calx, attracts phlogiston more strongly than either does when single; in proportion to its dephlogistication, and by union with other substances, its colour is either *blue, green, yellow, red, brown* or *black*; *blue*, is that which it acquires from the proportion of phlogiston, which it is enabled to retain by reason of its union with fixed alkalis; *green* arises from a mixture of the blue with the yellow calx of iron; *yellow* always arises from the prevalence of the calx of iron; *red*, from a slight phlogistication of the calx of manganese; *black*, from its thorough dephlogistication.

cation. Yet if the black calx be long roasted, it becomes *green*, which I think arises from the expulsion of fixed air, which leaves its phlogiston with the manganese, and thus produces a *blue*, which mixed with the yellow calx of iron, gives a *green*; *brown* arises from a mixture of the red and black calces of manganese. These observations I have extracted from Mr. *Scheele's* incomparable dissertation.

6. All these calces, of whatever colour they may be, communicate a *garnet* colour to glass of borax, when treated with a blow pipe, for being melted into a round globule, the surrounding atmosphere dephlogisticates them sufficiently to make them assume this colour.

7. Hence we may distinguish 3 principal varieties of the native calx of manganese, the white, the red, and the black.

I. VARIETY.

White Ore of Manganese.

8. This contains but a very small proportion of iron; it has been found by Mr. *Rinman* both in small white crystals, and in round masses in the cavities of quartz and adhering to glanzblend, rather less hard than limestone,

stone, of a sparry texture, and scarcely magnetic even after roasting, soluble with effervescence in nitrous acid, and affording a colourless solution, which solution, with mild alkalis, gave a white precipitate, and the precipitate, when heated, presently grew black; a sure criterion of manganese. *Mem. Stock.* 1765.

9. Mr. *Lapeirouse* found this white ore in the form of a spungy efflorescence, vegetating on the surface of some iron ores, particularly hæmatites.

10. It has been seen also by Mr. *Rinman* in the form of a calcareous spar, *of the colour of rosin*, and somewhat shining, in some places covered over with a sooty powder, and in thin pieces semi-transparent at the edges, and not hard enough to strike fire with steel; nitrous acid dissolves it almost intirely, with mild alkalis the solution gives a white precipitate, which blackens when heated. It consists of *manganese imbodied in zeolyte*, it melts *per se* with the blow pipe into a whitish grey porous slag, and with the addition of calcined borax gives a garnet coloured glass.

11. Many of white sparry iron ores may also be classed among the ores of manganese,

nese, as they contain more of it than of iron.

II. Variety.

Red Ore of Manganese.

12. It contains less fixed air, and is accompanied with more iron than the former variety, and also with calcareous or ponderous earth and silex. It is found either loose and semi-indurated in a matrix of calcareous spar, or talky shistus, or on hæmetites and other iron ores, or in heavy hard masses of a lamellar, radiated, or equable texture, or cryſtalized in pyramids, rhomboids, or short bright brittle needles. 15. *Roz.* 69.

III. Variety.

Black and Brown Ore of Manganese.

13. I place these together, as they differ but little; they are found either cryſtalized in the same form as the red ore, or in solid masses, some of which have a metallic appearance, others are dull, earthy, and mixed or embodied with quartz, or in a loose earthy form; their specific gravity is about 4,000 both, particularly the brown and the red are soluble in some measure by digeſtion in oil of vitriol, and the solution is at first reddish, but afterwards

afterwards becomes colourlefs, unlefs they contain a large proportion of iron. But the dephlogifticated nitrous acid does not act on them except fugar be added, and then this acid, as well as the concentrated vitriolic, operates a colourlefs folution, which with mild alkalis, gives a white precipitate of the fame nature as the firft variety; they contain more iron and lefs fixed air than the former varieties.

14. *Perigord Stone* belongs to this variety, it is of a dark grey colour like bafaltes or trapp, may be fcraped with a knife, yet is difficultly broken; when calcined it becomes of a reddifh brown colour and harder, but not magnetic. Its fpecific gravity is confiderable, it does not melt *per fe*, but with borax it affords an amethyftine glafs; nitrous acid fcarcely acts on it without the addition of fugar, this ftone feems alfo to contain argill, and fome portion of iron.

15. One of the moft remarkable ores of manganefe is that called *black wad*; it is of a dark brown colour, partly in powder and partly indurated, and brittle. If half a pound of this be dried before a fire, and afterwards fuffered to cool for about an hour, and then two ounces of lintfeed oil be gradually poured on it, mixing them loofely like barm with flour,

flour, little clots will be formed, and in something more than half an hour the whole will gradually grow hot, and at laſt burſt into a flame, as I have ſeen ſeveral times at the houſe of Sir *Joſeph Banks*. The temperature of the room where the experiment was made was about 50: the heat this ore was expoſed to while drying might be about 130.

16. According to Mr. *Wedgewood*'s analyſis 100 parts of black wad contain 43 of manganeſe, 43 of iron, 4,5 of lead, and 5 of mica.

17. To analyſe the abovementioned ores, they ſhould be firſt roaſted to dephlogiſticate, the calx of manganeſe, and iron if any, then treated with dephlogiſticated nitrous acid to diſſolve the earths; the reſiduum ſhould then be treated with nitrous acid and ſugar, by which means a colourleſs ſolution of manganeſe will be obtained, which being precipitated by aerated mineral alkali, will give a precipitate 100 gr. of which are equivalent to 100 of regulus of manganeſe.

18. Many ſpecies of iron ore contain manganeſe. To diſcover it, let the iron be diſſolved in ſome acid, and precipitated by the *Pruſſian* alkali; let the ſolution be poured off, and the precipitate digeſted in pure water;

Manganese.

water; the *Prussian* manganese will be dissolved, and the *Prussian* iron remain undissolved. See also Chap. 5. N°. 41 and 53.

Manganese in Vegetables.

19. " Manganese seems to be contained
" in the ashes of most vegetables, and to it
" the blue or greenish colour of calcined ve‑
" getable alkali is owing. These colours
" are generally attributed to the phlogiston
" of the alkali; but if so, they should not
" be found in fixed nitre, as the nitrous acid
" should carry off during its decomposition
" all the phlogiston; yet this alkali is always
" greenish, so that the colour seems to arise
" from the ashes of the charcoal with which
" the nitre was decomposed. If 3 parts of
" the alkali of tartar, 1 of sifted ashes, and
" $\frac{1}{8}$ of nitre be melted together, they form
" a dark green mass, which being dissolved
" in water affords a beautiful green solution,
" and this being filtered, on the addition of a
" few drops of oil of vitriol, becomes red,
" and after a few days a brown powder is
" deposited, which has the properties of
" manganese." *Scheele* 56 *Mem. Stock.*
1774, p. 189. The ashes of serpyllum contain very little of it, those of trees contain most. *Ibid.* 180.

CHAP. XVI.

Siderite.

1. The first distinct mention I find made of this substance is in the *Mineralogy* of Mr. *Monnet*, p. 384, printed in 1779; but the merit of discovering its nature is undoubtedly due to Mr. *Meyer* of *Stetin*, who, not contenting himself with vague generalities, developed its principal properties by a series of ingenious and well connected experiments published among the Memoirs of the philosophical society of *Berlin* for the year 1781 and 1782; some few of which he also mentioned in the Memoirs of the preceding year. Mr. *Bergman*, ignorant of what Mr. *Meyer* had done, arrived at the same conclusions nearly at the same time, as may be seen in the 3d volume of his works, and discovered some additional properties of this new semi-metallic substance. From these sources I have extracted the following account of it.

2. Siderite is principally found in iron of the first fusion or cast iron, and in the ores of coldshort iron. The manner of its extraction has been already mentioned, Chap. 5. N.º 46. A pound of cast iron sometimes affords about

Siderite.

about 12 drachms of this calx, whose natural colour is white, but it is generally tinged brown or yellow from a mixture of the calx of iron. Mr. *Bergman* purifies it by repeatedly abstracting the nitrous acid over it, which dephlogisticates the iron, and leaves the calx of siderite soluble in the mineral acids, but not in the acetous.

3. The solutions of it in the vitriolic and marine acids crystalize, though very difficultly; it rather tends to form a jelly, particularly if there be an excess of acid; the solution in the nitrous is reddish, and in the marine yellowish; all are slowly precipitable by water.

4. This calx is also in some measure soluble in water, but 1 part of it requires 1500 of boiling water for its solution.

5. Alkalis, both fixed and volatil, have some action on it, and acquire a brown tinge from it.

6. In the dry way it melts *per se* on charcoal, and is not volatil; it gives glass a green colour, except it meets phlogiston, and then the colour is brown.

7. It is reduced to a regulus by melting it with

with half its weight of borax in a crucible lined to the thickness of $\frac{1}{10}$ of an inch with a mixture of charcoal and a little clay, and exposing it to the fire of a smith's forge for three quarters of an hour.

8. The regulus is of a steel grey colour, not so hard as cobalt, exceeding brittle, not magnetic in small pieces, though slightly so when powdered. Its texture is granular; its specific gravity about 6,710.

9. Its fusibility is nearly as that of copper, and it seems to contain something more phlogiston than iron does; it is not volatil when heated.

10. It is very difficultly soluble in any acid, and requires the assistance of heat; after ebullition for some days the nitrous acid out of 5 grains dissolved only 4, aqua regia 4,2, dilute vitriolic acid 3,5, and the marine 3. Infusion of galls turns these solutions black; the *Prussian* alkali gives a dark blue precipitate, and common alkalis a white precipitate.

11. It precipitates gold, silver and copper very slowly from their solutions, and in their metallic form; but lead from nitrous acid in the form o a calx; it does not precipitate mercury from the nitrous acid.

12. It

12. It is itself precipitated from the nitrous acid in the form of a brown calx by zinc and iron. Copper seems to precipitate only a little dephlogisticated iron from it, to which a little of the white calx is united; lead also produces the same effect.

13. It does not detonate with nitre, though it alkalizes it, and is dephlogisticated by it.

14. It does not unite with sulphur.

15. It sublimes with sal ammoniac, and takes a yellow colour.

16. It does not amalgamate with mercury, but when in fusion it unites with iron, copper, or cobalt, but not with any other metal, except perhaps nickel, which has not been tried; it converts bar iron into the state of crude or cast iron, and when in a smaller proportion renders it *coldshort*.

CHAP. XXII.

Molybdena. Molybdena membranacea Cronst.
154. *Wasserbley of the Germans.*

1. It resembles plumbago, but its laminæ are larger, brighter, and when thin slightly flexible; it is of a lead colour, and does not

strike

strike fire with steel; its specific gravity is 4,569.

2. In an open fire it is almost intirely volatil and infusible. Microcosmic salt or borax scarcely affect it, but it is acted upon with much effervescence by mineral alkali, and with it forms a reddish mass, which smells of sulphur.

3. It is affected by no acid, but the nitrous and arsenical, both require the assistance of heat; the latter is converted into orpiment.

4. Mr. *Scheele* has found it to consist of an acid of a peculiar nature united to sulphur; a small proportion of iron is commonly found in it; but this seems merely fortuitous; 100 parts of it contain about 45 of acid, and 55 of sulphur.

5. It is decomposed either by detonation with nitre, or by solution in nitrous acid: this latter method is the readiest: for this purpose it is to be 5 times distilled, each time with 4 times its weight of spirit of nitre; a white calx at last remains, which is the molybdenous acid.

6. This acid is soluble in 570 times its weight

Molybdena.

weight of water in the temperature of 60; the solution reddens that of litmus, precipitates sulphur from the solution of liver of sulphur, &c. the specific gravity of the dry acid is 3,460. 3 *Bergm.* 127.

7. This acid is precipitable from its solution in water by the *Prussian* alkali, and also by tincture of galls the precipitate is reddish brown.

8. If this acid be distilled with three times its weight of sulphur, it re-produces molybdena.

9. The solution of this acid in water unites to fixed alkalis, and forms crystalizable salts; so it does with calcareous earth, magnesia, and argill: these last combinations are difficultly soluble; it acts also on the base metals, and with them assumes a bluish colour.

10. This solution precipitates silver, mercury, or lead from the nitrous acid, and lead from the marine, but not mercury.

It also precipitates barytes from the nitrous and marine acids, but no other earth. Molybdenous baroselenite is soluble in cold water.

11. This

11. This acid is itself soluble in the vitriolic acid with the assistance of heat, and the solution is blue when cold, though colourless while hot ; it is also soluble in the marine acid, but not in the nitrous.

12. Molybdenous tartar and ammoniac precipitate all metals from their solutions by a double affinity. Gold, sublimate corrosive, zinc and manganese, are precipitated *white*; iron or tin from the marine acid *brown*; cobalt *red*; copper *blue*.

13. Alum and calcareous earth white. *Scheele Mem. Stock,* 1778.

14. This acid has been lately reduced by Mr. *Hielm*, but the properties of the regulus thus obtained are not yet published.

CHAP. XVIII.

Of the Tungstenic Acid.

Though this acid, and the manner of obtaining it have been already mentioned, p. 38, yet as it is of a metallic nature, a few of its distinguishing properties may properly be inserted here.

1. Its solution in water reddens that of litmus;

litmus; with alkalis it forms cryftalizable falts; with barytes calcareous earth, and magnefia infoluble compounds.

2. This folution is precipitated white by the *Pruffian* alkali, and the precipitate is foluble in water.

3. It precipitates the folutions of vitriols of iron, zinc, copper, and the nitrous folutions of filver, mercury and lead, and that of lead in marine acid; all thefe precipitates are white: the folution of tin in marine acid is precipitated blue, but the folutions of gold and fublimate corrofive are not altered by it.

4. The folutions of chalk or alum are not altered by it, but that of barytes in the acetous acid is precipitated, and the precipitate is infoluble.

CHAP. XIX.

Saturnite.

The fubftance to which I ventured to give this name, is faid by Mr. *Monnet*, to be found in the lead mines of *Poullaoven* in *Brittany*, and is feparated from the lead ore during its torrefaction. According to him it refembles lead in its colour and fpecific gravity,

gravity, is soluble in the same acids, and with the same phænomena; but it is much more fusible, very brittle, easily scorified and volatilized, and refuses to mix with lead when in fusion. It were to be wished it was better examined.

CHAP. XX.

Reflexions on the nature of Cabalt, Nickel, and Manganese.

1. The principal reason why any simple substances are reckoned specifically different from each other, is their manifesting properties permanently different in the same circumstances, and every substance must be deemed simple, until it can be resolved into different principles, or formed out of them. Every other indication is at best a surmise grounded on mere possibility, but destitute of probability, and therefore inadmissable in any exact scientifical system; upon this foundation most chymists and mineralogists have admitted the abovementioned substances to a distinct rank among semi-metals. Yet as some others deservedly of great note, namely, Mr. *Pabst*, Mr. *Monnet*, and *Romé de Lisle*, have asserted, that all, or some or other of these semi-metals, are either modifications of iron, or compounds of some sort; I presume it will not be amiss before I conclude this treatise, to state

state the reasons they have alledged, and justify the opinion I have followed.

Of Cobalt.

2. With regard to cobalt, some have thought it to be nothing else but a compound of iron and arsenic, asserting that such a compound would communicate a blue colour to glass, but this pretension has been fully refuted by the experiments of Mr. *Brandt. Mem. Sued.* p. 46 and 47. and those of Mr. *Monnet. Diss. Des. Mett.* p. 279.

3. Others have thought that the tinging quality is produced in cobalt, merely by its union with arsenic, because it sometimes happens, that cobalt will not tinge, unless arsenic be added to it. But the true reason of this phænomenon is, that cobalt will not tinge unless it is dephlogisticated, nor even then unless it melts, and it sometimes happens that cobalt is too much dephlogisticated, and then it will not melt in the usual heat, without the addition of arsenic, which serves as a flux to it; for that arsenic is not otherwise essential to its tinging property is evident from this, that some cobalt ores, which tinge admirably well, are yet absolutely free from arsenic, such as the vitreous ore, *Sp. 2d.*

4. It is true, that in some circumstances glass may be tinged blue by iron, as Mr. *Gmelin* has learnedly shewn in the 5th part of Mr. *Crell's Chymical Journal*; but this iron is not transformed into cobalt; for if that glass be digested in aqua regia, the solution will not form a sympathetic ink; but, on the contrary, will manifest every property of iron; whereas glass tinged blue by cobalt will, when digested with aqua regia, afford sympathetic ink, and manifest the other distinctive characters of cobalt.

Nickel.

5. Mr. *Monnet* thinks that cobalt and nickel are one and the same metal, which when united to iron, exhibits the properties of, and is called *cobalt*, but when free from iron, is called *nickel*; so that nickel is the simple substance, and cobalt the compound. The solutions of cobalt he adds are red, merely on account of the iron, otherwise they would be green like those of nickel; the blue tinging matter he says is inherent in cobalt, but it cannot be developed without the addition of iron and arsenic. This opinion carries its own refutation with it, for common nickel always contains at least as much iron as cobalt does, and yet constantly gives glass a reddish yellow colour, and if ever the addition of arsenic

arsenic makes it give a blue tinge to glass, it is because it contains a portion of cobalt, which is not easily dephlogisticated, but remains in a reguline state, and while it remains in this state, it can give no colour to glass, but the addition of arsenic dephlogisticates this portion of cobalt, and thus enables it to unite to, and tinge glass, and this is so true, that the addition of nitre, which dephlogisticates still more powerfully than arsenic, produces the same effect, as Mr. *Bergman* has shewn in his elaborate dissertation on Nickel, 2 *Nov. Act. Ups.* p. 243. so that arsenic is no way necessary; and moreover it is absolutely false, that the addition of iron and arsenic will ever give nickel the properties of cobalt, as Mr. *Monnet* himself must well know. However, the reasons he alledges to prove the identity of these semi-metals are,

6. 1°· That cobalt and nickel are soluble in the same acids, and acted on by these acids in the same manner, all the difference being that the solutions of cobalt are red, and those of nickel green; a difference assuredly very great, and which no addition of iron and arsenic to nickel will alter, as it should according to his system; for let him combine iron and arsenic with nickel as he pleases, he will never make a substance whose solution in acids will be *red*, as that of cobalt is. But further, if

by

by *acids* he means the mineral acids and the acetous, then he may as well say that bismuth is the same substance as cobalt and nickel, for it is acted upon by these acids in nearly the same manner, but if he means the long tribe of other acids, the assertion is not true, since the tartarous acid for instance does not act on nickel, whereas it does on cobalt.

7. 2^{ly}. Because though the ores of Nickel become *green* by calcination, and those of cobalt, *blue*, yet if the calcination of the nickel be continued, its calx will become *brown*; but I do not see how this change to a reddish brown, approximates nickel to cobalt, any more than the green colour does, for it is equally different from the blue or chocolate colour of cobalt, and it appears from Mr. *Bergman's* experiments, that the green colour arises from a mixture of arsenic, for when nickel is thoroughly free from it, its calces are brown.

8. 3dly. Because nickel long exposed to the air, contains a green rust, as does cobalt But this appearance would as well indicate copper.

9. 4^{thly}. Because both nickel and cobalt unite with the same metals. He probably forgot

forgot that cobalt and bismuth will not unite, nor will cobalt and silver, or cobalt and lead, whereas nickel will unite to any of them when well purified from cobalt, and with bismuth, even without such purification.

10. 5^{thly}. Because according to *Cronsted* himself, nickel will give a blue colour to borax. But Mr. *Bergman* has shewn, that when it is well purified from cobalt, it will give a hyacinthine, and not a blue tinge to borax. Mr. *Monnet* adds, that cobalt, melted with quartz and alkali, gives a *greenish* brown glass in some circumstances, and quotes *Brandt*, but *Brandt* says the colour was *reddish* brown, and in effect this colour should be expected from the species of cobaltic ore he examined, which was loaded with iron, and from the manner in which the experiment was conducted, the cobalt being too much dephlogisticated.

11. Lastly, he observes that the cobalt is always magnetic; but it is to be observed, that this magnetism constantly decreases in proportion as it is freed from iron, and yet the cobalt remains in full possession of all its properties, therefore its properties do not depend on the presence of iron, and if it were perfectly free from iron (a state of purity to which Mr. *Monch* says he has reduced it. 3 *Crell.* p. 164) it would not

not be in the leaft magnetic; befides this argument would fubvert Mr. *Monnet*'s own opinion, for nickel is alfo always magnetic.

12. Mr. *Rome de Lifle* thinks that nickel confifts of iron, cobalt and copper intimately united :* although Mr. *Bergman* has demonftrated that this opinion is deftitute of any proof, either fynthetic or analytic; for, in the firft place, he mixed thefe fubftances in various proportions, but could produce nothing that refembled nickel; and, in the 2d place, he fhewed that copper is very feldom mixed with it, and when it is, may eafily be feparated, and cobalt alfo may be feparated though more difficultly. But Mr. *Romé* looks on the blue colour which volatil alkalis produce in the folutions of nickel, as an evident fign of its containing copper. To make this proof of any weight, we muft affume this principle; *that two different metals cannot give the fame colour to the fame menftruum*, which is evidently falfe, for gold and platina give the fame colour to aqua regia, to fay nothing of the various metals, whofe folutions in nitrous acid are colourlefs. The only confequence ftrictly deducible from the colour of a menftruum is purely negative; namely, *that it does not*

* Chryftilographie, p. 91.

fingly

fingly contain any *fubftance*, which is known to communicate a different colour to that menftruum in the fame circumftances; for there is fcarce any one property of any fubftance that may not be communicable to fome other fubftance, as it is only the aggregate of all their properties that fully diftinguifhes fubftances from each other.

13. He further adds, that nickel cannot be looked upon as a diftinct femi-metal, becaufe it cannot be thoroughly purified from iron. What ftrefs fhould be laid on this argument, we fhall prefently confider in treating of manganefe; but in the mean time we may obferve that it is far from being clear that nickel can never be purified from iron; for the only ground of this fufpicion is, that the pureft nickel is magnetic; but this muft be deemed infufficient, unlefs it be taken for granted that magnetifm is a property inherent in iron only, and incommunicable to all other poffible metallic fubftances, as we know it is to thofe that are already known; a pofition which feems to me fully contradicted in the cafe of nickel; for when it is purified as much as poffible from iron, it becomes *more* inftead of *lefs* magnetic, and even acquires what iron does not, the properties of a magnet. What hinders us then from allowing magnetifm, like the property of giv-

ing a blue colour to alkalis, to be common to thofe different metallic fubftances in which we find it?

Manganefe.

According to Mr. *Romé* this femi-metal is a mixture of iron, zinc and cobalt: that it contains iron is not denied; but it is afferted, that befides iron it contains a peculiar femi-metal, whofe properties are independent of the prefence of iron, fince they are abfolutely different from thofe of iron, and every alloy of iron with any other known metallic fubftance, and are fo much the more apparent, as the portion of iron it contains is diminifhed. Neverthelefs, Mr. *Romé* objects that the regulus of manganefe can never be totally freed from iron, and that all the experiments hitherto made upon it being made on a mixed femi-metal, the properties difcovered by thefe experiments fhould be deemed thofe of a mixed, and not thofe of a fimple fubftance. But the fallacy of this reafoning will readily appear, if it be confidered that, though until lately, platina could not be obtained perfectly free from iron; yet the moft judicious chymifts in Europe, *Lewis*, *Margraaf*, *Scheffer*, *Macquer* and *Baumé*, were of opinion that it was a peculiar diftinct metallic fubftance; and at this day regulus of antimony and tin are never abfolutely free from

from iron, yet no one dreams of attributing their peculiar properties to an alloy of iron, and any other metal; and indeed if this manner of reasoning were of any weight, no properties could be attributed to any simple substance; for what substance can be procured absolutely pure? When was water rigorously pure ever found or procured, or gold of 24 carats? Unless therefore we can produce by art a compound similar to that which we presume to be a mixture, or shew some good reason why such a compound cannot be artificially produced, or unless we can decompose such substance, and thereby destroy its peculiar properties, or at least alter them by the substraction of any one of its supposed constituent parts, we must look upon the supposition that such substance is essentially a *compound*, as groundless relatively to the present state of our knowledge, on which alone, and not on mere possibilities, we can rationally found any assertion. The word *modification* has been strangely abused on this occasion. Cobalt, nickel and manganese, have been said to be only modifications of iron; but as long as it is not known wherein that modification consists, this word presents no idea whatsoever, and any other insignificant word may as well be used. If it be said that it denotes *iron with the addition of some unknown substance*, then it would follow at least,

least, that by diminishing the proportion of iron, the specific properties of the compound would be altered, which is not true with respect to these semi-metals, for the freer they are from iron, the more perfectly they manifest their peculiar properties; so that in every sense this assertion is either false or unintelligible.

With respect to zinc and cobalt, there is not the least foundation for suspecting, much less affirming, their existence in regulus of manganese, as they are never found even in the ore of manganese, except fortuitously; but, on the contrary, this ore is most frequently found without a particle of either; nor does the regulus shew any property that approximates it more to them than to other metallic substances, but, on the contrary, many that belong to no other, nor to any compound of any other metallic substances.

APPENDIX

APPENDIX III.

Geological Obſervations.

Mountains:

ELEVATIONS, conſiſting chiefly of clay, ſand or gravel, are called *Hills*, thoſe that conſiſt chiefly of ſtone are by mineralogiſts called *Mountains*. As they are the chief repoſitories of minerals, and particularly of metallic ores, I ſhall here relate the moſt intereſting obſervations relative to them that have occurred to me, or that have been made by others.

Mountains may be conſidered either with a view to their antiquity and origin, their height, or their ſtructure.

Of the Antiquity and Origin of Mountains.

In this point of view mountains are divided into *primæval*, that is, of equal date with the formation of the globe, and ſecondary, or *alluvial*; ſome add even *tertiary*; but this diſtinction I think ſuperfluous.

Among the primæval, thoſe that conſiſt of granite hold the firſt place. The higheſt mountains, and moſt extenſive ridges in every part of the globe, are granitical. Thus the *Alps* and *Pyrenees* are the loftieſt in *Europe*, and particularly ſuch of them as conſiſt of granite, the *Altaiſchan*, *Uralian* and *Caucaſus* in *Aſia*, and the *Andes* in *America*. From them the greateſt rivers derive their origin. The higheſt of them never contain metallic ores, but ſome of the lower contain veins of copper or tin, as thoſe of *Saxony*, *Sileſia* and *Cornwall*. The granitic ſtones next the ore always abound in mica; petrefactions are never found in them.

Many of the granite mountains of *Aſia* and *America* form large plat-forms at about half their height, from which ſeveral lofty ſpires ariſe. No ſuch plat-forms have been obſerved in the *Alps* or *Pyrenees*.

That the formation of theſe mountains preceded that of vegetables and animals is juſtly inferred from their containing no organic remains either in the form of petrifaction or impreſſion, from their bulk, extenſion and connection, which ſeem too conſiderable to be aſcribed to ſubſequent cauſes, and from their uſe and neceſſity for the production of rivers, without which it is hard to ſuppoſe that the world had exiſted at any period ſince the creation of animals. Moſt naturaliſts are at preſent agreed that granites

were

were formed by cryftallization. This operation probably took place after the formation of the atmofphere, (which in the hiftory of the creation is called the firmament) and the gradual excavation of the bed of the ocean; foon after which, it is faid, that by the command of God (that is, by virtue of the laws of nature which he eftablifhed) *the dry land appeared*; for by means of the evaporation of part of the waters into the atmofphere, and the gradual retreat of the remainder, the various fpecies of earths before diffolved or diffufed through this mighty mafs, were difpofed to coalefce, and among thefe the *filiceous* muft have been the firft, as they are the leaft foluble: but as they have an affinity to other earths with which they were mixed, fome of thefe muft alfo have united with them in various proportions, and thus have formed in diftinct maffes the felt fpar, fhoerl and mica, which compofe the granite. Calcareous earth enters very fparingly into the compofition of this ftone; but as it is found in fhoerl, which is frequently a component part of granite, it follows that it muft be one of the primitive earths, and not entirely derived from marine exuviæ as many imagine. Quartz can never be fuppofed to be a product of fire, for in a very low heat it burfts, cracks, and lofes its tranfparency, and in the higheft we can produce, it is infufible;

so that in every essential point it is totally unlike to glass to which some have compared it. As granite contains earths of every genus, we may conclude that all the simple earths are coeval with the creation. This observation does not preclude further researches into their composition; for though water undoubtedly dates from the creation, yet some late experiments shew it to be a compound; their simplicity may be only relative to the present state of our knowledge.

Mountains, which consist of *lime-stone* or *marble* of a granular or scaly texture, and not disposed in strata, seem also to have preceded the creation of animals, for no organic traces are found in them. Also those that consist of stones of the *argillaceous* genus, and of the 6th compound species of the siliceous genus, seem to be primæval, as they contain no organic remains: these often consist of parallel strata of unequal thickness, and the lower are harder and less thick than the upper, whence the lower seem to have been first formed, and the upper latter. They are the principal seat of metallic substances, whose ores run across the strata in all directions; hence they are by the Germans called *Gang geburge*, and by the French *Montagnes à filons*. Coal is never found in them.

It is little to be doubted, but that submarine volcanos preceded not only the creation of animals, but also the separation of dry land from the waters, the Mosaic expression, *Let there be Light*, seems to me to denote the consequences of those laws of nature to which volcanos owe their origin. The specific gravity of the globe exceeds 3 or 4 times that of water, and consequently its proportion of earth is greater than that of water; but at the creation the mass of water as specifically lighter, lay for the most part at the surface, until by the excavation of the bed of the ocean, and by evaporation, it made way for the appearance of dry land. Hence the interior regions of the globe, were never so overwhelmed with water, but volcanos might be formed within them, as they are at this day under the sea. The flame of these fires being adapted to excite the sensation of light, sufficiently authorised Moses to call it by that name, and the period during which it existed by that of *Day*, in contradistinction to the period of darkness which preceded and succeeded it. Mr. *Giraud de Soulavie* has distinctly proved the existence of these primæval volcanos, in various parts of his Natural History of the *South* of *France*.

Alluvial mountains are evidently of posterior formation, as they contain petrefactions and

and other vestiges of organic substances, they are always stratified.

The principal granitic ridges are flanked by argillaceous, as these are by alluvial mountains.

Of the height of Mountains.

There is no circumstance relating to mountains, that excites the surprise, or interests the curiosity of mankind to a greater degree than their height; hence many methods have been devised to determine it. The trigonometrical is the most antient, and in many cases exact, but it is often imperfect, and in some cases impracticable; the barometrical also remained for a long time imperfect, until the celebrated Mr. *De Luc*, with indefatigable industry, and uncommon sagacity, brought it to a degree of accuracy, scarce to be expected. Some improvements have lately been made in it by Sir *George Shuckburgh*, and the calculation has been rendered still more simple by Mr. *Magellan*.

In this method the elevation of mountains is determined by the different heights of 2 columns of mercury, one at the top and the other at the bottom of the mountain, the degree

gree of heat of each being equal, or reduced to an equality, and the common temperature of the atmofphere being given. Two barometers are therefore ufed, and each has a thermometer annexed to it. The degree of heat to which both barometers are reduced, is 55° of Fahrenheit, yet if either of the barometers be at 30 inches, and the thermometer attached to it at 55, no reduction need be made in that barometer; but if either barometer be at 30, and the thermometer attached to it below 55°, we muft add the expanfion the mercury would have by the heat of 55°, or if it be above 55° we muft fubtract the excefs of expanfion it gains by that heat.* Now every degree of Fahrenheit produces an expanfion, of, 00304 of the barometrical inch, when the barometer is at 30, therefore when the thermometer is at n degrees below or above 55° we muft add in the former, or fubtract in the latter cafe, 0,00304 n to, or from the barometrical height. But if the mercury in the barometers ftand above or below 30 inches, then let the correction be found as if the mercury were at 30, and let it be denoted by c, the correction fought by x and the barometrical height h, then $\frac{hc}{30} = x$. The thermometers fhould go alike, or if not, the difference fhould be obferved and fubtracted.

* The fractions to be added or fubtracted, are marked on a feparate fcale, called the fcale of correction.

The barometrical heights, of both barometers being thus corrected, the logarithm of the number of inches at which the mercury in the upper stands, is to be substracted from the logarithm of that of the lower; the difference between the 4 first decimal figures on the left gives *nearly* the number of fathoms, as that of the two last decimals does of the parts of a fathom between the upper and lower barometers, which being multiplied into 6, gives the number of feet and parts of a foot.

I said *nearly*, for this height is not exact, except when the mean temperature of the atmosphere is $31°,24$ of Fahrenheit.

The mean temperature of the atmosphere is the arithmetical mean between the degrees, marked by two *detached* thermometers, one above, and the other below, both being held for about an hour in the shade.

When this medium is $31°,24$, the above method is just, and requires no further correction, but if the medium exceeds, or falls short of $31°,24$ that difference must be found, suppose it $=d$.

The approximate height must now be corrected by multiplying it in feet, into the fraction 0,00243, let the product $=p$, then

pd

Geological Observations.

pd added to the approximate height, if the mean temperature be above 31°,24, or subſtracted from that height, if the mean temperature be below 31,24 gives the true height.

The following example will make the calculation more intelligible, the inſtruments on the top of the mountain are denoted by *A*, and thoſe at the bottom by *B*.

OBSERVATIONS.

Barometer A	25,19 Inches.
Its attached thermometer	46°
Detached thermometer A	39,5

Barometer B at the ſame time	29,4
Attached thermometer	50
Detached ditto	45°

CALCULATION.

Here the lower barometer ſtands below 30 inches, and its attached thermometer below 55° namely at 50. then $n = 5$ and $,00304 \times 5 = ,01520$ this would be the correction to be added if the barometer were at 30, but as it is at 29,4 then

$$\frac{b\,c}{30} = \frac{,29,4 \times ,01520}{30} = \frac{,44688}{30} = ,01489 = x$$

which

which is to be added to 29,4 $\left.\begin{array}{r}29,4000\\+,0148\end{array}\right\}=$
29,415 its corrected height

Again the upper barometer is at 25,19 inches, and its attached thermometer at 46 then $n=9$. and $c=,02736$ and $\dfrac{b\,c}{30}=\dfrac{25,19\times 02736}{30}$
$=,02297=x$ and $25,19+02297=25,21297$ or in round numbers 25,213 as its corrected height.

Now the logarithm of 29,415 is 1,468568, and the log. of 25,213 is 1,401624, whose
difference is - - - $\begin{array}{r}4685,68\\4016,24\\\hline 669,44\end{array}$

The difference of the 4 first figures on the left, gives the number of fathoms, and is therefore separated by a comma from the last, which gives the decimal parts of a fathom, and 669,44, × 6 = 4016,664 feet, this is the approximate height.

The mean temperature is next to be found. The detached thermometer A was at 39,5, and the detached thermometer B at 45, now then
39,5

$39,5 + 45 = 84,5$ and $\frac{84,5}{2} = 42,25$, which is therefore the mean temperature of the atmosphere; the difference between this and $31,24 = 11,01 = d$.

The fraction ,00243 is now to be multiplied into 4016,664, the product is 9,7604 which multiplied into $d = 107,462$, and as the mean temperature is above 31,24. pd is to be added to the approximate height then $4016,66 + 107,46 = 4124,12$ feet, the true corrected height.

Some of the moſt remarkable mountains, whoſe heights have been taken with tolerable accuracy are,

In America.

Engliſh feet above the level of the ſea.

Chimboraço	20575,8 or 3,89 miles.
El Coraçon	15783
The town of Quito	9242

In Africa.

Teneriffe	11022 De Borda 13 *Roz.*
Pico Ruivo in Madeira	5141 *Phil. tranſ.* 1765.

In Europe.

Mont Blanc, higheſt of the Alps 15672 Sir G. Shuckburgh
Phil. tr. 1777.
Veſuvius in 1776 - - 3938 Sauſſure.
Ætna - - - - 10954
Canigou, one of the Pyrenees 9214
St. Bartelemi in pays de Foix 7565
Mont d'Or in Auvergne - - 6696
Puy de Dome - - - 5221
Hecla - - - - 5000 Von Troil.

The height of the Aſiatic mountains has never been accurately determined. Mr. *Bergman* remarks, that the ſphericity of the earth is no more altered by the height of the higheſt mountain, than that of a globe of 2 feet in diameter, would be by an elevation of the ſize of a grain of ſand.

The line of congelation in ſummer, under the Æquator, is at the height of 15400 feet; at the entrance of the temperate zone, 13428; on *Teneriffe*, in latitude 28, at about 1000; in *Auvergne*, in latitude 45, at 6740 nearly; with us, in latitude 52, it is probably at 5740. The greateſt height hitherto aſcended, is 15783 feet; in *Peru*, vegetation ceaſes at the height of 14697 feet, and on the *Alps*, at 9585, Mr. *Sauſſure* found the air leſs pure at 3834 feet; Mr. *D'Arcet* obſerved, that on the

the *Pic de midi* (one of the Pyrenees, lower than *Conigou*) falt of tartar remained dry for an hour and a half, though it immediately moiftened at the bottom of the mountain. The vapor of marine acid was alfo invifible on the fummit. The electric and magnetic powers were as ftrong as on the plain. 8 *Roz.* 403.

Of the Structure of Mountains.

Mountains confidered as to their ftructure, are divided into *intire*, *ftratified*, and *confufed*.

Intire mountains are formed of huge maffes of ftone, without any regular fiffure, and moftly homogenous; they confift chiefly of granite, fometimes of gneifs, fhiftus, flagftone, fandftone, limeftone, gypfum, porphyry, ferpentine, or trapp. Some in *Sweden* and *Norway* confift of iron.

Stratified mountains are thofe whofe mafs is regularly divided by joints or fiffures; thefe ftrata are confidered in relation to the angle which their fiffures make with the horizon and meridian, with refpect to the former they are called horizontal, rifing, or dipping. With regard to the latter, they are faid to run to this or that point fo many degrees;

they are most commonly parallel to eachother, and rise or fall with the mountain.

The strata of which mountains consist, are either *homogeneous* or *heterogeneous*.

Homogenous stratified mountains consist chiefly of stones of the argillaceous genus, as shisti, hornstones, flagstones, or of the fissile compound species of the siliceous genus, as gneifs, and metallic rock, or of both, the one behind the other. Sometimes of primæval limestone, that is, limestone of a granular or scaly texture, in which no animal vestiges appear. This limestone reposes on the argillaceous or siliceous strata; sometimes the argillaceous are covered with masses of granite, and sometimes with lava.

These mountains, as already observed, are the chief seat of metallic ores, particularly those of gneifs, metallic rock, and hornstone. When they are covered with limestone, the ore is generally between the limestone and the argillaceous stones. These ores run in veins and not in strata. The calcareous rarely contain any ore, when they do, it is either iron, copper, lead, or Mercury. Petrefactions

tions are found upon, but not in thefe mountains.

Heterogenous, or compound ftratified mountains *, confift of alternate ftrata of various fpecies of ftones, earths or fands either of the calcareous or argillaceous genus, or both, or metallic ores, and fometimes lava, as toad-ftone, &c. The lime-ftone is always of the laminar, and not of the granular or fcaly kind, and when it contains any ore, this is placed between its laminæ; it is very feldom that ftones of the filiceous genus form any ftratum in thefe mountains, except lavas; but the ftrata are frequently interrupted by filiceous maffes; fuch as jafper, porphyry, granite, &c. thefe may be called *ftops* †. Coal, bitumen, petrifications and organic impreffions, are found in thefe mountains; alfo falts, calamine, gold in the fandy ftrata, iron in intire ftrata or neftways, copper in the ftrata, lead ore, fingly or mixed with copper, (it fometimes fhoots through the ftrata in fmall veins,) cobalt ore in the ftops, pyrites every where; it fometimes conftitutes whole ftrata; the matrixes of thefe ores are chiefly of the calcareous or barytic genera, rarely quartz, and never mica.

* *Flotzgeburge.*   † *Klancken, kamme, Rucken Weck-fel.* I am not acquainted with the correfpondent *Englifh* technical terms.

There are other mountains analogous to these, which yet cannot properly be called stratified, as they consist only of three immense masses; the lowest granite, the middle of the argillaceous genus, and the uppermost of lime-stone. When they are metalliferous, as they generally are, the metallic ores are found in the argillaceous part, or between it and the calcareous; these ores form veins or bellies, and not strata; these may be called *triplicate* mountains.

Confused mountains; that is, of a confused or promiscuous structure, consist of stones of all sorts heaped together without any order; their interstices are filled with sand, clay and mica; they scarce ever contain any ore.

Of Volcanos.

Volcanos, or burning mountains, are peculiar to no climate, and have been observed in every quarter of the globe: they have no necessary or regular connection with other mountains, but they seem to have some with the sea, for they are generally placed in its neighbourhood. It is true that antient extinguished volcanos have lately been discovered in the inland parts of most countries; but this is one of the many proofs that the sea at some remote period covered those countries.

tries. Sub-marine volcanos have often been obferved even in our own times.

These mountains are of all heights, some so low as 450 feet, as that in *Tanna* *, but they generally form lofty spires, internally shaped like an inverted cone placed on a broader basis. This cone is called the crater of the volcano, as through it the lava generally passes, though sometimes it bursts from the sides, and even from the bottom of the mountain; sometimes the crater falls in and is effaced; sometimes in extinguished volcanos it is filled with water, and forms those lakes that are observed on the summit of some mountains.

Both the crater and basis of many volcanic mountains consist of lava either intire or decomposed, nearly as low as the level of the sea, but they finally rest either upon granite, as the volcanos of *Peru*, or on shistus, as the extinguished volcanos of *Hesse* and *Bohemia*, or on lime-stone, as those of *Silesia*, the *Vicentine Alps*, and *Vesuvius*. The decomposed and undecomposed lavas form irregular strata that are never parallel to each other. No ore is found in these mountains, except iron, of which lava contains from 20 to 25 per cent.

* *Foster*, 143.

and some detached fragments of copper, antimonial and arsenical ores.

If we consider the immense quantity of matter thrown up at different periods by volcanic mountains, without lessening their apparent bulk *, we must conclude the seat of these fires to be several miles, perhaps hundreds of miles, below the level of the sea; and as iron makes from $\frac{1}{7}$ to $\frac{1}{4}$ of all these ejections, we may infer that the interior parts of the earth consist chiefly of this metal, its ores, or stones that contain it, whose greater or lesser dephlogistication in different parts may be the cause of the variation of magnetic direction.

The origin of these fires is not easily accounted for. It is well known that martial pyrites, being moistened, will acquire heat; but that this heat should burst into actual flame, the concourse of open air is absolutely requisite; however, if we suppose the heated pyrites to have been in contact with black wad and petrol, we may suppose the flame to arise, as we see it produced by art from the desiccation of that substance, and its mixture with the mineral oil. That ore when heated affords dephlogisticated air,

* Mr. *Gerhard* computes that *Vesuvius* has ejected from the year 79 to the year 1783, 309658161 cubic feet. 2 *Mineral. Gesch.* §. 87.

of which a very small quantity is sufficient to produce flame: this flame once produced, may be supported by dephlogisticated air from other ores, which Dr. *Priestly* has shewn to afford it, and the phlogiston may be supplied by pyrites, bituminous shistus, bitumen and coal; marl, shistus, horn-stone, shoerl, with a further addition of iron from the pyrites, are the true sources of the melted matter or lava. The explosion and eruption of this melted matter proceeds, in all probability, from the access of a large quantity of water, which either enters through some crack in the bottom of the sea, or from sources in the earth; if the mass of water so admitted be sufficiently great, it will extinguish the subterraneous fire; if not, it will suddenly be converted into vapour, whose elastic force is known to be several thousand times greater than that of gunpowder; if the superincumbent weight be too great, it may cause earthquakes, but will propel the melted matter latterally towards the mouth of the volcano, where, meeting with least resistance, it will expel it, together with all the unmelted stony masses it meets in its passage. It is easy to conceive that before the dense melted matter is ejected, the dilated air of the volcano will first be forced out, and carry with it the ashes and looser stones adhering to the sides and crater of the volcano, as has been observed,

observed, and elegantly described by our modern *Pliny* Sir *William Hamilton*.

The substances ejected by volcanos are, phlogisticated, fixed, and inflammable air, water, ashes, pumicestones, stones that have undergone no fusion, and lava.

The water proceeds partly from that contained in the volcano, partly from the condensed vapors, and partly perhaps from the intimate union of the phlogiston and dephlogisticated air; an union which some late experiments shew to be productive of water in certain circumstances. Part of the ashes is plentifully moistened with this water, and forms *tufa traass*, &c.

Stones of all sorts and sizes, even of 10 feet in diameter, are projected by volcanos, and sometimes to great distances: hence probably those solitary masses of granite, which are sometimes met with in lime-stone countries.

Lavas, in their passage through the volcano and its caverns, and during their flowing, necessarily involve various sorts of stone, which are not therefore products of fire, though found in lava; such as quartz, spar, shoerl, &c. and thus various porphyries and
pudding-

pudding-stones are found, which have lava for their ground.

Basaltes, and in many instances shoerl, seem to me to owe their origin both to fire and water: they seem to have been at first a lava, but this lava, while in a liquid state being immersed in water, was so diffused or dissolved in it with the assistance of heat, as to crystalize when cold, or coalesce into regular forms. That basaltes is not the result of mere fusion appears by a comparison of its form with its texture; its form, it being crystalized, should be the effect of a thin fusion, but in that case its texture should be glassy; whereas it is merely earthy and devoid of cavities. Hence we may understand how it comes to pass that lava perfectly vitrified, and even water, are sometimes found inclosed in basaltes. *Mon. Mineral.* 511. *Von Troil,* 285.

The immense masses of lava ejected by volcanos, presenting but a relatively small surface to the atmosphere, are many years in cooling, and many hundreds of years are required for their decomposition; this decomposition is quicker or slower as they have been more or less perfectly melted. According to the observations of Sir *William Hamilton,* the lava of *Vesuvius* forms one or two feet of mould in 1000 years; this bed of mould being

being afterwards covered with fresh lava, and this, after mouldering by that of still latter eruptions, affords some ground for calculating the age of the volcano at least within certain limits.

The beds of lava are deepest and narrowest in the proximity of the crater, and broader and shallower as they are more distant, unless some valley intervenes; pumicestone and ashes lie still more distant. From these observations extinguished volcanos are traced. Many excellent investigations of this sort may be seen in Mr. *Soulavie*'s history of the south of *France*.

Basaltic mountains (common in *Sweden*) seem to owe their origin to sub-marine volcanos.

Petrifications.

The most remarkable observations relative to petrifactions are,

1st. That those of shells are found on or near the surface of the earth; those of fish deeper, and those of wood deepest. Shells in *specie* are found in immense quantities at considerable depths.

2dly. That those organic substances that resist

fift putrefaction moft are frequently found petrified; fuch as fhells and the harder fpecies of woods: on the contrary, thofe that are apteft to putrefy are rarely found petrified, as fifh, and the fofter parts of animals, &c.

3$^{dly.}$ That they are moft commonly found in ftrata of marl, chalk, lime-ftone or clay, feldom in fand-ftone, ftill more rarely in gypfum, but never in gneifs, granite, bafaltes or fhoerl; but they fometimes occur among pyrites, and ores of iron, copper and filver, and almoft always confift of that fpecies of earth, ftone, or other mineral that furrounds them, fometimes of filex, agate, or carnelian.

4$^{thly.}$ That they are found in climates where their originals could not have exifted.

5$^{thly.}$ That thofe found in flate or clay are compreffed and flattened.

Of Metallic Ores.

Iron ore is the only one that forms intire mountains, all other ores form but an inconfiderable part of the mountain in which they are found.

Ores either run parallel to the ftony ftrata,
or

or run across them in all directions; these last are called *veins*.

The course of veins, with relation to the meridian, is called their *direction*, and with relation to the horizon is called their *inclination*.

Their direction, in the language of miners, is denoted by *hours*; the horizontal circle being divided into twice 12 hours, 12 from south to north, and 12 from north to south: east and west directions are therefore denoted by 6 o'clock.

Inconsiderable veins that diverge from the principal are called *slips*; considerable masses of ore that have no great length are called *bellies* or *stock-works*; so are also accumulated veins or thick bodies of ore formed by the junction of several veins.

The stones which fill the cavities that form the veins are called the matrix (gang) of the ore; the rocks that lie over the veins are called the *roof*; those that lie under them the *floor*, and by some the *hading*; the matrix is almost always a finer species of stone than the surrounding rocks, though of the same genus; even the rocks themselves are finer grained as they approach the vein.

There

There is no matrix peculiarly appropriated to any metal; it has only been remarked, that tin is generally found among stones of the siliceous genus, and lead very frequently among those of the calcareous.

There is no certain sign from which the existence of an ore in any mountain may be inferred, except the vestiges of it in the beds of torrents or mineral waters, and the structure of the mountain itself, of which enough has been already said.

Of Hot Springs.

Mr. *Tiffington* has remarked, that waters flowing through a blue marl filled with nodules of pyrites are warm; Mr. *Guettard* has also observed, that all the hot mineral springs of *France* flow from shistus: hence there is no occasion to derive their heat from any subterraneous volcano.

TABLE.

TABLE I.

The Quantity of Metal in a Reguline State afforded by 100 Grains of different Metallic Calces, and to which consequently they are respectively equivalent.

100 Grains – – – – –	Grains.
Brown calx of iron afford of regulus – – –	from 79 to 89 grs.
Red ditto – – –	from 71,4 to 78
Brown calx of copper	from 84 to 86,5
Minium – – – – –	89
Calx of tin – – – –	96
Precipitate per se – –	92
Flowers of zinc – –	85,5
Calx of bismuth – –	98
Grey calx of antimony	96
White calx of manganese	54

Hence the quantity of calx, which 100 parts of any of these metals would afford, is easily found; thus 100 gr. of lead would afford 113 of minium for $\div$ 89. 100 : : 100 113.

TABLE

TABLE II.

Of the Weight and Colour of Metallic and Earthy Precipitates, extracted with some Alterations and Additions from the 2d vol. of Mr. Bergman.

100 Grains.	Precipitated by	Weight.	Colour.
GOLD.	Aerated Min. Alkali	106 Gr.	Yellowish.
	Caustic Ditto - -	110	Darker, retains more acid than the former.
	Prussian - - -	- -	Yellowish or bluish from Iron, not total.
SILVER. In Nitrous Acid	Aerated, &c. - -	129	White.
	Caustic - - -	112	White.
	Prussian - - -	145	Brick colour, or if dilute, flesh colour.
	Marine Acid - -	133	White cloud or clots.
COPPER. Nitrous Acid	Aerated - - -	194	Bluish green.
	Caustic - - -	158	Greyish brown.
	Prussian - - -	530	Dark red.
IRON. Vitriolic or Marine Acid	Aerated - - -	225	Greenish brown, and soon after yellowish.
	Caustic - - -	170	Darker brown.
	Prussian - - -	590	Blue.

(400)

TABLE II. *Continued.*

100 Grains.	Precipitated by	Weigh.	Colour.
TIN.	Aerated	131	White.
Aqua Regia, or	Cauſtic	130	White.
Marine Acid	Pruſſian	250	Dark green, and ſoon after blue.
LEAD.	Aerated	132	White.
Nitrous Acid	Cauſtic	116	White.
	Pruſſian		Greeniſh yellow, and after ſome time white.
	Vitriolic Acid	143	Or if well waſhed, 137. White grains.
MERCURY.	Aerated	110	Brick colour.
Nitrous Acid	Cauſtic	104	Yellower.
	Pruſſian		White and yellow, with ſpots of green.
	Vitriolic Acid	130	Or 119 if waſhed. White.
ZINC.	Aerated	193	⎱ Dull white.
Nitrous Acid	Cauſtic	161	⎰
	Pruſſian	495	Reddiſh yellow, and after ſometime whitiſh yellow.
Regulus of Anti-	Aerated	140	⎱ Dull white.
mony.	Cauſtic	138	⎰
	Pruſſian	138	Blue, eaſily re-diſſolved by exceſs, and then green.

(401)

Bismuth. Nitrous Acid	Aerated Cauftic	130 125	} White,
	Pruffian	180	Reddifh yellow.
	Water	113	White.
Nickel. Nitrous Acid	Aerated Cauftic	135 128	} Whitifh green.
	Pruffian	250	Dirty reddifh yellow, or red and greenifh yellow.
Cobalt. Nitrous Acid	Aerated Alkali Cauftic	162 140	} Greenifh pale red.
	Pruffian	142	Blue, greyer than that of iron.
Arsenic. Marine Acid, or Aqua Regia	Aerated Cauftic		} White, imperfect.
	Pruffian	180	Green and yellow mixed.
Manganese. Nitrous Acid	Aerated Cauftic	180 168	} Brownifh red when dephlog'd or white if phlogifticated
	Pruffian	150	Dirty bluifh grey, and after fome time, brownifh grey.
Earths. Barytes Nitrous Acid Marine Acetous	} Pruffian	150	Reddifh white. Greenifh white. Yellowifh and greenifh white.

D d

TABLE II. Continued.

100 Grains.	Precipitated by	Weigh.	Colour.
Pure Lime	Aerated Alkali	181,8	
	Cauſtic	130	
Magneſia	Aerated	222	
	Cauſtic	118	
	Cauſtic Vol.	110	

100 Grains regulus of antimony, dephlogiſticated by nitrous acid, weigh 138 grains.
100 Grains tin, dephlogiſticated by nitrous acid, weigh 140 grains.

REMARKS.

The precipitates are generally ſuppoſed to be well waſhed in diſtilled water, and dried in a heat of 212 of Fahrenheit, to which they are expoſed for 10 minutes.

The precipitate of biſmuth by *Pruſſian* alkali, is re-diſſoluble in hot nitrous acid. That of lead is not.

The quantity of *Pruſſian* alkali neceſſary to precipitate barytes from the acetous acid, is to that neceſſary to precipitate iron from the marine, as 1 to 14 nearly.

TABLE III.

Of the Proportion of Ingredients in Earths and Stones.

Calcareous Genus.

100 Parts.	Calcar.	Argill.	Silex.	Magn	Wat.	Iron.
Calcareous Spar	55	— —	— —	—	11	—a
Gypsum	32	— —	— —	—	38	—b
Fluor	57	— —	— —	—	—	—c
Tungsten	50	— —	— —	—	—	—d
Compound Spar	60	— —	— —	35	—	5e
Cruetzenwald Stone	75	— —	— —	12	—	3f
Calcareous Marle	50 to 75	20 to 30	20 to 30	—	—	—g
Margodes	50	32	15	—	—	2
Stellated Spar	66	— —	30	—	—	3
Calcareous Grit or Sand Stone }	50	— —	— —	—	—	—h
Swine Stone	95	— —	— —	—	—	—i
Pyritaceous Limest.	75	14	— —	—	—	4k
Martial Tungsten	— —	— —	— —	—	—	50l

a And 34 Fixed Air.   *b* And 30 Vitriolic Acid.   *c* 43 Acid and Water.   *d* 50 Acid and Iron.   *e* Both Earths mild.   *f* Ditto.   *g* And Water.   *h* Or more. Remainder, Silex, Argill, and Iron.   *i* And Petrol, remainder, Argill and Iron.   *k* And 7 Quartz and Sulphur, that is, 25 Pyrites.   *l* By the dry way only 30, and 50 Tungsten.

Barytic Genus.

100 Parts.

Mild Barytes   78 Earth, 20 Fixed Air, 2 Barofelenite.
Barofelenite   84 Earth, 13 Vitriolic Acid, and 3 Water.
Hepatic Stone   33 Barofelenite, 33 Silex, 22 Allum, 7 Gypsum, 5 Petrol.

TABLE III. *continued.*

Muriatic Genus.

100 Parts.	Silex.	Calc.	Magnesia.	Argill	Water.	I on.
Mild magnesia	—	—	48	—	22	—*
Keffekil	50	—	50	—	—	—
Steatites	80	—	17	2	—	1
Argillaceous steatites	72	—	17	11	—	—
Chalk of Briançon	70	—	17	11	—	—†
Soap Rock	70	—	17	13	—	—
Asbestos	63	11	20	4	—	2‡
Martial abestos	62	,12	13,7	1,7	—	10,6
Suber montanum	59	11	24	2,4	—	3,6‖
Amianthus	64	6,9	18,6	3,3	—	1,2§
Serpentine	45	—	23	18	12	3
Talc Muscovy	50	—	45	5	—	—
Talc Venetian	a larger portion of argill and smaller of magnesia.					

Note, The magnesia and calcareous earths are in a mild state in all the above stones.

* At a medium and 30 fixed air.   † And 2 of talc.   ‡ At a medium.
‖ At a medium.   § And 6 barytes.

Argillaceous Genus.

	Silex.	Argill	Calcareous	Magnesia.	Iron.	Water.
Pure clay dry	63	37*	—	—	—	—
Argillaceous marl dry	46	27	25 †	—	—	—
Fuller's earth	53	18	5	3	4	17‡
Pouzzolana	57	20	6	—	20	—
Tripoli	90	7	—	—	3	—
Pure mica	38	28	—	20	14 ‖	—
Martial mica	34,5	25,5	—	18	22	—
Roof slate or shistus	46	26	4 mild	8 mild	14	—
Flagst. or argill. shist.	36	56	—	—	4	—
Horn-stone	37	22	2	16	23	—
Killas	60	25	—	9	6	—
Toadstone	63	14	7	—	16	—
Zeolyte	60	20	8	—	—	12§
Pitch-stone	65	16	—	—	5	14 ¶
Gronsten	Horn-stone and mica, or horn-stone and shorl.					
Stellsten	Mica, quartz and argill.					
Binda	Horn-stone, mica, shorl, quartz, and pyrites.					
Growan	Argill, mica and quartz.					

* At a medium when perfectly dry, 63 siliceous.   † Mild at a medium.
‡ And marine acid at a medium.   ‖ White calx of iron.
§ At a medium.   ¶ And air.

Vitreous copper ore—10 or 12 fulphur, and 90 of copper.
Azure ore—20 to 30 iron, from 40 to 60 of copper, the remainder fulphur.
Yellow copper ore—pyrites, fulphur, and from 4 to 30 parts of copper.
Grey copper ore—arfenic, pyrites, from 35 to 60 copper, and a little filver.
Blendofe copper ore—pyrites, pfeudo galena, from 18 to 30 copper.
Shiftofe copper ore—fchiftus, fulphur, from 6 to 10 of copper.

---

100 Parts.   *Iron.*

Steel ore—from 60 to 80 iron.
Black eifen rahm—74 plumbago, 26 iron.
Sparry iron ore—38 calcareous earth, 24 manganefe, and 38 iron.
Flos ferri—65 calcareous earth, and 35 calx of iron.
Magnetic fand of *Virginia*—about 50 of iron.
Hæmatites—from 40 to 80 of iron.
Grey iron ore—fiderite, and from 40 to 66 of iron.
Highland argillaceous ore—from 30 to 66 of iron.
Ditto *fwampy*—fiderite, and 36 of iron.
Siliceous ore—25 to 30 of iron.

100 Parts.   *Tin.*

Black tin ore—80 tin, some iron.
Red ditto—more of iron than of tin.
Sulphurated tin—40 per cent. sulphur, a little copper, the remainder tin.

---

100 Parts.   *Lead.*

White lead ore—a little iron, argill or calcareous earth, 80 to 90 of tin.
Red ditto—more iron, argill, 80 or 90 of lead.
Green ditto—still more iron, seldom copper.
Bluish ditto—a little copper.
Vitriol of ditto—about 70 of lead.
Galena—from 15 to 25 of sulphur, from 0,01 to 1,5 or 2 of silver, from 60 to 85 of lead, besides quartz and iron.
Antimonial lead ore—antimony, from 0,08 to 0,16 silver, and from 40 to 50 of lead.
Pyritous lead ore——pyrites, 18 to 20 of lead.
Red lead spar—realgar, a little silver, and 43 of lead.

100 Parts.   *Mercury.*

Native calx of mercury—9 fixed air, and 91 mercury.
Vitriol and marine falts of ditto—About 70 mercury.
Cinnabar—20 Sulphur, and 80 mercury.
Pyritous ore of mercury—Cobalt, arfenic, pyrites, 1 of mercury.

---

100 Parts.   *Zinc.*

Vitreous Ore, Zinc, Spar—28 Aerial acid, 6 water, 1 iron, and 65 calx of zinc.
Tutanego—Iron, argill, and from 60 to 90 of zinc.
Calamine—Iron, clay, rarely calcareous earth or lead, 30 to 84 calx of ditto.
Zeolytic ore—Quartz, water, and about 36 calx of zinc.
Blende, pfedogalena blue—8 iron, 4 copper, 26 fulphur, 4 water, 6 filex, and 52 zinc.
Ditto black—1 Arfenic, 9 iron, 6 lead, 29 fulphur, 6 water, 4 filex, and 45 zinc.
Ditto red—5 Iron, 17 fulphur, 5 water, 5 argill, 24 quartz, and 44 zinc.
Ditto, phofphoric—5 Iron, 20 fulphur, 4 fparry acid, 6 water, 1 filex, and 64 zinc.
Ditto grey—Galena, petrol, fulphur, 24 zinc.
100

100 Parts   *Regulus of Antimony.*

Antimony—26 Sulphur, and 74 regulus.
Arsenicated ditto—The same as the plumose silver ore.

---

100 Parts   *Regulus of Arsenic.*

Orpiment—10 Sulphur, and 90 arsenic.
Realgar—16 Sulphur, and 84 arsenic.

---

100 Parts.   *Manganese.*

Sparry iron ore—50 Calcareous earth, 22 iron, and 28 calx of manganese.

---

100 Parts.
Molybdena—45 Acid, 55 sulphur.

F I N I S.

www.ingramcontent.com/pod-product-compliance
Lightning Source LLC
Chambersburg PA
CBHW051732300426
44115CB00007B/534